GOD'S
GENERALS

Other Books By Richard A. Gabriel

The Madness of Alexander the Great (2015)
Between Flesh and Steel: Military Medicine From The Middle Ages to the War in Afghanistan (2013)
Man and Wound in the Ancient World (2012)
Hannibal: The Military Biography of Rome's Greatest Enemy (2011)
Philip II of Macedonia: Greater Than Alexander (2010)
Thutmose III: Egypt's Greatest Warrior King (2009)
Scipio Africanus: Rome's Greatest General (2008)
Muhammad: Islam's First Great General (2007)
The Warrior's Way: A Treatise on Military Ethics (2006)
Soldiers' Lives: Military Life and War in Antiquity: 4,000 B.C.E. to 1453 C.E. (2006)
Jesus The Egyptian: The Origins of Christianity and the Psychology of Christ (2005)
Ancient Empires at War, 3 vols. (2005)
Subotai The Valiant: Genghis Khan's Greatest General (2004)
Lion of the Sun (2003)
The Military History of Ancient Israel (2003)
Great Armies of Antiquity (2002)
Sebastian's Cross (2002)
Gods Of Our Fathers: The Memory of Egypt in Judaism and Christianity (2001)
Warrior Pharaoh (2001)
Great Captains of Antiquity (2000)
Great Battles of Antiquity (1994)
A Short History of War: Evolution of Warfare and Weapons (1994)
History of Military Medicine: Ancient Times to the Middle Ages (1992)
History of Military Medicine: Renaissance to the Present (1992)
From Sumer To Rome: The Military Capabilities of Ancient Armies (1991)
The Culture of War: Invention and Early Development (1990)
The Painful Field: Psychiatric Dimensions of Modern War (1988)
No More Heroes: Madness and Psychiatry in War (1987)
The Last Centurion (French, 1987)
Military Psychiatry: A Comparative Perspective (1986)
Soviet Military Psychiatry (1986)
Military Incompetence: Why The US Military Doesn't Win (1985)
Operation Peace For Galilee: The Israeli-PLO War in Lebanon (1985)
The Antagonists: An Assessment of the Soviet and American Soldier (1984)
The Mind of the Soviet Fighting Man (1984)
Fighting Armies: NATO and the Warsaw Pact (1983)
Fighting Armies: Antagonists of the Middle East (1983)
Fighting Armies: Armies of the Third World (1983)
To Serve With Honor: A Treatise on Military Ethics (1982)
The New Red Legions: An Attitudinal Portrait of the Soviet Soldier (1980)
The New Red Legions: A Survey Data Sourcebook (1980)
Managers and Gladiators: Directions of Change in the Army (1978)
Crisis in Command: Mismanagement in the Army (1978)
Ethnic Groups in America (1978)
Program Evaluation: A Social Science Approach (1978)
The Ethnic Factor in the Urban Polity (1973)
The Environment: Critical Factors in Strategy Development (1973)

GOD'S
GENERALS

THE MILITARY LIVES
OF MOSES, BUDDHA, AND MUHAMMAD

RICHARD A. GABRIEL

Skyhorse Publishing

Contents

List of Figures and Maps

Figures

Maps

In Memoriam

Jacqueline Brandt Weingartner
1922-2015

"Sunt lacrimae rerum et mentem
mortalia tangunt"

"These are the tears of things and
our mortality cuts to the heart"

------ Aeneas

And For My Beloved Susan
Whose Smile Entices and Eyes Beguile

Introduction

It is one of the more interesting curiosities of military history that the founders of three of the four 'great religions' – Judaism, Buddhism, and Islam – were also accomplished field generals with extensive experience in commanding men in battle. Moses, the founder of Judaism, commanded a tribal army that sacked an Egyptian supply depot, outmanoeuvred the Egyptians in a desert campaign, fought the Amelekites to a draw near Rephidim, created and trained the first Israelite national army at Sinai, defeated the Ammonites on the plain of Jahaz, destroyed fortified cities in the Jordan Valley, and left his successor, Joshua, a large, well-equipped, and professionally led army with which to attack Canaan. Muhammad, the founder of Islam, was a soldier too. In a single decade, he fought eight major battles, led eighteen raids, and planned thirty-eight military operations. He was wounded twice, and twice had his positions overrun before rallying his troops to victory. Muhammad was also a military theorist, organizational reformer, strategic thinker, operational level combat commander, revolutionary, the inventor of the theory of insurgency and history's first successful practitioner of it. Siddhartha Gautama, the Buddha, and founder of Buddhism, was the son of an Aryan warrior chief and trained soldier who witnessed so much battlefield carnage that he suffered a psychological collapse. The experience of war was central to the lives of these three great men.

If the experiences of these men in war had not been significant, it is possible that their achievements as religious leaders might never have occurred. For all three generals, war and religion were so closely intertwined in their personalities that it is difficult to discern where the influence of one ended and the other began. This book attempts to do just that, and explores the military experiences of Moses, the Buddha, and Muhammad, and the role their war experiences played in their lives.

It is always difficult to be objective about the life of the founder of a religion. His personality and the events of his life are blurred by an aura of the miraculous, enhanced almost inevitably by the needs of his followers to believe. The earliest biographers, those closest to his lifetime, are often preoccupied not with historical fact as much as with glorifying in every way the memory of one they believe to have been the Messenger of God or even God himself. The result is a rich accretion of myth and miracle, mysterious portents and heavenly signs, of residues from other religions and traditions. The biographies of saviours and messiahs cannot usually pass as history. They are rather the propaganda of an expanding faith. It is the task of the historian to locate and explicate the truth that lies behind the myth. At the root of the effort rests the historian's faith that the task can be accomplished at all.

This book deals with the *military* lives of Moses, Buddha and Muhammad and, as such, is a work of military history and not a work of religion or theology. As history, the social, economic and cultural environments in which each of the generals lived are addressed insofar as they had an important influence on their military lives. This, of course, includes their religious experiences. But their religious experiences are addressed only when they are relevant to military history. Muhammad's reform of the marriage laws, for example, that permitted each man four wives, was mostly motivated by the need to find husbands to care for the widows and orphans of his troops killed at the battle of Badr. In another example, Moses' crossing of the Reed Sea is more accurately seen as the crossing of a water obstacle at night rather than a divine intervention in which God parted the sea. A number of events in the lives of the generals that have often been treated as religious or even miraculous in nature can be just as easily understood as events with purely military causes, objectives and explanations. The author has made every effort to avoid religious analysis, judgements or conclusions, elements that have sometimes made previous biographies of our subjects unreliable. I repeat, this is a work of military history, not religion.

The fundamental sources from which the military lives of Moses, the Buddha, and Mohammed can be reconstructed are the Old Testament, especially the books of Exodus, Numbers, and Deuteronomy that contain the most details of Moses's life; the texts of the Pali Canon that contain the oldest, if not the most complete account of Buddha's life, and the Jaina texts; the Qur'an (Koran) and Ibn Ishaq's monumental *Life of Muhammed* written less than a hundred years after Muhammad's death.[1] Although the Bible, Pali Canon, and Qur'an are generally regarded as religious texts, nothing prohibits them from being read as epics that contain kernels of historical truth that can be understood by the military historian. Thus, for example, while Exodus identifies the 'pillar of fire' as being a divine instrument guided by Yahweh to lead the Israelites out of Egypt, nothing prohibits the historian from understanding it to be the usual means by which Egyptians commanded their armies to pitch or break camp, nor from noting that when Alexander the Great learned of the practice after conquering Egypt, he quickly adopted it for use by the Macedonian army. The Qur'an records that when on the verge of defeat in one of his battles, Muhammed was rescued by a flock of black-clad angels who attacked his adversary in the flanks at just the right time. The military historian is likely to see in the tale one of Muhammad's tribal allies dressed in their traditional black robes arriving in the nick of time to rescue the Prophet.

The basic sources upon which this work relies, though generally regarded as essentially religious texts, can be alternately examined as historical sources of information and analyzed and compared with what we know of warfare at the time from other secondary sources. As noted, the basic sources are the original accounts that provide us with the details of the lives of the three generals found in the religious texts. In addition, Ibn Ishaq's history of Muhammad's life can be regarded as an original source, if by original sources we at least mean that the materials ought to have been written as close as possible to the events they record. Ibn Ishaq wrote only ninety years after the events he recorded. Compared to the 'original' sources often cited by ancient historians in the West, Ibn Ishaq's work is almost contemporaneous with the events themselves. Plutarch, for example, wrote about events that occurred 200 to 600 years before he lived; Arrian's history of Alexander was written 500 years after Alexander's death; Curtius' history of Alexander was written between 300 and 500 years after the events it records; and Livy wrote of events that occurred two centuries before he was born. Only a few ancient historians – Tacitus, Polybius, and Suetonius to name the most obvious – wrote about events that actually took place during their lifetimes. By any fair standard of proximity to events, Ibn Ishaq's work qualifies as an original source.

The ability to understand a religious text from an historical perspective requires that one not read it at all as a religious text. The axiom that 'the presumption of knowledge is the enemy of discovery' is applicable here. If one regards a religious text as exactly that, one is likely to be blinded by claims of the divine to other perspectives that might have been revealed when examining the information contained within. Thus, if the Qur'an's account of Muhammad's own description of the physical symptoms he experienced when he heard the voices of God is read as a religious text, a physician is likely to overlook the fact that these symptoms are identical to those of malaria, a disease endemic to the oases of Arabia. The analysis of religious texts from an historical perspective requires a constant assessment of religious-based claims and events insofar as they might be explainable on a more empirical basis. This does not require the historian to reject the religious explanation as true or false. It only requires that the event may be explicable in more limited, that is historical, terms.

Having hopefully set aside the question of religious bias or antagonism, one might ask why write a book dealing with the military lives of the founders of the three great religions when it is obvious that hundreds of millions of the various faithful already believe that the accounts presented in the religious texts are truthful accounts of their lives? The simplest answer is that most readers are unaware that Moses, the Buddha and Muhammad were soldiers who can be shown to be competent military commanders quite apart from the influence of divine interventions that the religious texts presume. An analysis of their military lives apart from the issue of divine intervention not only affords the reader a new perspective regarding the accounts in the religious texts, but allows the reader considerable insight into the nature of warfare and military technique particular to the time when each of the great generals lived and fought.

To the historian, war is an artefact strongly influenced and shaped by the social order, the culture, and era in which it is fought. The culture that gave rise to the military exploits of Moses was radically different from the one that gave rise to those of Muhammad, and both are radically different from the Sakya-Aryan warrior culture that shaped the actions of the Buddha. To understand the military lives of our three generals, it is necessary to understand the socio-cultural context and the period in which they lived. An understanding of this larger context must rely heavily upon what are often referred to as 'secondary' source materials. Fortunately, there is a substantial secondary literature written by biblical scholars, Muslim historians and Indian scholars available on all three of our subjects through which the larger context of each of their lives can be bought to bear on the analysis. An important goal of this book is to provide the reader with an understanding of the larger context that shaped the lives of the three generals.

Always of interest to those of us who study war and its practitioners in an historical context are the lessons that can be gleaned from an analysis of war and its commanders. This book attempts to assess what might be called the influence of war upon the religious thinking of our three generals, as well as those aspects of their respective religious doctrines that can reasonably be said to have affected the course of military history. As is often the case, it is surprising how much might be learned from the experiences of those who have gone before us.

Chapter 1

Moses: Israel's First General

The oldest fragments of the Bible may have been written down as early as 1000 BC and are contained in the Book of Exodus. Before that, the story of the Israelite Exodus existed only as an oral history passed from one generation to the next by tribal storytellers. The account of the Exodus became the central founding myth of the Israelites, explaining the origins of a distinct people and the establishment of a unique monotheistic religion. Over the next 600 years, the Bible was rewritten and redacted by no fewer than four major authors known to biblical scholars as the Yahwist (the earliest), Elohist, the Priestly source and the Deuteronomist. Each of these redactors rewrote segments of the original story in response to the challenges faced by the Israelites at the time of the redaction. The result was that some of the information that appears in the earliest books reflects the historical realities at the time of redaction.

Many of the elements inserted by the redactors found their way into the Book of Exodus. Thus, the claim of slavery in Egypt and the Israelites forced to make bricks 'without straw' to build Pharaoh's new city probably came from the Israelites' Babylonian experience, where both slavery and making mud bricks were common. Neither was found in Egypt. Slavery was not institutionalized in ancient Egypt and the pharaohs constructed their cities, monuments, and tombs of stone, not mud brick. It was probably not until after the Israelites returned from the Babylonian Captivity in the sixth century BC (597–538 BC), that the Bible as we know it was finalized. Whatever else it is, the Bible is a disorganized collage of legend, history, law, propaganda, politics, poetry, prayer, ethics, hygiene practices, genealogy, military tactics, dietary advice and even carpentry instructions.[1] Trying to tease the historical story of Moses and his military life from this bundle of tales is a challenge.

Moses The Man

Next to Yahweh, Moses is the most intriguing character of the Old Testament. Held in awe as the founder of one of the world's great religions, respected as a national patriot who led his people out of slavery and the subject of endless writings and speculations, Moses has become a figure of history. And yet there is scant evidence beyond the Bible itself that the man ever existed. Whoever he was, Moses is regarded as the founder of Yahwehism and, ultimately, Judaism, a claim that may be accepted in the absence of any other explanation to the contrary.

The Bible tells us that Moses was born in Egypt to Israelite parents. His father was Amram, a man who married his aunt, Jochebed, in clear violation of the law against incest found in the Book of Leviticus. Much effort has been expended by theologians and religious historians to explain away this 'inbreeding characteristic', also found among the Patriarchs. Both Abraham and Isaac, for example, passed off their wives as their sisters.[2] The idea that the founder of a great religion should have been the product of incest is so embarrassing that one wonders why the later compilers of the Exodus saga included it, unless there was some truth to it. Its importance is that it supports the claim that Moses was born an Israelite and that he was not, as is sometimes argued, an Egyptian.

We have no knowledge of where within Egypt Moses was born. The claim that he was set adrift in a basket on the waters of the Nile to be found by Pharaoh's daughter and raised at court can safely be ignored. The story is clearly a fabrication and contains elements that are common to the birth myths of other heroes of the ancient world. The birth myth of Sargon, the great Akkadian king who ruled in Mesopotamia in the third millennium BC, is so close to the Moses tale that some scholars believe that the Exodus compilers simply cut and pasted the story of Sargon into the Old Testament. The Sargon text appears below:

> Sargon, the mighty king, king of Agade, am I
> My mother was a changeling, my father I knew not....
> My changeling mother conceived me, in secret she bore me.
> She set me in a basket of rushes, with bitumen she sealed my lid.
> She cast me into the river which rose not over me.
> The river bore me up and carried me to Akki, the drawer of water...
> Akki, the drawer of water, took me as his son and reared me.[3]

Sargon comes to the attention of the king and becomes his cupbearer. Introduced to court life, he becomes invaluable and is made king.

If we accept another element of the Moses saga that he was born close to the court of Pharaoh, it may have been that he was born among the Israelites living in and around Raamses and Pithom during the time of the Oppression. Ramses II ruled for sixty-seven years, and if he was the pharaoh of the Oppression, Moses could have been born just before Ramses' reign and still had sufficient time to lead the Exodus under Merneptah, Ramses' son and heir. If so, then from beginning to end, Moses would have been 72 years old, close to the 80 years claimed for him at the time of the Exodus.

One of the reasons why Moses was sometimes thought to be an Egyptian is that his name is Egyptian. 'Moses' is the Greek translation of the Egyptian word '*mose*', meaning child, and is an abridgement of an usually more complete theophoric name such as Ptahmose (child of Ptah) or Amunmose (child of Amun). The name is a common one found on many Egyptian graves. It may seem curious that an Israelite couple should give their child an Egyptian name. But there is considerable evidence that some Israelites acculturated to Egyptian manners and ways, part of which was taking Egyptian names for their children. Moses, a fourth-generation Israelite resident in Egypt, probably was given an Egyptian name by his parents for similar reasons. Possessing an Egyptian name suggests that Moses' family had already acculturated to some degree. It does not, however, prove that Moses was an Egyptian.

If Moses was an Israelite, one would think that he would be able to speak his ethnic tongue. We do not know what language the Israelites spoke. That it was some semitic tongue that dated back to the Patriarchal Period is almost certain. It was not, however, Hebrew. It was only after their arrival in Canaan, while still retaining some elements of their old language, that the Israelites developed a form of speech that eventually became biblical Hebrew. Hebrew seems to have grown out of a dialect of the northwestern Semitic languages spoken by the Canaanites.[4] There is no reason to expect that the Israelites lost their language while in Egypt, but it is not unlikely that the more acculturated among them may have lost considerable fluency in the same manner that second generation American ethnics often understand the language of their parents and speak a few words of it, but have difficulty making themselves understood in the native tongue. This would explain why the Bible says Moses spoke with '*aral sefatayim*' or 'an uncircumcised lip'. This is often taken to mean that Moses suffered from some speech impediment, or that he stammered. More likely Moses spoke 'like a foreigner', that is his poor command of the Israelite tongue made it difficult for him to communicate with his Israelite kinsmen. Moses was likely an acculturated Israelite who had lost fluency with his native tongue and spoke it with an Egyptian accent.

The Bible tells us that Moses was adopted by Pharaoh's daughter, educated at his court, and grew to be a 'prince of Egypt'. None of this is rooted in biblical evidence, for the Bible reveals nothing at all about Moses' childhood experience or his education.[5] The Bible says only that 'the man Moses was exceedingly important in the land of Egypt'.[6] This description hints that Moses may have been some sort of leader in Egypt, either of his own people or as a governmental official of some authority. The Egyptian government often educated the children of foreigners in state schools as a way of insuring that they had someone to deal with directly on ethnic questions. If Moses was educated in this manner, he would have been sent to one of the Houses of Life near the palace, a scriptorium where reading and writing were taught, and where Egyptian history and religion were also subjects. He would have lived at the scriptorium and would have attended between the ages of 8 and 12 years. These circumstances may have contributed to the tradition that Moses was educated at the court of Pharaoh. To his countrymen, however, Moses would have appeared as an Egyptian nobleman wearing fine clothes and speaking Egyptian, even as he struggled with his own tongue.

We are not to imagine, however, that Moses rose in this manner from some lowly position. More likely, his family already had attained some status in Egyptian and Israelite society. Otherwise, it is difficult to imagine how any of these opportunities would have been offered to him. He was, then, most likely the son of an Israelite family that was already very much acculturated to Egyptian ways. The Bible states clearly that in outward appearance Moses was an Egyptian. When Jethro's daughters encountered Moses at the well after he fled from Egypt, they ran home and told their father that an 'Egyptian saved us from the interference of the shepherds'.[7] Biblical scholars suggest that Moses may have been wearing Egyptian clothes, or that his speech was Egyptian, or that he spoke the Israelite tongue with a heavy accent, all marks of an acculturated Israelite.

Martin Buber denies that Moses was an Egyptian, but concedes that the evidence of his education and the story of his Egyptian appearance, language, and education in some way 'at court', suggest strongly that Moses may have derived from a largely Egyptianized segment of his people.[8] This segment was most probably the leadership elite of the group, those who like Joseph before them had become virtually Egyptians, even as they remained leaders of their less-assimilated brethren. It is only if Moses was a member of the Israelite leadership class that his return to Egypt from his successful escape after murdering the Egyptian overseer makes any sense. Only a leader would have felt an obligation to return, or expected that he would be followed by the people he left behind.

Elements of Moses' behaviour are worth examining insofar as they shed light on his personality. One of the more interesting elements is Moses' bloodthirsty and violent nature. I am not referring here to the murder and mayhem committed by Moses at the command of Yahweh, itself terrible enough, but rather to the violence and killing that Moses committed at his own initiative in the absence of Yahweh's directives. History first encounters Moses as an adult when he murders an Egyptian overseer. This was no act of rage. It was, instead, clearly premeditated murder. The Bible says, 'he looked this way and that, and seeing there was no one about, he struck the Egyptian down'.[9] Moses showed no sign of panic. Instead, he coolly dragged the dead man away and 'hid his body in the sand'. Moses then calmly went about his business and even returned to the scene of the crime, where he learned his Israelite brethren knew about the crime and might betray him. After he learned that Pharaoh knew of the murder and 'seeks to slay him', Moses fled.[10] Moses' behaviour was that of a man not easily upset by violence, and was a portent of his willingness to use it whenever it suited his purpose.

Another violent incident occurred when Moses returned from Mount Sinai to discover the Israelites worshiping a golden calf. Having convinced Yahweh not to exterminate the Israelites for their sin, Moses took it upon himself to punish them. Moses called upon his Levite praetorian guard and instructed them: 'Put ye every man his sword upon his thigh, and go to and from gate to gate throughout the camp, and slay every man his brother, and every man his companion, and every man his neighbour.'[11] The Levites were Moses' clansmen, and formed the police force that Moses used time and again to keep his people in line. Interestingly, it is only among the Levites that we find Israelite men with Egyptian names.[12] Phinehas, the commander of the expedition that exterminated the Moabites, for example, was a Levite with an Egyptian name, as was Hur, and even Moses' sister, Miriam. Three thousand Israelites were put to death that day, and then only after Moses had crushed the idol into powder, mixed it with water, and forced the apostates to drink it before being killed.

The next murderous outburst came when the Israelites were camped on the border of Moab and Canaan. Some Israelite men took up with the 'daughters of Moab', taking them as concubines and fornicating with them. Moses ordered the death of every Israelite man who 'committed harlotry with the daughters of Moab'.[13] Some of the Midianite women had apparently joined the Moabites in seducing the Israelites. The Bible says Yahweh ordered Moses to exterminate the Midianites, a particularly cruel command since Moses' wife, Zipporah, and father-in-law, Jethro, were Midianites. Moses was being asked to kill his blood clansmen and he complied without hesitation or pity. He gave command of the expedition to the religious zealot, Phinehas, son of the high priest. Moses ordered Phinehas to exterminate the Midianites, specifically no one was to be left alive.

Phinehas attacked the Midianites with a cruel vengeance. But even this cold *apparatchik* could not bring himself to slaughter all the women and children, even as he slew every Midianite male. When Moses saw that Phinehas had spared the helpless, he flew into a rage. 'Have ye saved all the women alive?' Moses then ordered everyone but the virgins to be killed. 'Now therefore kill every male among the little ones, and kill every woman that hath known man by lying with him.'[14] The young virgins were turned over to Moses' troops to do with them as they wished. The slaughter and rape were so hideous that the officers of the army that had committed the outrage turned their share of booty over to Moses 'to make atonement for our souls before the Lord'.[15] It might be noted that while the Moabites were slain because of their sexual proclivities, the Midianites were slaughtered because they seduced the Israelites into worshiping idols, that is, they were killed for religious reasons. It was Moses who ordered the first religious genocide in recorded history.[16]

Another aspect of Moses' personality was his flair for the dramatic, for the mysterious ritual or gesture that confounds the comprehension of his clansman at almost every turn. His encounter with Yahweh on Sinai may have left him with some sort of disfigurement. Exodus says that 'the children of Israel saw the face of Moses, that the skin of Moses' face sent forth beams'.[17] A more likely explanation of Moses' condition is that he may have been afflicted by one of the six plagues that the Bible says the Israelites suffered on the desert trek, plagues that the text tells us killed nearly forty-thousand people in all. Whatever disfigured Moses must have left a serious facial injury that encouraged Moses to cover it up.

From that moment on Moses always wore a mask, removing it only when he spoke with Yahweh in the 'tent of meeting'. The effect of walking around the Israelite camp with a mask covering his face no doubt marked Moses as a mysterious man somehow chosen of God. Interestingly, the word used in the Bible to denote the mask that Moses wore is *masweh*. Often translated as veil, this word also means a mask of the kind commonly worn by pagan priests when addressing their gods.[18] To further mystify his actions, Moses ordered the 'tent of meeting' moved to the centre of the camp and mounted an armed guard around it comprised of his Levite clansman. If anyone came near the sacred tent, 'the common man who draweth nigh shall be put to death'.[19] Moses had arranged the circumstances of his leadership so that he alone remained the only connection between the people and their god.

Ritual as a mechanism of personal power is nothing new and Moses may have found himself in a difficult spot when it came to keeping the Israelites in line. He may have had desperate need for recognizable ritual to rally his followers. Some of these he may have recalled from the old Israelite rituals, as when he fashioned the magic-soaked ritual of Passover with its sacrifice of the lamb and smearing of blood on the door posts of the Israelites so that Yahweh would know his own people as he went about exterminating the Egyptians.[20] Others he may have adopted from Egyptian rituals, as when 'Moses made a serpent of brass, and set it upon the pole, and it came to pass that if a serpent had bitten any man, when he looked unto the serpent of brass, he lived.'[21]

It is intriguing that Moses may not have known how to perform a ritual sacrifice in the old Israelite manner. When the time came to perform the first sacrifice to Yahweh, it was not Moses who performed it. When the knife cut through the animal's flesh, its blood spilled upon the altar and the flesh was offered to the flame, it was Jethro, the old Midianite pagan priest and Moses' father-in-law, who offered the sacrifice.[22] Showmanship is the stock in trade of any successful leader, secular or religious, and Moses knew how to mix magic, mystery and mastery with the best of them to convince the crowd. As Will Durant put it, 'poetry embroidered magic and transformed it into theology'.[23]

The portrait of Moses that emerges from the historian's examination of the Bible is that of an Egyptianized Israelite at home with the norms of the dominant culture that provided him with a successful life, but someone substantially separated from his original ethnic group and culture. In these circumstances, Moses may have become what social psychologists call a 'marginal man', a person who belongs neither to his original culture nor to the one to which he aspired, but brings elements of both to his personality and behaviour. Moses' knowledge of the norms of the ethnic culture from which he came, like his declining language fluency, was probably not substantial. In this regard, Moses was no different from the thousands of sons and daughters of immigrants in America in modern times.

But the murder of the Egyptian overseer and Pharaoh's efforts to bring him to justice forced Moses to flee, leaving behind the life and position he had enjoyed in Egypt. Now, rejected by the society he had sought to join, Moses sought refuge among his own kind and fled to the Midianites, his mother's tribe. Here he was taken in, married an ethnic woman and settled down to a new life as a tender of livestock. There, under the instruction of Jethro, he became reacquainted with the rituals and beliefs of the Semitic religious tradition. It was Jethro, the pagan priest and Moses' father-in-law, who also taught him the ways of the shepherd and how to live off the land in the desert, training that would serve Moses in good stead later on.

Two minor aspects of Moses the man emerge from the military historian's reading of the biblical text. The Bible says Moses was 40 years old when he killed the Egyptian taskmaster, and 80 years old when he returned to lead the Israelites out of Egypt. Both claims can be safely dismissed. Longevity in antiquity was a very rare event. The average life span in Egypt was approximately thirty-eight years.[24] Of a hundred children born, half died before age 5. Of the fifty survivors, twenty-seven died before age 25, nine others died by age 35, and six lived to age 50. Only three of the original one hundred children lived to see age 60.[25] It is statistically improbable that Moses lived to age 80 or, if he did, that he would have been able to withstand the rigours of the desert trek. All that can be said is that he must have been considerably younger than what the Bible asserts.

Of somewhat more importance is the question of Moses' circumcision. Given the great importance that circumcision came to have in later Judaism, it is strange in the extreme that the Bible does not tell us that Moses was circumcised. The original significance of circumcision among the Israelites is elusive, for the Bible is clearly opposed to every practice of scarification and mutilation of the body, including tattooing, on the grounds of pagan idolatry.[26] Circumcision was a well-established Egyptian practice and not, as sometimes believed, a Mesopotamian practice.[27] Much of the evidence points to the Israelites having acquired the practice in Egypt.[28] Egyptian circumcision was performed on some 13-year-old males to mark their passage into adulthood, but does not seem to have been universally practised by all classes. A letter written by an Egyptian military conscript in the twenty-third century BC, suggests that circumcision in Egypt was associated with military service in that conscripts (and we may assume officers) were circumcised as part of the oath of service taken to serve Pharaoh, who was regarded as their divine warrior god.[29] Joshua probably had opportunity to witness such displays while in Egypt, and may have adopted the Egyptian ceremony for the Israelite army for the same reasons.

The text notes that all of the males of *military age* who had come out of Egypt had been circumcised, but all of them had died by the time Joshua was prepared to lead the Israelites into Canaan.[30] None of those born on the trek and now of military age had been circumcised.[31] While preparing for the invasion at Gilgal, Joshua officiated at the circumcision of the Israelite troops, thereby endowing the ceremony with a distinctly military character. In Egypt and Israel, it seems the ceremony of circumcision was associated with military service and with a covenant between the soldier and Yahweh or Pharaoh.[32]

The Exodus: An Historical Perspective

To comprehend Exodus as military history, it is necessary to understand the social and military history of the Israelite tribes during their sojourn in Egypt. The Israelite saga has portrayed the Israelites in Egypt as slaves and herd-tending nomads when they were probably neither. The Israelite historical-theological tradition has lent credence to the belief that the Israelites were slaves in Egypt. S. H. Isserlin notes that the saga of the Israelites that suggests they were slaves is very unusual among the sagas of peoples of the Middle East. All others – Egyptian, Sumerian, Babylonian, Assyrian, Hittite, etc – claim that their peoples and kings were descended from or created by gods. Only the Israelites claim that they are descended from slaves, a claim so unusual that it has led theologians and cultural historians to conclude that it was probably true.[33] As so often happens, once a question has been answered, especially by well-regarded experts, further inquiry ceases and contrary evidence is disregarded. What evidence there is, however, suggests strongly that the Israelites in Egypt were not slaves at all.

The Hebrew text of Exodus 1:13–14 offers a significantly different view of the Israelites than is presented in later Christian translations of the Bible. In the original Hebrew, the text says:

> The Egyptians ruthlessly imposed upon the Israelites the various labours that they made them perform. Ruthlessly they made life bitter for them with harsh labour at mortar and bricks and with all sorts of tasks in the field.

Note that there is no mention of slavery in the Hebrew text. The Hebrew term used to describe the Israelites at their labours is *avadim* that in an obscure and irregular usage can connote slaves, but which more commonly translates as 'workmen' or 'workers' or even 'servants'.[34] The linguistic argument is not conclusive, however. More convincing is the historical fact that slavery was never an Egyptian institution, even during the New Kingdom when foreigners lived in the country in large numbers.[35] Slavery did make a brief appearance during the Greek occupation of the third to first century BC, when the Greeks introduced house slaves, but the practice never caught on among Egyptians themselves.

Three factors worked against the development of slavery in Egypt. First, with a population of 7–9,000,000 people at the time of the Exodus there was never a shortage of manpower for any military or governmental project. It was the shortage of manpower that forced the use of slavery in other empires of the period, most notably Babylon and Assyria. Egypt had a surplus of people to man her army and to staff any governmental construction project with ease. Second, Egypt was a highly developed administrative state that possessed the ability to organize and deploy manpower for social tasks on a colossal scale. In this manner Egypt was able to construct and maintain a national irrigation system that ran for 700 miles, and to sustain it for more than 2,000 years! Third, both Egyptian religion and law forbade slavery, just as it extended equal legal and religious standing to women and children.[36] As Rostovtzeff notes, Egyptian peasants had legal rights under the law which, when violated, often led to labour strikes. If working conditions on the land or construction project became overly harsh, workers would strike and take refuge in the religious temples, where the legal right of sanctuary prohibited employers and police from following.[37] It is puzzling, then, that the Israelites should have remembered being enslaved in a country that did not practice slavery on any scale.

If not slavery, then what did the Israelites experience? The answer is just what the Hebrew text tells us: physical labour. The Egyptians often employed corvée labour to construct their great temples, government buildings and military forts, as well as to maintain the irrigation system. This labour was usually performed by military conscripts who did not meet the standards for assignment to combat or regular force units, or by the regular agricultural employees on temple and pharaonic estates. In the Egyptian army of the New Kingdom these conscripts would sometimes be supplemented by civilian labourers: the corvée. These civilian workers were not slaves nor impressed against their will. Most government construction in Egypt took place during the inundation, the three-month period of the Nile flood that began in September and ended in November. Agriculture was impossible during this period and the land was full of unemployed workers. These temporarily unemployed agricultural workers were hired at local construction projects as a way of keeping them fed. That these workers were not slaves is evident from texts which show military doctors assigned to the construction crews to look after the workers' health and treat their injuries. Considerable attention was paid to the workers' diet to keep them fit and healthy.[38]

Corvée labour had a long tradition in Egypt and was used to construct the great pyramid tombs. Although it is commonly believed that the pyramids were constructed by thousands of slaves, in fact it was corvée workers who built them and were paid to do so. Not unlike medieval Christians who willingly worked on building the great European cathedrals as a religious duty, so it was with the corvée workers who built the great pyramids to keep the bodies of their divine pharaohs secure. It is possible, then, that the Israelites were forced to undertake a period of corvée labour for reasons to be examined shortly.

In Exodus we find them at forced labour making bricks for Pharaoh's new city in the Delta. This period became known in the biblical saga as the Oppression, and portrays the Israelites 'in bondage' or as slaves. The 'enslavement' came to form a central event in the Israelite saga, for it was supposedly to escape from bondage that the Israelites followed Moses into the wilderness and became the chosen people of Yahweh. But if the Israelites in Egypt were not slaves, who were they, and why did they come to regard a temporary period of corvée labour so resentfully? The answer lies in understanding the Israelites not as a tribe of Bedouin animal herders, but as a much more complex social entity: the *habiru*.

The discovery of the Amarna Letters introduced the world to a group of people that the Egyptians called *apiru* or, in Akkadian, *habiru*, described as a wandering group of Asiatics in Palestine and Syria with whom the Egyptians were quite familiar.[39] They are portrayed sometimes as brigands, sometimes as fighting against Egyptian troops, sometimes as ethnic units serving within the Egyptian army, as tenders of cattle, and as being skilled vintners and stone cutters.[40] The obvious similarity of the words '*habiru*' and 'Hebrew' led some scholars to suggest that the *habiru* might be the Israelites, appearing for the first time in an historical source outside the Bible.[41] While the *habiru* were indeed an important factor in Egyptian and Israelite history, further research has clearly resolved that they were not the Hebrews.[42]

'*Habiru*' was not a designation for an ethnic or racial group, but described a class of wandering peoples in Palestine and Syria who came into frequent contact with the Egyptians after the establishment of the New Kingdom. The ethnic mingling so characteristic of the *habiru* is evident among the Israelites as well. Exodus 12:38 says: 'also many foreigners went up with them, and flock and herd...very heavy cattle'. The term for 'foreigners' is '*erev rav*' or 'mixed multitude' or 'mixture', and is a rare construction. It seems to imply concubines, half-breeds, and other persons who joined the group. It may also refer to the Egyptian wives, husbands, relatives, and children acquired by the Israelites during their stay in Egypt. Later, in Numbers 11:4 when the people agitated against Moses for lack of food, the term used to describe the non-Israelites among them is '*hasaphsuph*', or 'riff-raff'.[43]

The ethnically mixed character of the Israelites of the Exodus is reflected more clearly in the foreign names of the group's leadership. Moses himself, of course, has an Egyptian name. But so do Hophni, Phinehas, Hur, Merari, and Miriam, Moses' sister.[44] Hur is Moses' sacral assistant and Phinehas an important priest chosen to lead the army in its murderous attack against the Midianites. The Merari clan are one of the Levite sub-clans who keep the Tabernacle. Even Joshua, whose surname was bin Nun, has an Egyptian name. The fact that such important personages possessed Egyptian names testifies to the multi-ethnic character of the Israelites of the Exodus. It also suggests that it was the welding of this diverse group to the monotheistic belief in Yahweh, more than ethnic identity, that forged the national identity of the Israelites during the desert trek.

Habiru also appears to mean 'wanderers', 'outcasts', 'bandits', or 'passers-by'.[45] They are described in Egyptian documents as 'the miserable stranger...He does not dwell in the same spot, his feet are always wandering. From the days of Horus [from time immemorial] he battles, he does not conquer, and is not conquered.'[46] The *habiru* comprised larger groups than Bedouin, and their social structure was vastly more complex. Its members possessed far more skills beyond animal husbandry. Gottwald is insistent that the Israelites were not Bedouin or simple flock-tenders.[47] Rather they were pastoralists comprised of stock breeders, agriculturalists, soldiers, merchants, construction workers, skilled government employees and even fishermen.[48] Martin Buber suggests that they were not a tribe in the usual sense of the term, but a group of tribes united in loose confederation, so that their name was connected to a common way of life or social interaction rather than an ethnic designation.

They were mostly Semites, but not all, a people without a country disassociated from national identity, united now and again in common journeys for pasture or plunder. Buber describes them as 'semi-nomadic herdsmen who become freebooters if the chance arises'.[49] Gottwald suggests that the Israelites possessed the *habiru* quality of being agriculturalists. He notes that during the desert trek the Israelites fondly recall their diet in Egypt as including fish, melons, cucumbers, leeks, onions, and garlic, all of which require at least some agricultural expertise to produce.[50] The Israelites also show expertise in stock breeding. When Moses asks Pharaoh for permission to journey three days into the desert to sacrifice to Yahweh, it suggests that at least some of the Israelite community regularly moved out into the Sinai steppe to herd and pasture their flocks. There is also reasonable evidence to suggest that much of Israelite stock breeding was neither nomadic nor even quasi-nomadic. The many references to large cattle herds as well as to 'large cattle', that is oxen that do not move for seasonal pasturing, imply that some segments of the Israelites were tied to the land by their large bovine herds.[51] This would make sense in light of the fact that Goshen (and Pharaoh's Succoth estates nearby) were excellent cattle raising country. The large store cities (logistics depots) and military garrisons near and in Goshen would have been steady customers for meat and hides.

As long as life remained good, the *habiru* were content to remain where they were. At times, they would remain near a town for a considerable period so that the best among them rose in the affairs of the town (or even the country, as seems to have been the case with Joseph, who became Pharaoh's vizier), holding governing positions. Some became mercenaries or overseers of public works. Buber notes that this life required 'a peculiar mix of pastoral and military virtues'.[52] The *habiru* were much more than seasonal Bedouin in search of grasslands for their flocks. They represented an amalgamation of many skills and occupations, including soldiery and governance. 'They were a people settled in the irrigated region of Goshen, where they gardened, fished, and grazed flocks and herds, their sheep and goats being taken into the steppe during the winter rains.'[53] And they were armed to the teeth.

There were other reasons why the *habiru* might remain in an area for long periods, and that was because they had become clients of the host kingdom and performed valuable military service. The *habiru* community possessed a military arm, so that the line between the *habiru* military and its agriculturalists, herdsmen, or tradesmen was indistinct, each seeing the others as a part of the same community.[54] When *habiru* soldiers were hired by a Canaanite king to protect a certain region, their kinsmen would follow and settle the area. Sometimes these soldiers moved into an existing village or town and settled down for a long period, intermarrying and becoming leaders of the community, as David and his *habiru* brigands did in Ziklag. It was 'in such settings that early Israel took its rise'.[55]

Habiru military units within Canaan seem to have been employed in three ways: (1) as mercenaries in the role of auxiliary infantry to augment the armies of the Canaanite city-states. There is sufficient evidence that such units served in the armies of Egypt during the New Kingdom as well; (2) as client freebooters to harass the frontiers of rival city-states, a role that required that some form of political legitimacy be extended to them; and (3) as proto-allies where the entire *habiru* group with its wide array of occupations was settled on some land along with the soldiers, with the understanding that they protect the land against the client's enemies.[56] The *habiru*, then, 'operated as armed groups, semi-independent in the feudal structure, available for hire, as auxiliary troops or resourceful in carrying out freebooting, either on their own or at the instigation of one city-state against another'.[57]

The *habiru* were often settled in lands on the borders of a state that were in dispute, or where they might come under attack. It was this type of arrangement that seems to have been made between David and his *habiru* freebooters and the Philistine prince when David and his men and their families were settled in the border town of Ziklag in return for agreeing to defend it against the raids of the Amalekites. Under these circumstances, the *habiru* military units remained independent and under the control of their own commanders, even though they might receive weapons and supplies from the client king. It may have been precisely this kind of arrangement that Pharaoh made with Joseph out of gratitude for the latter's service in interpreting the king's dreams and avoiding famine for Egypt.

Genesis 47:6 tells us that 'Pharaoh spake unto Joseph', saying that 'the land of Egypt is before thee; in the best of the land make thy father and thy brethren to dwell; in the land of Goshen let them dwell.' The land of Goshen (modern Wadi Tumilat) is a fertile valley in the eastern Egyptian Delta that leads directly from the heart of the Delta to a break in the chain of the modern Bitter Lakes. A major road runs through Goshen that in ancient times continued on through a series of fortifications, the famous Wall of Princes, and the major fortress at Taru, called the Gate of the Barbarians. Beyond these fortifications the road joined the ancient caravan trail leading to Beersheba. This axis of advance from the desert leading to the heart of the Delta cities was the traditional route of invasion from the east, the route used by the Hyksos. Settled in Goshen, the Israelites were settled along one of Egypt's most vulnerable and strategic avenues of advance, Their settlement in that area would have made no sense unless they were expected to use their military capabilities in its defence.

Habiru military contingents could be formidable combat assets. Their primary skills seem to have been conducting operations in rough terrain, where they were experts at hit-and-run raids, ambush, and surprise attack. Their reputation was that of tough military professionals, often the equal of elite units in regular national armies.[58] The Amarna Letters make clear that as Egyptian control in Canaan weakened, *habiru* units were used more frequently by the Canaanite kings to further weaken Egyptian influence. Seti I (1315–1300 BC) was forced to deal frequently with *habiru* raids on Egyptian outposts in Canaan. In 1310 he sent an army to Beth-shean to deal with the problem, but met with mixed success. *Habiru* units could be of sufficient size and expertise to cause difficulties even for a major power like Egypt. David's *habiru* army numbered 600 men. A similar *habiru* force is listed on a document from Alalakh as comprising 1,436 men, 80 of which were charioteers. An additional 1,006 soldiers of the same force are described as *shananu*, probably light archers and infantry.[59] Another text recalls that the city of Zallul, north of Carchemish on the Euphrates, was stormed and captured by a *habiru* force of 2,000 men.

The Bible gives us no indication as to the military strength or capability of the Israelite *habiru* in Egypt. If the Israelites followed the typical *habiru* pattern of social organization, then it is reasonable to conclude that they possessed a military arm central to the main social order itself. If the pattern holds as typical of the military arms of other *habiru*, then it is reasonable to expect that the Israelite military arm was comprised of military professionals, sufficiently armed and experienced in war to protect the social order from its enemies. Under these circumstances, it would have made sound military sense for Pharaoh to have settled them across one of the most likely avenues of advance leading from the desert into the Delta and Egypt's heartland. The area of Goshen and the Wall of Princes were among the most heavily fortified and manned in all Egypt, and any Israelite troops stationed in this area would likely have served as augmented units, a role they traditionally performed in the armies of the Canaanite kings.

The preponderance of scholarship suggests that the Israelites arrived in Egypt probably during the New Kingdom, sometime around the time of Amenhotep III (1417–1378 BC) during whose reign the Amarna Letters were produced. If so, then the story of Joseph as advisor to Pharaoh fits well with the Amarna Age, specifically with the time of Akhenaten himself, so that the 'Amarna age would provide a more satisfactory background for it [the story of Joseph] than any other age of which we have knowledge.'[60] It was Pharaoh Akhenaten who introduced a strict monotheism to Egypt. His violent destruction of the old religious establishment, its shrines, temples and priesthood, caused a degree of social, economic and political turbulence equal to that of the French Revolution. While it remains a matter for speculation, it is possible that the traditional monotheism of the Israelites and of their leader, Joseph, was one of the factors that might have recommended Joseph and his people to Pharaoh. Joseph's ability to interpret dreams and his proven administrative experience not withstanding, it remains possible that the Israelite belief in a single god may have also served to make the Israelites acceptable to the 'god-intoxicated' Egyptian king.

The establishment of the Egyptian empire had opened up Egypt's borders to foreign visitors more than ever before, and evidence from reliefs, monuments and texts suggests a greatly increased presence of Semites in Egyptian governmental and military life. That the Israelites were among these Semites seems probable. Redford supports this view when he notes that even before Akhenaten there is evidence that many Asiatics had achieved important positions in Egyptian society. Texts and reliefs show Asiatics in the priesthood, police, palace bureaucracy, the military and the foreign office. In addition to Asiatic soldiers, military units, and charioteers, Buber notes other Semites who rose to high office working for pharaoh. These include the minister of Syrian affairs responsible for granaries. Another Semite was described as the 'highest mouth of the whole land' (a political advisor?), who is shown being awarded the 'golden chain' and being driven through the streets in a carriage.[63] It is not unlikely, then, that the story of Joseph may be substantially true, the tale of an Israelite tribal leader who rose to great heights and used his position to help his people. The Pharaoh under whom Joseph was most likely to have risen, Rowley asserts, was Akhenaten.[64]

Under these circumstances it is not unreasonable to suggest that Israelite military men might also have risen to important positions within the Egyptian military, more so if Akhenaten had a particular military use for them. Akhenaten intended to exterminate all traces of the old religious order and replace it with a new god and theology. His campaign of destruction was conducted on such a large scale and so thoroughly accomplished that it could not have been carried out without the support of a large military force to deal with the considerable resistance and violence that occurred. An inscription on the tomb of Tutankhamen, Akhenaten's successor, describes the destruction as he found it:

> The temples of the gods and goddesses were desolated from Elephantine as far as the marshes of the Delta... their sanctuaries were like that which has never been, and their houses were foot-worn paths.[65]

Every temple from Elephantine to Syria was destroyed, and the statues of the gods desecrated.

After the initial shock had passed, it was to be expected that the Amun priests would rally the people at their temples and shrines to oppose the defacers. Military units would have been required to surround the temples and control the angry crowds. Violent confrontations and killings must have been commonplace. Although commanded by professional officers, the ranks of the army were comprised of conscripts and it is likely that their willingness to carry out the murder of their own gods was problematic. Harsh discipline might have been required at times to stiffen the resolve of the troops. More importantly, there is evidence that special military units of non-Egyptian troops were used in the defacement campaign, perhaps to avoid strong resistance among the Egyptian soldiery.

It is in this context that the reliefs found in Akhenaten's new capital need to be understood. These reliefs show the constant presence of the military, and portray Akhenaten as a vigorous military commander.[66] In almost every portrayal the king is shown wearing the Blue Crown of war or the Nubian wig, the characteristic military headdress of the New Kingdom.[67] The city itself is an armed camp, complete with watch towers, within which the king and his soldiers are shown engaged in marching, chariotry, and military exercises.[68] Most interesting is the substantial presence of military detachments comprised of troops whose features suggest Semitic and African origin.[69] Schulman identifies them from their physical features as Nubian, Libyan, and Syro-Palestinian (i.e, Semites).[70] These units may have constituted a foreign legion or even a mercenary praetorian guard that would have shown little hesitation in carrying out Pharaoh's campaign against the Egyptian gods. Although these units bear a striking resemblance to *habiru* units, the features of the soldiers in the reliefs are Semitic, the timing with the Joseph story is correct, and the monotheism of the Israelites fits nicely with that of the new Pharaoh, there is no conclusive evidence that any of these units were Israelites. The probability that they were, however, cannot be entirely excluded and explains a number of events that occurred later during the Exodus.

It might be valuable to summarize what has been said so far. First, the Israelites in Egypt were neither slaves nor nomads, but *habiru*, with a confederational form of social organization much more diversified and sociologically complex than that of Bedouin, nomads, or seasonal stock breeding communities. Second, like other *habiru*, the Israelites possessed a military arm comprised of experienced military professionals who often hired themselves out as mercenaries. Third, the settlement of the Israelites in Goshen, a part of Egypt's borderland vulnerable to military attack, in exchange for their military participation in its defence as augmented units to the regular Egyptian units, is a typical pattern of *habiru* military employment found elsewhere, most often in Canaan. Fourth, sufficient scholarly evidence places the Israelites in Egypt shortly before or during the reign of Akhenaten and his violent campaign to enforce monotheism upon Egypt. Fifth, special military units comprised of non-Egyptians, including Semites, were used to enforce Akhenaten's program of religious monotheism. The utilization of Israelite *habiru* units in Akhenaten's pogrom, therefore, cannot be completely rejected.

From the death of Joseph to the appearance of Moses, the Bible is silent concerning the activities of the Israelites in Egypt. The death of Tutankhamun had put an end to the bloodline of the Eighteenth Dynasty. Beginning with Ay, Egypt was ruled by a succession of competent military men. Horemheb (1344–1317 BC), who succeeded Ay, chose Ramses I as his successor, a soldier from the northeast corner of the Delta who had risen no higher than a 'captain of troops', but must have been well known to the king. Ramses I (1317–1315 BC) was already an old man when he assumed power and died within two years, leaving the throne to his son, Seti I (1315–1300 BC), also trained as a soldier. Seti passed the sceptre to his son, Ramses II (1300–1232 BC), who ruled for sixty-seven years, and was probably the Meror of the Bible, who set the Israelites to corvée labour.[71] Ramses' son, Merneptah (1232–1222 BC), followed him and was probably the Pharaoh of the Exodus.[72]

The first mention of the Israelites as a people in any source outside the Bible occurs in the fifth year of the reign of Merneptah who, after suppressing rebellions in Canaan, erected a stele to his victory which included the following inscription:

Israel is desolated, his seed is not. Palestine has become a widow for Egypt. All lands are united, they are pacified. Everyone that is turbulent is bound by king Merneptah.[73]

The hieroglyph used in the text to denote Israel is the hieroglyph denoting a people or tribe, not a settled nation, suggesting that at this time, approximately 1235 BC, the Israelites had moved into Canaan but had yet to conquer it sufficiently to form a stable social order of their own. This fits reasonably well with Albright's conclusion that the approximate date of the Israelite conquest of Canaan, as deduced from the date of the first wave of destruction visited upon Canaanite towns, occurred sometime between 1250 and 1150 BC.[74]

The story of the Israelites in Egypt continues when we find them hard at forced labour making bricks for Pharaoh's new city in the Delta. The obvious question is: how did this state of affairs come about? Why was a respected and valued military ally reduced to corvée labour? The answer seems clear enough from *Exodus* 1:8–10:

A new king arose over Egypt who did not know Joseph. And he said to his people, 'Look, the Israelite people are much too numerous for us. Let us deal shrewdly with them, so that they may not increase; otherwise in the event of war they may join our enemies in fighting against us and rise from the ground.'

It is probable that this new pharaoh 'who did not know Joseph' was Seti I.

Almost immediately after Seti became king, Canaan flared into open revolt, forcing him to lead an army into the area to put it down. He met with only limited success and was barely able to hold onto Beth-Shean, Megiddo, and Rehebn. As always, Egypt's enemies were the Canaanite princes, this time assisted by large bands of *habiru* who joined the revolt.[75] At the same time, the entire Middle East was struck by a terrible drought and famine that set populations in motion in search of relief. As in time's past, it was to Egypt that these populations tried to flee. These conditions continued into Ramses' reign, when Egypt was attacked twice by foreign invaders. The conditions were so terrible throughout the area that the thirteenth century BC has been called 'the end of the Bronze Age', when all the major civilizations, except Egypt, collapsed or were destroyed.[76] Coming as all these events did in the aftermath of the religious upheaval and destruction caused by Ankenaten, Egypt's kings must have been highly suspicious of foreigners of any kind.

It may have been this revolt that prompted Seti to begin construction of a new city and summer capital in the Nile Delta, the great city of Raamses mentioned in the Bible. The city, called the 'dwelling of the lion' by the Egyptians, was an important supply base and military fortress to protect the main avenue of advance that led from Canaan to the Delta cities. Although designed for defence, the city could also be used along with Sharuhen, further east, as a springboard for a sudden military strike against Canaan. It was here and at Pithom, eight miles away, that the Israelites were put to work.[77] Although it was Ramses II who completed the work on the cities and thus gained the title of Pharaoh of the Oppression, it was almost certainly Seti who first set the Israelites to work. But why would Seti oppress the Israelites?

The Bible says that the Israelites had become 'too numerous'. What this might mean in a country of 7–9,000,000 people is unclear. It is unlikely that numbers alone were sufficient cause for action against the Israelites. However, their presence in even relatively large numbers in Goshen during the time of Seti's, then Ramses II's and then Merneptah's troubles with the Canaanite rebels may have led Egypt's kings to see the Israelites as a potential fifth column in the midst of a vital military sector. The Canaanite rebels were being openly supported by the *habiru* in the highlands there, sufficient reason to give any military commander cause to doubt the loyalty of their fellow 'cousins' in Egypt. Moreover, the location of the Israelites in Goshen might rightly have concerned Seti from a military perspective. The two roads leading from the Palestine-Egyptian border at Oar passed directly through the Wadi Tumilat and Goshen.[78] It was to protect this route that the city of Raamses was constructed. Any military commander with a tactical sense would have been concerned that such an important axis of advance passed through the territory of a people who might have more in common with the enemy than with Egypt.[79] If so, Seti may have forced the Israelites into corvée service to remove them as a factor in the tactical equation.

There may have been another reason for Seti's action against the Israelites. Seti was a deeply religious man who valued the old gods that Akhenaten had attempted to destroy.[80] Although it had been fifty-seven years since Akhenaten's death, the temples and shrines he destroyed were still in terrible disrepair. Seti set about rebuilding the holy places and restoring the mutilated inscriptions and statues. He toured the land inspecting the damage and when he came to Abydos and saw the destruction of Osiris' great shrine, he wept at what the heretics had done.[81] The king's strong reverence for the old gods and his anger at Akhenaten's destruction may have led him to develop a suspicion for anything connected with the heretic king. If the Israelites had maintained their monotheism after Akhenaten's death, if they had served as praetorians in the king's foreign guard employed to destroy the old temples and if, somehow, the Israelites came to Seti's attention, then Seti's religious fervour might have prompted him to punish the Israelites for the sins of their fathers.

While serving in Pharaoh's army as mercenaries, Israelite officers and other high-ranking members of the Israelite community would have been exempt from corvée labour. If, under Seti, the military men of the community were now forced to perform physical labour, it would have been regarded as a deprivation of their former high social status and an insult. Under these conditions, it is not unreasonable that they might have come to regard forced manual labour as little better than slavery. Even if the Israelite officers remained exempt, the sight of their families and relatives forced to labour might have been too much to bear. Over time, the military men might have found the condition intolerable and decided to leave Egypt at the first opportunity. The story of Moses suggests that the Israelites took the initiative in provoking a situation where they would be permitted to leave Egypt.

Yet another historically significant event may have contributed to the Egyptian expulsion of the Israelites. The ancient Egyptians were great archivists and kept prodigious records of events, although no official Egyptian record of the Exodus has survived. When the Greek king Ptolemy II (283–246 BC) instructed Manetho, the Egyptian high priest of Heliopolis, to construct a history of Egypt so that the Greeks might learn of the country's past, Manetho was able to assemble four thousand years of Egyptian history – the *Aegyptiaca* – in short order from the records kept in the temple libraries.[82] It is to Manetho (Egyptian name: 'Truth of Toth') that we owe our first knowledge of the pre-dynastic and early dynastic history of Egypt and of the earliest king lists. Archeological and historical research has shown Manetho's account of these early events to be substantively accurate.

Manetho's account says that Moses, whom he calls Osarsiph, was a renegade heretic priest and follower of Akhenaten who led a group of lepers in the practice of the heretical religion. Manetho records their deportation by Egyptian authorities to prevent them from spreading their disease to others. Even the Bible seems to support Manetho's claim that the Israelites were expelled when in *Exodus* 12:39 it says that 'because they had been expelled from Egypt and could not tarry...' Historians agree that Manetho's story was probably based upon then existing Egyptian records now lost, or a very old oral saga.[83] In either case, the story circulated in many different versions among ancient chroniclers, suggesting that Manetho was sharing a widespread tradition.[84]

Manetho's account cannot be easily dismissed, for it squares nicely with other events that lend it support. Sometime around 1322 BC, the entire Middle East, Turkey, and the Aegean was struck by a devastating plague that lasted twenty years.[85] A Hittite attack in the Bekaa Valley captured hundreds of Egyptian soldiers, transporting them back to the Hittite homeland. Shortly thereafter, the plague broke out, spread widely and killed both Suppiluliuma, the king of the Hittites, and his son.[86] This may be the plague that Manetho is referring to. Manetho says the plague occurred '153 years before the founding of Carthage', which places the Egyptian outbreak around the same time as the Hittite plague. Judged from its symptoms, the plague was probably tularemia ('rabbit fever'), caused initially by ticks.[87] Infected humans can transmit the disease through damaged skin, mucous membranes and inhalation. Handling infected animals or ingesting infected water, soil or food can also cause infection.[88] The mortality rate ranges between five and fifteen per cent, but is three times higher in patients with typhoidal symptoms.[89]

Manetho identifies the expelled group as 'lepers', the usual description in antiquity for a number of diseases that involved some sort of skin affliction. He places their number at 110,000, a far more probable number than the 600,000 claimed in the biblical text. Once infected with tularemia, the face and eyes redden and become inflamed. The inflamation spreads to the lymph nodes, which enlarge and suppurate, mimicking the 'buboes' of bubonic plague. This last symptom is exactly what Manetho describes when he notes in his account that those expelled 'had buboes in their groin'.[90] It is possible that Manetho is describing the expulsion of the Israelites by the Egyptians.

Moses the General

It is against the foregoing background that Moses' actions as a military man can be most properly understood. In his regard, I have argued that there is sufficient reason for questioning the claim that the Israelites in Egypt were slaves or stock-breeding Bedouin. I have proposed instead that they were *habiru*, and that as part of that community they possessed an experienced and proficient military arm for their own defence or as mercenaries for Canaanite and Egyptian kings. Seen in this light, the adventures of the Israelites as described in Exodus take on new meaning. What follows is an examination of the Exodus from this new perspective that analyses a number of events described therein from the perspective of a military historian trying to make sense of the Moses tale in military terms.

To help the reader see the story with a soldier's eye, it is useful if the reader could set aside any reliance upon divine explanations for these events and see them instead from the perspectives of a combat field commander. Where I thought it helpful, I have attributed the military commands of Yahweh and Moses as reported in the Hebrew text to Moses alone. Hopefully, this simple literary device will help the reader see that these commands often make surprisingly good military sense.

Exodus has been presented to the world mostly by theologians and religious historians and not military historians, with the result that Exodus has been largely overlooked as a significant source of military history. Yet even a cursory examination of Exodus reveals more than a few examples of the military art practised with an expertise sufficient to hold the attention of any serious student of strategy and tactics. Seen from a military perspective, The Exodus is the saga of a people equipped and familiar with weapons, led by experienced and tactically proficient commanders, who were not Egyptian slaves and whose military proficiency and operational capability improved greatly during the desert trek until, with remarkable clarity of strategic aim, they were able to achieve their ultimate objective of conquering the land of Canaan.

The military tenor of Exodus is obvious from the very beginning of the saga where the text employs the language of military terms and metaphors to describe the departure of the Israelites from Egypt. Exodus 13:19 states clearly that the Israelites were armed when they departed: 'Now the Israelites went up armed out of Egypt.' The term *hamushim* is used to denote the condition of being armed.[91] The traditional view of the Israelites as slaves does not, of course, accord very well with the use of this term, since armed slaves would make no sense. This has led some scholars to interpret *hamushim* as meaning 'equipped', in the sense of the Israelites being adequately prepared and provisioned for their journey.[92] But the Exodus text is quite clear that the Israelites were *not* well-equipped. Exodus 12:39 tells us that 'because they had been expelled from Egypt and could not tarry...they had made no provisioning for themselves'.

The use of *hamushim* to mean 'equipped' is an uncommon usage. More commonly, *hamushim* means armed. While there are any number of roots from which the word might be derived, none make sense in the context of the Exodus text that is not of some implied military meaning. Moreover, the word has come down to us with its original military meaning intact, that is, as 'armed'. As William Propp notes, 'the majority rendering, "well girted, armed, equipped," fits all attestations well enough and has been adopted into modern Hebrew'.[93]

Other terms and metaphors in the Exodus text also suggest a military dimension to the Israelite tribes on the eve of their departure. Exodus 12:37, for example, tells us that 'Israel's sons set forth from Raamses to Succoth, about 600,000 footmen – the males besides the dependants.' The term employed for 'footmen' is *ragli*, literally 'he of the leg'.[94] It is a term that is ordinarily used as a singular collective noun connoting not just *people* on foot, but *soldiers* on foot. In short, *ragli* means infantry.[95] The text goes on to describe how this infantry was organized. Exodus 12:41 describes the infantry units as being formed into brigades: 'And it happened at the end of thirty years and four hundred years, and it happened on the bone (body) of this day, all Yahweh's brigades went out from the land of Egypt.' The English translation retains this sense of a military formation when it translates the same verse as meaning: 'In battle array, the Israelites marched out of Egypt.' It seems reasonable, then, that as the Israelite *habiru* prepared to depart from Egypt they did so with their weapons in hand and their military elements formed up in march formations, conditions that cannot reasonably be attributed to slaves, but which fit nicely with their identification as *habiru*.

The Israelite's possession of weapons (sickle-swords, socket axes, daggers, spears, bows, etc.) is of considerable importance. Weapons of this period were made of bronze. The tin required to cast bronze weapons was very expensive and at this early date came only from two sources, northern Germany and Afghanistan. The expense of bronze weapons was so great that their cost was a serious limitation on the size of military contingents that could be armed with them.[96]

Only the great powers could afford large military establishments. As allied forces, the Israelites may have been issued Egyptian weapons while in service, and may have refused to relinquish them when assigned to corvée labour. Or, perhaps, the Israelite military was not required to do corvée labour, and kept their weapons, while other Israelites served in Pharaoh's construction battalions. The Israelites who left Egypt could hardly have been both slaves and armed at the same time.

No sooner had the Israelites set their feet upon the road out of Egypt than the presence of a keen military mind made itself evident in the choice of which route the Israelites would follow. Exodus 13:17–18 reveals the mind of a sound strategist as he plans his escape.

> Now when Pharaoh let the people go, Moses did not lead them by way of the land of the Philistines, although it was nearer; for Moses said, 'The people may have a change of heart when they see war, and return to Egypt.' So Moses led the people roundabout, by way of the wilderness at the Sea of Reeds.

The 'way of the land of the Philistines' is a reference to the coastal road running from Sinai north to Mount Carmel, known to the Egyptians as the Way of Horus and, later, to the Romans as the Via Maris. Its designation in Exodus as passing through the land of the Philistines is a later redaction by the text's author who was writing after the Philistine arrival in the area to place the route in a context his audience would understand.

Moses' decision to avoid the coastal road was based on sound military considerations. The road was well guarded by Egyptian fortresses and strong points. If Moses was concerned about avoiding the Egyptian authorities, then the coastal road could not be used. Moreover, the Canaanite towns and cities along the coastal route were protected by formidable military forces, some including other *habiru* serving as mercenaries to Canaanite kings. These armies would have to be dealt with if the coastal route were chosen, an unacceptable risk to a people whose years of peaceful living in Goshen may have dulled their fighting spirit. The text implies that the Israelites may not have been psychologically prepared for war when it tells us the 'people may have a change of heart when they see war, and return to Egypt'. Under these conditions, Moses' decision to avoid the coastal road and lead the Israelites 'roundabout, by way of the wilderness' makes excellent military sense.

Having received permission to leave Egypt, why would Moses be concerned about the Egyptians? Why would the Israelite commander have reason to believe that Pharaoh might suddenly change his mind about letting the people go? The reason offered by the text is unconvincing, telling us only that Pharaoh changed his mind, but not why. Exodus 14:5–6 tells us

> When the king of Egypt was told that the people had fled, Pharaoh and his courtiers had a change of heart about the people and said, 'What is this we have done, releasing Israel from our service.' He ordered his chariot and took his men with him [and gave chase to the Israelites].

But could there have been other reasons why Pharaoh changed his mind? A clue may lie in the description in Exodus 14:8 that the Israelites were 'departing defiantly, boldly.' It is important to recall that the *habiru* were not only mercenaries, but brigands and freebooters as well who could quickly turn from allies to looters if the circumstances required. Exodus 12:39 tells us that the Israelites were forced to leave in a hurry and could not make adequate provisions for their journey. To lead the Israelites into the desert without sufficient provisions was to face almost certain death.

The Israelites in Goshen were surrounded by the very provisions they required. Both Raamses and Pithom were 'store cities', major logistics depots for the Egyptian army in the Delta. The route from Goshen to the desert took the Israelites through Succoth, one of Pharaoh's largest cattle estates, and the land of Goshen contained many smaller agricultural and stock-breeding settlements as well.

Everything the Israelites needed was there for the taking. It is a reasonable hypothesis that the Israelites might have sacked one of the towns or even the king's estate on the way out of the country to provision themselves for the long desert trek.

Exodus 12:35–36 tells the outrageous tale of how Moses proposed to solve the provision shortage by simply asking the Egyptians for them! Thus:

> The Israelites had done Moses' bidding and borrowed from the Egyptians objects of silver and gold, and clothing. And the Lord had disposed the Egyptians favourably toward the people, and they let them have their request; thus they stripped the Egyptians.

It is, of course, not plausible that the Egyptians would have provided food, clothing, gold, and silver for the asking. Far more likely is that Israelite brigands took them at sword point. The Hebrew word used to describe what happened to the Egyptians is *nitzeyl*. Although translated as 'stripped', it is usually translated as 'despoiled', so that the Israelites 'despoiled Egypt'. The connotation is clearly that the Egyptians were relieved of the provisions that the Israelites needed against their will.

Relieving the Egyptians of their gold and silver at the same time certainly sounds like a robbery. Later, in the desert, when Yahweh commands that the people construct a tabernacle and tent for him to live in, he orders that it be constructed of gold, silver, precious stones, and other valuable materials. When Moses asks the people to provide these valuable materials and objects for this sacred purpose, they respond by giving him so much gold and silver that Moses had to tell them to stop! Perhaps carrying all this heavy, useless, booty through the desert was such a burden that they were glad to be rid of it. But if the news of an Israelite sack of an Egyptian town reached Pharaoh's ears, it would surely qualify as the Israelites having departed 'defiantly' and may have provoked him to try to punish them. Perhaps this is why Moses feared that the Egyptian authorities might change their minds.

Taking a clue from Manetho, however, leads us to a very different interpretation of Pharaoh's sending troops after the Israelites. Exodus 14:6–7 tells us that Pharaoh sent '600 chosen chariots, and all the chariots of Egypt, and captains over all of them' to pursue the Israelites. Interestingly, the numbers ring true. An Egyptian combined arms division numbered 6,500 men, three brigades of one thousand infantry each and two brigades of archers, each comprised of one thousand men. Organic to the division was a chariot brigade of 500 chariots organized into 25 machines per platoon, 50 machines per company, and 150 machines per battalion.[97] With 600 chariots, the Egyptian force that took out after the Israelites may have been a division-strength unit. This size force was not sufficient to force the return of the 110,000 armed Israelites that Manetho estimates. But if the mission of the Egyptian division was to make sure that the Israelites did indeed leave Egypt, then a single combined arms division was adequate.

Pillar of Fire and Smoke

The Israelites began their march along the well-travelled road leading from Raamses to the edge of the desert. The first day's march, about 10 miles, brought them to Succoth. The end of the next day found them in Etham, about 8 miles from Succoth. All along the way the Israelites were accompanied by a strange phenomenon, a pillar of cloud and a pillar of fire. Exodus 13:20–22 describes it this way.

> They set out from Succoth, and encamped at Etham, at the edge of the wilderness. The Lord went before them in a pillar of cloud by day, to guide them along the way, and in a pillar of fire by night, to give them light, that they might travel day and night. The pillar of cloud by day and the pillar of fire by night did not depart from before the people.

Again and again throughout the journey of the Israelites the pillars appear. Miraculous explanations aside, the pillars appear to have two functions: first, to guide the Israelites as they move over unfamiliar terrain; second, to signal the Israelites when to camp and when to break camp. And so Exodus 40:36–37 tells us,

> When the cloud lifted from the tabernacle, the Israelites would set out on their various journeys; but if the cloud did not lift, they would not set out until such times as it did lift.

Numbers 9:17–18 is even more explicit.

> And whenever the cloud lifted from the tent, the Israelites set out accordingly; and at the spot where the cloud settled, there the Israelites would make camp. At the command of Moses the Israelites broke camp, and at the command of Moses they made camp.

What the pillar of cloud and fire appears to be is a signal to the assembled multitude to encamp or break camp, and in that regard is not so much a divine totem but a practical device to improve Moses' command and control over his followers.

The same signaling device is found in the writings of Quintus Curtius, a Roman historian. In his *History of Alexander*, Curtius describes how after conquering Egypt and returning to Babylon Alexander prepared his army for movement further east. These preparations included a number of changes in his regular methods of command and control. As Curtius tells it, 'in the military discipline handed down by his predecessors Alexander made many changes of the greatest advantage'.[98] Curtius goes on to describe one of these changes.

> When he [Alexander] wished to move his camp, he used to give the signal with the trumpet, the sound of which was often not readily enough heard amid the noise made by the

bustling soldiers; therefore he set up a pole (*perticam*) on top of the general's tent, which could be clearly seen from all sides, and from this lofty signal, visible to all alike, was watched for fire by night, smoke by day [*ignis noctu fumus interdieu*].[99]

Until very modern times, Arab caravans, including those making their way to the *hajj*, were commonly preceded by a signal brazier of some sort.[100] The Egyptian origins, if any, of this military practice are yet to be examined. Here it is sufficient to note that Alexander adopted a similar device for similar purpose after he had spent considerable time in Egypt where he learned of it.

Was the pillar of fire and smoke some sort of Egyptian military signalling device, as Alexander's use of it implies? Was there one pillar of cloud and fire or two pillars, one for cloud and one for fire? The expert opinion is that the text implies two pillars.[101] The text uses the word *anan* which translates as 'cloud', but certainly connotes 'smoke' as well. Thus, the pillar of cloud is really a pillar of smoke. Just such a device is portrayed in the reliefs in the Luxor Temple depicting Ramses II military camp at the Battle of Kadesh. A drawing of the lower left hand panel is reproduced below.

Standing behind Ramses as he sits upon his throne are two figures, each holding a long straight pole. Atop one of the poles appears to be a portrayal of a brazier in full flame. The other figure is holding a second pole atop which sits the bottom half of a brazier, partially covered with some sort of top. A brazier covered in this manner would dampen the flame and produce smoke. The item atop the second pole closely resembles the hieroglyph for 'flame', that is a clay pot or brazier without a top. The item atop the taller pole is more problematic, since only the bottom is similar to the brazier while the top might well represent flames emanating from it. In one of the Amarna reliefs of a marching military unit, a similar item is in evidence. In this one, the flames emanating from the centre are much clearer. Below both poles are two smaller figures of men, each looking up at the tops of the poles. In their hands are narrow

Figure 1.   Portion (lower left panel) of the Reliefs of the Luxor Temple Depiction of Ramses' II Military Camp at the Battle of Kadesh.[102]

fans with which they appear to be fanning air over the flame and brazier. If the Ramses relief is indeed portraying a covered brazier and one in full flame, then it might be an Egyptian portrayal of the pillar of smoke and fire described in Exodus.

There is one more tantalizing clue as to the device's Egyptian origins. When Pharaoh's chariots approached the Israelite camp near the Reed Sea, they saw the pillar of smoke change into a pillar of fire and shift position. But these 'miraculous' events produced no reaction at all on the part of the Egyptian commanders and soldiers, and the Egyptians calmly went into their night encampment and waited for dawn. This suggests that the Egyptians were observing something which they had often seen before, an enemy commander's signal for his troops to encamp for the night. As we shall see, Moses depended upon Pharaoh's troops seeing just that.

Crossing the Reed Sea

Perhaps no event in Exodus has captured the imagination more than the Israelite crossing of the Reed Sea. Despite scores of scholarly articles over the last two centuries seeking to prove that this or that location was the site of the event, the event itself has not undergone significant scrutiny from the perspective of military technique. When examined in this manner, however, it is clear that what happened at the Reed Sea was a tactical manoeuvre known and practised routinely by ancient and modern troop commanders: the night crossing of a water obstacle. Crossing a water obstacle at night is one of the most dangerous and difficult of small-unit tactical manoeuvres. The success of the Israelite commanders in executing an operation of this type is proof that the military arm of the Israelites had reached a high level of military operational capability even before they left Egypt.

The Israelites had lived in Goshen for a long time and were familiar with the area, including the marshy tract of land where the fertile land met the desert. For years they had taken their herds down the same road they were travelling now to pasture them in the Sinai steppe during the rainy season, a time when the Nile's flood inundated the land of Goshen and the rest of Egypt.[103] The main road led directly from the edge of Goshen to a road junction where it joined the old road to Beersheba. It was probably down this road that Moses asked Pharaoh for permission to take his people into the desert so that they might sacrifice to Yahweh.[104] As mercenaries serving in Goshen, Israelite commanders would have been well aware of the locations of Egyptian fortresses and strongpoints as well as the strength and disposition of Egyptian troop garrisons. These garrisons protected the fords and bridges that made movement through the great salt marsh possible. There were at least four major fortresses on the border, one of which, probably

Taru, stood at the junction where the main road met the desert.[105] There were scores of other guarded bridges, fords, shallow crossing points et cetera throughout the area. In describing the location of the Israelites, Exodus 14:2–3 tells us the Israelite camp was located 'between Migdol and the sea'. The term *migdol* means tower or fort, and probably refers to the Egyptian fortress guarding the road junction noted above.

It is pointless to attempt to locate the exact place where the Israelites crossed the Reed Sea. Suffice it to say that the terrain where Goshen met the desert was marshy and wet, deep in places and shallow in others, neither sea nor lake, yet subject to strong tidal flows. The tidal flows of the general area are attested to in antiquity. Strabo seems to be describing them when he notes that during his stay 'in Egypt the sea rose so high near Pelusium and Mount Cassius as to overflow the land and to convert the mountain into an island'.[106] That the marshy terrain was dangerous to ground troops is clear from the description offered by Diodorus Siculus, a first century CE Greek historian, who records that during Xerxes' invasion of Egypt in 340 BC, a unit of his army drowned in the place.[107] It is not difficult to imagine a company of Persian troops walking across a shallow muddy flat only to be trapped and drowned when the tide suddenly came in. As Moses marched the Israelites down the road to the desert, he had the advantage of knowing the enemy troop dispositions and how to navigate the marshy terrain.

Moses must have been aware that the Israelite column would have to pass directly beneath the Egyptian fortress that guarded the road junction. As one of the four major fortresses of the area, the Egyptian garrison would have been large and well-armed. Moses depended upon a peaceful passage. If he had to fight his way through, the results would be a catastrophe, for his people were no match for the Egyptian professionals. Perhaps this was when a message reached Moses that Pharaoh's troops had already left Raamses and were fast closing in on the road behind him, trapping him between them and the Egyptian fortress to his front. If he remained where he was,

Moses would find himself caught between the classic 'hammer and anvil'. With the Egyptian garrison to his front and Pharaoh's chariots closing from behind, the situation was already desperate. In a few hours it would be hopeless.

The Bible says Moses assembled his commanders. 'Tell the Israelites to turn back and encamp before Pi-hahiroth, between Migdol and the sea, before Baal-Zephon; you shall encamp facing it, by the sea.'[108] The order must have struck some of the Israelite commanders as insane, for Moses had just instructed the Israelite column to leave the road and head directly into the desert! With no chance of forcing his way through the Egyptian fortress to his front, Moses manoeuvred to neutralize its tactical significance by moving his people south and west, away from the garrison. In a single stroke the Israelites had escaped from between the hammer and anvil, and removed the anvil from the strategic equation completely.

One might well imagine some headstrong young officer voicing his complaint. 'But General, there is no way out of the desert. Pharaoh's chariots can manoeuvre easily on the flat ground and cut us to pieces. Why, sir, are we moving further into the desert?' Exodus 14:3 tells us what was in Moses' mind when it explains, 'Pharaoh will say of the Israelites, "They are astray in the land; the wilderness has closed in on them".' It is a basic axiom of war to deceive the enemy as to your intentions, to mislead him into thinking one thing while you prepare to do the opposite. Here Exodus provides us with an example of tactical deception at its best. Moses intends to convince Pharaoh that the Israelites are lost when, in fact, having lived in Goshen for many years, they know exactly where they are. Moses knows the terrain better than Pharaoh and his troops do!

The Israelites turned south and west and marched into the desert. When they had reached a place sufficiently distant from the Egyptian fortress (the *migdol*) and where the firm ground to their front met the watery marsh to their rear, the Israelites encamped and waited for the Egyptian chariots to arrive. Egyptian units always moved with reconnaissance chariot screens and scouts to their front, and it is possible that the Israelite manoeuvre was observed by these scouts and reported to the Egyptian commander. Probably aware that he was being watched, Moses tried to deceive the Egyptians further. Exodus 14:19 tells us 'the pillar of cloud shifted from in front of them and took up a place behind them, and it came between the army of the Egyptians and the army of Israel'. Moses moved his command tent and its characteristic signal, the pillar of smoke atop a pole, around *behind* the Israelite column to strengthen the impression that the Israelites were facing in a direction of march leading deeper into the desert. The object was to convince the Egyptians of what their scouts had already told them, that the Israelites were indeed 'astray in the land'.

It must have been near dusk when the Egyptians arrived and they went immediately into camp. From the Egyptian camp it looked like the Israelites were facing in a direction of march that would take them deeper into the desert. There could be no doubt about this because the Israelite command tent and its signal pillar leading the Israelite column were facing the Egyptian camp. Facing in this direction, it looked like the Israelites were not leaving Egypt, but looking for a place to settle still within the country. Behind the Israelites lay the tidal salt marsh. To the right and rear of the Israelite camp, at a distance of several miles (two hours march), was the Egyptian fortress. Moses had given up any idea of trying to reach the road to Beersheba. As dusk gave way to darkness, the pillar of smoke atop the Israelite signal standard gave way to bright flame and 'the pillar lit up the night, so that the one [camp] could not come near the other all through the night.'[109]

Moses carried out his plan while the Egyptians slept. The bright flame atop the pillar drew the attention of the Egyptian observers, blocking their ability to see behind it. When training in night discipline, modern soldiers are taught that any bright object at night affects the cones and rods of the eye, making the eye physically incapable of seeing in the dark behind the light. Once exposed to a bright light in the darkness, it can require almost thirty minutes for the eye to readjust. Moses could safely manoeuvre his troops behind the light as long as the direction of movement was to the rear of the

Israelite encampment. For all practical purposes, the Egyptians were blind.

Now the *ruah qadim* or 'forward wind' began to blow. It was springtime, the time of the sirocco winds that blew out of the eastern desert with terrific force and terrible noise. Because the Israelites oriented themselves for religious reasons toward the sunrise, the translation of *ruah qadim* as east wind, the forward direction, is correct.[110] The term also realistically translates as 'hot desert wind', or a sirocco.[111] The wind grew stronger and the noise increased until it was difficult to hear. Now the Egyptians were deaf as well. The shallow water covering the sandbar just below the surface began to move as the strong tide flowed out to sea. With the desert wind pushing from the southeast and the tide pulling it northward, the water was gone in a short time and the ground dry and hard enough to hold the weight of man and animals. Perhaps Moses had been born in Goshen or hunted birds in the marshes or some of his followers (Joshua?) had served as an Israelite auxiliary in the area where they may have noticed the effect of the sirocco and tide upon the shallow wetlands. If so, like Wellington at Waterloo, perhaps he had kept this piece of ground in his pocket for a long time. With the land bridge now exposed, Moses ordered the Israelites to withdraw across the marsh during the night and gain the open desert on the other side.

In Exodus, the tale of the crossing is framed in theological metaphor.

> Then Moses held out his arm over the sea and the Lord drove back the sea with a strong east wind all that night, and turned the sea into dry ground. The waters were split, and the Israelites went into the sea on dry ground, the waters forming a wall for them on their right and on their left.[112]

Still, even the theological metaphor contains many of the elements necessary to a more military explanation, that is, the execution of a

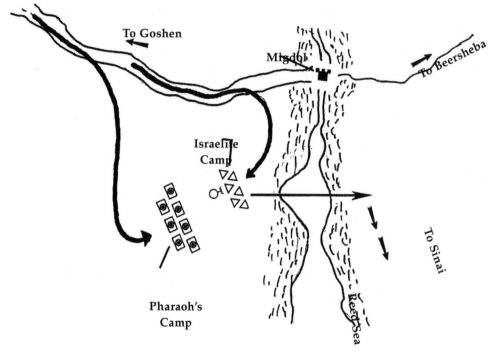

Figure 2. Night Crossing of the Reed Sea

night water crossing. Exodus 14:24 tells us that the Egyptian pursuit began 'at the morning watch', or shortly after daybreak. With the Israelites watching safely from the other side of the marsh, the Egyptians appear to have attempted to follow them across the dry bed of the marsh, but the wheels of their chariots became 'locked' so 'that they moved forward with difficulty'.[113] This seems to be nothing more mysterious than chariot wheels caught in the mud. While struggling to free their machines, 'the waters turned back and covered the chariots and the horsemen'. Perhaps the tide came in and some of the Egyptian troops and horses drowned.

The Bible says that every Egyptian died in the Sea of Reeds. Exodus 12:28 tells that 'not one man remained alive'. The death of an entire Egyptian division of 6,000 men at the hands of a band of Israelite foreigners would hardly have gone unrecorded by the Egyptians or someone else outside the Bible, and cannot be taken as true. But if we recall Manetho's version of the Israelite saga as the *expulsion* of the Israelites, the story makes somewhat more sense. The Egyptian troops were sent not to retrieve the Israelites, but to ensure that they left Egypt. Once across the Sea of Reeds, the Israelites were beyond the border of the country and in the desert; there would have been no need for the Egyptians to pursue them any further. To sustain the tale of their voluntary flight instead of expulsion, the biblical authors had to explain why the Egyptians did not pursue them into the desert. Thus, the authors killed off the Egyptian force by having them drown at the Sea of Reeds while in the act of pursuing the Israelites.

The Israelites had crossed the marsh and gained the desert. The original plan had been to leave Egypt and return to the land of Canaan. Given the original direction of march, the Israelites had probably intended to cross out of Egypt at the road junction where the old road met Goshen and follow it on to Beersheba, the road that Jacob had probably taken when he came to Egypt and which remained a well-worn caravan track until modern times, and led directly into Canaan.[114] To return to their original route, however, would have required them to turn north to gain the Beersheba road, a route that would have taken them perilously close to the Egyptian fortress at the junction of the Beersheba-Goshen road, the same *migdol* that they had avoided when they turned into the desert. Egyptian reconnaissance chariots regularly patrolled the area along the road and might easily discover the Israelites and bring them under attack. Moses could not know whether the Egyptian mission was to ensure their departure or to eliminate them. Moses decided to do the unexpected and turned not toward the land of Canaan, but away from it. Exodus 15:22: 'Then Moses caused Israel to set out from the Sea of Reeds. They went into the wilderness of Shur.' And so began the great desert trek of the Israelites in their attempt to return to the promised land.

Skirmish with the Amalekites

Moses' decision to turn south and east into the desert was calculated to take advantage of his knowledge of the terrain over which the

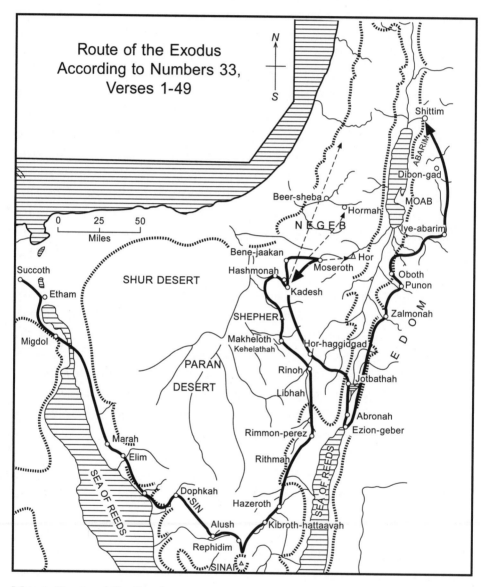

Map 1. Route of the Exodus

Israelites would have to travel. We ought not to believe that Moses and the Israelites simply 'wandered' from one place to another only to stumble upon Sinai and then Kadesh-Barnea. The texts tell us differently. Moses had spent years among the Midianites tending flocks in the Sinai desert, an occupation that would surely have equipped him with a knowledge of the desert and where the important water and pasturage sources were located. Moreover, the text informs us that the Israelites were aided by Midianite guides 'who serve as eyes for Israel'. These hardy desert Bedouin also instructed the Israelites how to 'encamp in the wilderness', that is how to live off the land. The fact that the Israelites required such instruction, moreover, is further evidence that they were not nomadic desert peoples themselves, but *habiru*.

Little more than a month after crossing the Reed Sea, and somewhere in the Sinai near Rephidim, the Israelites were attacked by the Amalekites and forced to fight their first battle. The text suggests an engagement that occurred in two phases. The first was an ambush in which the Amalekites caught the Israelites in column of march and attacked their rear. Deuteronomy 25:17–19 describes the ambush.

> Remember what the Amalek did to you on your journey, after you left Egypt – how, undeterred by fear of God, he surprised you on the march, when you were famished and weary, and cut down all the stragglers in your rear.

The Amalekites broke off the attack on the column's rear, probably due to nightfall, and waited to engage them again in the morning.

This respite gave Moses time to plan his defence. Moses placed command of the Israelite fighting men in the hands of a young troop commander named Joshua. 'Moses said to Joshua, "Pick some men for us, and go out and do battle with Amalek".'[117] Moses explained the plan that he devised during the night. 'Tomorrow I will station myself on the top of the hill, with the rod of God in my hand.'[118] Here we see the ancient dictum that effective commanders must be seen by their soldiers. Egyptian pharaohs were always portrayed as leading their troops in battle, as was Alexander. Caesar wore a red cloak so his men could easily identify him during battle and, in modern times, both George S. Patton (who seriously contemplated wearing a red cloak!) and Irwin Rommel were both known for their presence on the battlefield in plain sight of their soldiers. The text tells us that for the entire day Moses stood in plain view on the hill overlooking the battle 'until the sun set', while on the battlefield below 'Joshua overwhelmed the people of Amalek with the edge of the sword.'[119] This was the first Israelite victory by force of arms.

The skirmish with the Amalekites shows that there can be no doubt now that the Israelites are armed, and they are armed, at least, with the sword. The sword is the sickle-sword, the basic second weapon of the Egyptian spear infantryman, called the *khopesh* or 'foreleg' of an animal by the Egyptians. The weapon was so completely identified with the Egyptian army that the *khopesh* replaced the mace as the symbol of pharaonic authority.[120] The straight sword had not yet made its appearance in Canaan or Egypt, and would not do so in any numbers for at least 200 years. Where, then, did the Israelites acquire this weaponry in sufficient numbers if they were not, as the text tells us they were, already possessed of them *before* they left Egypt? Given the expense and difficulty of bronze manufacture, especially so for a people on the move, we may safely rule out the Israelites having manufactured the weapons after they left Egypt.

The armies of Egypt during the New Kingdom were conscript armies led by professional officers and supported by a national arms industry. Conscripts were taken into the army, issued weapons, trained and sent to their units. When their tour of duty was over, the weapons and other equipment (shoes, shields, helmets, belts, canteen, etc) were returned to army supply depots for reuse. If the Israelites at Rephidim were armed with standard-issue Egyptian weapons, this could only be because they were issued them during their mercenary service while in Egypt. When they fell out of favour with Pharaoh, there may have been some thought given to disarming them. No doubt the Egyptian army could have accomplished this task, but probably only at a bloody cost. Perhaps it was simply easier to permit the former mercenaries to leave Egypt and take their weapons with them. Thus it might have been that the Israelites went up out of Egypt armed.

The selection of Joshua to command the troops in battle prompts the question of why he was chosen. He was young, came from no distinguished lineage, and is not shown to have any other special credentials that would qualify him for command. In the absence of other qualifications, it is likely that the choice of Joshua to command might have been based upon his reputation as a competent fighter and commander among the Israelite mercenaries acquired when he served with Pharaoh's armies in Egypt. In this sense Joshua might have come to Moses' attention because of his already established reputation as a warrior.

As Mendenhall points out, the *habiru* form of 'customary military organization' had no permanent command authority or central political organization that could enforce appointed officers upon troops who did not know them.[121] The *habiru* form of military organization is the same as that found in the *Iliad* and characterized Israelite armies during the later periods of Joshua and the Judges. As in the *Iliad*, each leader in battle commanded troops of his own tribe or clan. Combat leaders were appointed because of their reputations as proven soldiers demonstrated in full view of their peers.[122] It was the same system used by the Arab caliphates from the 6th to the 8th century CE and, most recently, it is the system of combat command employed by Afghani warlords.

Until the incident at Rephidim, Moses had avoided having to set his troops to battle. There, as the text tells us, his column was ambushed from the rear. The main body of the column might have taken refuge in narrow terrain with hills on either side. Moses remained with the main body and assigned a unit of soldiers under Joshua's command to take positions in the rear of the column and prevent further attacks. Then Moses positioned himself on the top of the hill so his men could see him and take courage. The Amalekites could also see Moses, probably giving them pause to wonder whether he had additional troops carefully hidden out of sight that might outflank or take the ambushers from the rear. Once more Moses was attempting to deceive his opponent, this time psychologically.

The admittedly speculative scenario outlined above has the advantage of showcasing the operational capabilities of the Amalekites and the Israelites. We might imagine that Joshua took up positions at the rear of the Israelite column, while its main body took refuge behind his soldiers in a narrow defile, protected by hills on either side. The hills, if only moderately steep, would have prevented any Amalekite flanking attack or envelopment. Arranged in phalanx, Joshua's spear-and-shield infantry would have offered an impenetrable wall of spear points, the first rank kneeling with their spear butts stuck in the ground and points elevated at 45 degrees, the second rank standing with its spears levelled. Behind the heavy spearmen were Joshua's archers, armed with the Egyptian composite bow of greater range and penetrating power than the simple bow of the Amalekites. Behind the archers, deployed upon both sides of the hills to get a better view, were the slingers capable of throwing stone shot the size of a tennis ball three hundred yards or more. The Amalekites could rush at the wall of spears time and again, only to pull up short as long as the Israelite infantry held fast. Every Amalekite attack would be subject to long-range slinger fire before it ever reached the wall of spears and shields. Once in close, Joshua's archers could pick off individual targets.

Exodus 17:12–13 tells us that the battle lasted until sunset, and that 'Joshua overwhelmed the people of Amalek with the edge of the sword'. It is clear, however, that from a defensive position Joshua could have done no such thing, since at any time the Amalekites could have broken off the attack on Joshua's fixed position and given up the fight. An Israelite infantry force could not have pursued and 'overwhelmed' the Amalekite force with any hope of success. The text offers us a clue as to what might have happened. The word used in the Hebrew text is *chalash* which means 'weakened' and also 'overcome', but the latter only in the sense of being overcome by weariness or weakness, not by force of arms. The more common meaning of *chalash* is 'exhausted', meaning in the current context that Joshua exhausted the Amalekites.[123] This is exactly what we might expect from any infantry force that threw itself again and again against a stubborn wall of disciplined infantry, only to expose itself to archer and slinger fire as it did so. Sooner or later the enemy commander would have concluded that he could not carry the day, broke of the assault, and turned for home.

Joshua and his men fought well that day, with Joshua living up to his reputation as a brave and resourceful warrior. Moses must have been pleased, for from that day forward we find Joshua always at Moses' side until the day came when Joshua replaced Moses himself and led the Israelites into the Promised Land. As Moses' second-in-command, whatever changes in the structure, organization, weapons and tactics that were made in the Israelite military during the Exodus might well have been accomplished under some of Joshua's influence and that of other experienced Israelite commanders. As we shall see shortly, the Israelite army that emerged from Sinai and later from Kadesh-Barnea was very different from the one that left Egypt.

Moses' new army

To this point I have argued that the Israelite *habiru* who left Egypt and made their way to Mount Sinai possessed a military arm of some type that they employed in self-defence, as brigands, or as mercenaries in the service of Egyptian kings. While it was possible to offer some reasonable assumptions about the weapons and tactics employed by this force, the text of Exodus tells us nothing about its size, organization, or structure. All this changes after the Israelites arrive at Mount Sinai and encamp there. Much of this time was spent putting their religious and military houses in order. Part of the effort was to create an organized army. Numbers 1:2–4 tells us that Moses

> took the sum of the congregation of the children of Israel,
> after their families, by the house of their father, with the

number of their names, every male by their polls; from
20 years old and upward, all that are able to go forth
to war in Israel; thou and Aaron shall number them by
their armies. And with you there shall be a man of every
tribe; everyone head of the house of their fathers.

Until now, the Israelite community's military arm was comprised
of professional warriors in a manner similar to David's band of
600 *habiru* fighters in the service of the Philistine king. These
soldiers were not drawn from any tribal or family levy applicable
to the entire community. They were military professionals, like
the warriors of the *Iliad*, and not conscripts.

At Sinai, Moses completely reformed the Israelite military arm,
for the first time introducing a tribal and lineage levy from which
conscripts were to be drawn. The new system surely integrated
the professionals within it as well, selecting the best as troop
commanders. The old professional corps lived on in Israelite
memory, however. Deuteronomy 2:14 recalls that prior to the
assault on the Transjordan thirty-eight years after the Exodus,
'the whole generation of soldiers had perished from the camp',
no doubt a reference to the professional warriors who had led
and protected the Israelites in the days before the tribal militia.
While we have no idea as to the size of the Israelite military
arm prior to its reconstitution at Sinai, it is certain that the new
arrangement increased the size of the army considerably by
making the manpower of the entire community available for
military service for the first time. It was at Sinai that the modern
Israeli Defence Force finds the first evidence of its existence as a
citizen army in which all eligible males of the community must
serve.

The census ordered by Moses to serve as the basis for conscription
presents problems for the military historian in that the numbers of
men eligible for service listed by tribe comes to 605,550, suspiciously
close to the 600,000 Israelites that supposedly comprised the original
Exodus population. The second census as recorded in Numbers 26
arrives at a figure of 601,730. Both estimates are clearly not possible,

even though they may have been for Egypt with its population of almost 10,000,000. Both estimates are calculated in the text by examining the census lists that record what appears to be the number of men available from each tribe multiplied by the number of units, each of which is assumed to mean a unit of 1,000 men strong, or an *eleph*.[124] The confusion and numerical inflation results from the use of the term *eleph* to mean 1,000 men. It later came to mean exactly that during the time of the monarchy, when there were indeed military units of 1,000 men called *alaphim*. The authors of Numbers were writing during or shortly after the time of the monarchy and were familiar with the monarchy's military system and its 1,000-man units. When they reconstructed the census lists in Numbers 1 and 26, they used *eleph* to mean 1,000, thus multiplying the number of units by that number and producing extraordinarily high numbers.[125]

Mendenhall argues that the numbers listed in the Exodus census texts are accurate, but miscalculated. While the term *eleph* surely meant 1,000 during monarchical times, in Exodus times it did not. An *eleph* as understood by the Exodus census-takers did not mean a military or tactical unit of 1,000 men, but a population unit or subsection of the tribe. The *eleph* was a social unit from which a certain number of fighting men were to be drawn to make up the total number of soldiers required from each tribe.[126] Read this way, the census lists can be adjusted to appear as they do in the table below.

If the number of *alaphim* are divided into the total number of men to be levied from each tribe, one arrives at the total strength of the Israelite army in Sinai as being between 5,000 and 5,500.[127] This number tallies well with our knowledge of the size of other military forces of the period. The city of Mari, for example, could raise 4,000 troops, while Shamsi-Adad of Assyria put ten thousand men in the field, and the kingdom of Eshnunna 6,000 men.[128] It must be kept in mind that prior to the Iron Age, the major limitation on the size of armies was not usually available manpower, but the expense of equipment, especially bronze weapons and chariots, that were incredibly costly.[129] The use of the *eleph* for calculating

Figure 3. Recalulated Size of Israelite Units (elef) by Tribe and Estimate of Size of Israelite Army (Numbers: 1 and 26)

Tribe	Numbers 1		Numbers 26		I Chron 12	
	Units	Men	Units	Men	Units	Men
Reuben	46	500	43	750	(40)	xxx
Simeon	59	300	22	200	7	100
Gad	45	650	40	500	(40)	xxx
Judah	74	600	76	500	6	800
Issachar	54	400	64	300		200 rd'fim and their men
Zebulun	57	400	60	500	50	xxx
Ephraim	40	500	32	500	20	800
Manasseh (Half-tribe)	32	200	52	700	18 (40)	xxx xxx
Benjamin	35	400	45	600	3	xxx
Dan	62	700	64	400	28	600
Asher	41	500	53	400	40	xxx
Naphtali	53	400	45	400	37	1000 šārīmn
TOTALS	598	5550	596	5750	329	2300

Source: George E. Mendenhall, "The Census Lists of Numbers 1 an 26" *Journal of Biblical Literature* 77 (1958): 52-66.

military recruitment as well as Moses' division of the people for judicial purposes into units of thousands, hundreds, fifties, and tens point to a major conclusion: the basis for Israelite political/ military organization was not lineage, but territorial organization. Lineage was of lesser importance, since the social organization of early Israel was based on territorial divisions, as was the military draft.[130]

The revised census figures permit an estimate as to the size of the overall Israelite community at Sinai. Israelite men became eligible for military service at age 20, the same age for military service in Egypt.[131] We do not know until what age soldiers remained in service, but with the average age of death around 40 years, it was unlikely that one could get more than ten good years, perhaps fifteen at the extreme, out of a soldier. If the 5,000 or so calculated by the census in Numbers are taken to represent between 20 per cent of the population of the entire community, then the size of the Israelite community that arrived a Sinai was about 25,000 people, far less than the 600,000 mentioned in the texts.[132] The larger figure may be safely excluded on the grounds that the logistics of supporting such a large number of people on the march stagger the imagination.

Even the smaller number of 25,000 people presents one with difficult, although not impossible, logistical problems in keeping the Israelites alive on their march through Sinai. The logistical tables of modern armies calculate that in the climate of the Middle East a soldier requires 3,402 calories a day and 70 grams of protein to sustain him in *minimal* nutritional condition. The standard military ration of the ancient world of three pounds of wheat per person per day provided only 2,025 calories per day, insufficient to maintain even minimal nutritional requirements for very long.[133] Normal water requirements are 5 quarts of water per day, but under desert climatic conditions both the United States Army and the Israeli Defence Force plan for 9 quarts a day as a minimal requirement.[134] Oxen and cattle need to be fed and watered as well. A cow requires 8.3 kg of fodder a day and 9 litres of water.[135] Calculated as a daily logistical burden, then, the Israelite logistical officers would have had to provide 60,000 pounds of wheat, 1400 kg or 3,080 pounds of protein (usually meat), and 140,000 quarts of water a day just to keep 25,000 people alive. The animals would have to graze where they could and, eventually, die or be slaughtered for food.

The Exodus text mentions severe shortages of food and water, implying that the Israelites must have eaten whatever animals they took with them out of Egypt. Even large herds of cattle, sheep, and goats would have been quickly exhausted with limited pasturage and water to keep the animals alive. With no supply train, nor anyone from whom to purchase supplies along the route, whatever grain supplies the Israelites carried with them would have been quickly consumed. The biblical tradition itself notes that a whole generation of the original population died in the wilderness, suggesting high losses to thirst and starvation. In addition, the text records several outbreaks of disease in which thousands die each time.[136] Several additional thousands were killed in Moses' various purges. Under these harsh conditions, a loss rate of more than 50 per cent is not unimaginable over, say, two years. If the Israelites at Sinai numbered somewhere around 25,000 people, it is possible that the group that left Egypt numbered somewhere around the 100,000 that Manetho records. Given that the death rate on the march would have been highest among the old and weakest, most of those who survived the trek would have been of an age where they could reproduce another generation at a higher fertility rate than usual. Within the forty years recorded by the biblical tradition, the Israelites could have mostly regained their population strength.

It is likely that it was the skirmish at Rephidim that brought the question of reorganizing the Israelite military arm to Moses' attention. He had already decided to make Joshua his second-in-command, but how might the other experienced officers be used to best advantage? The answer was to establish a quasi-military judicial system that guaranteed these officers important social positions and established ethical qualifications for appointment. So began the system of Judges that governed Israelite society for the next 200 years. Exodus 18:25–26 tells us that:

> Moses selected men of competence from all Israel and set them heads over the people – rulers of thousands, rulers of hundreds, rulers of fifties, and rulers of tens. And they would judge the people at any time; the difficult matters they would bring to Moses, and all small matters they would judge themselves.

This first Israelite judicial system has a decidedly quasi-military caste, one that may have as its first intention the organization of Israelite society along more structured military lines. The later period of the Judges reveals that all the *sopets* (judges) were military chiefs first and judicial officers second.

The way the Exodus text describes the offices of the system and the men who held them suggests that Moses may have imposed a quasi-military chain-of-command upon the judicial system by using military men as judicial officers.[137] The text uses the term *sar* for 'rulers' and *sophet* for 'judges', and always distinguishes between them. *Sar* is a term most commonly associated with appointed military command, and was used later to describe the appointed military commanders of Saul, David, and Solomon, while *sophet* connotes only a judicial officer. The text tells us that the appointees were 'rulers of thousands, rulers of hundreds, rulers of fifties, and rulers of tens', that is military commanders, who also 'judge the people at any time'.

There is additional evidence that the judges were military men. In describing the qualifications of the judges Exodus 18:21 says 'you shall seek out from among all the people men of competence who fear God, trustworthy men who spurn ill-gotten gain'. The term used for 'men of competence' is *Is hayil*, which commonly connotes a warrior or military commander as well as a rich man or citizen of social influence.[138] Taken along with the term *sar*, it is reasonable to suggest that Israel's first judicial officers were appointed because they were experienced military men of sound character. The linking of sound character to military command and judicial appointment provides us with the first clear statement in history of the importance of military ethics to leadership, a tradition found in the modern Israeli Defence Force's military ethical tradition of *tohar haneshek*.[139]

When the Israelites camped at Sinai, the outline of a new civil-military organizational structure was put in place so that further reforms could proceed. When Moses reorganized the military manpower system by extending military service to the entire Israelite community, the military-judicial structure devised previously provided a ready-made command and organizational structure through which the new manpower system could operate. This system persisted through Joshua's conquest of Canaan and the Period of the Judges, until Saul reformed it and, finally, David and Solomon replaced it.

The building of a national army in Sinai included a renewed stress on martial spirit and courage, qualities that needed to be instilled in the new conscripts. When Moses addressed the assembled people as recorded in Leviticus 26:36–37, he warned of the terrible punishments he would inflict upon them if they did not obey his rules. One of these punishments was that the Israelites would be known as cowards.

> Those of you who survive in the land of their enemies
> I will make so fainthearted that, if leaves rustle behind
> them, they will flee headlong, as if from the sword,
> though no one pursues them; stumbling over one another
> as if to escape a weapon, while no one is after them – so
> helpless will you be to take a stand against your foes!

This is a classic example of the 'death rather than dishonour' speech that has been given to new soldiers by commanders ever since armies first crawled upon the land. One can easily imagine it being given to a group of modern IDF soldiers who are about to begin their conscript military service.

Moses' actions at Sinai regarding his military reforms reveals a person who had an expert understanding of the human dimensions of war. One element of this human dimension is morale, and Deuteronomy 20:1–4 notes the moral strength that can clearly result from the soldier's faith in God. Be that as it may, troop commanders are very practical men, and it is clear that the Israelite officers also possessed a keen understanding of the psychology of war. In World War II, American divisions about to be sent into combat were repeatedly culled to remove potential psychiatric casualties from the ranks.[140] Israelite military commanders seem to have done the same thing. Deuteronomy 20:5–9 instructs troop commanders to remove certain kinds of people from the fighting ranks precisely because they were not likely to fight well.

> The officials shall address the troops as follows: 'Is there anyone who has built a new house but has not dedicated it? Let him go back to his home, lest he die in battle and another dedicate it. Is there anyone who has planted a vineyard but has never harvested it? Let him go back to his home, lest he die in battle and another harvest it. Is there anyone who has paid the bride-price for a wife, but who has not yet married her? Let him go back to his home, lest he die in battle and another marry her. The officials shall go on addressing the troops and say, 'Is there anyone afraid and disheartened? Let him go back to his home, lest the courage of his comrades flag like his.' When the officials have finished addressing the troops, army commanders shall assume command of the troops.

All of the conditions noted above are most likely to affect young men, the new conscripts called to war, and not the more seasoned military professionals that comprised the warriors of the old *habiru*. The new army of Israel was now a national army and had to deal with the same problems of morale, fighting spirit and psychiatric collapse that have afflicted conscript armies from time immemorial. In requiring troop commanders to examine their troops according to a list of conditions that could reduce troop morale and fighting spirit, the Israelites may have introduced the first practical method of military psychiatric screening.[141]

The practical bent of the Israelite commanders at Sinai is further evident in what appears to be the world's oldest manual on field hygiene, the instructions found in Leviticus and Deuteronomy. Disease and epidemic were the scourge of ancient armies, often causing more deaths and casualties than weapons.[142] The hygienic instructions contained in Leviticus and Deuteronomy make clear that Moses and his commanders were aware of disease and contagion, and prescribed a number of hygienic practices to keep the camp and the army from falling victim to disease. Some of the rules, such as those dealing with menstruating women or dietary restrictions, were based on religious requirements. But others have a strong pragmatic effect. The diagnosis and treatment of leprosy, rash or discharge (infection?) as detailed in Leviticus, for example, require that the afflicted soldier remain outside the camp for seven days to prevent contagion. Even on the march the soldier must remain outside the main column, making do as best he can. To treat or inspect the infected soldier the priest must go outside the camp, avoiding the risk of contagion if the soldier were to be brought to the priest. The Israelites also recognized that disease may also spread through objects like clothing, blankets, woven material and even saddles. All of these items had to be washed before the recovered soldier was permitted to rejoin the camp. The constant injunctions to wash one's hands before eating or after toileting and to wash one's clothes frequently are also excellent military hygienic practices.

Additional hygiene practices were more directly related to military life. Deuteronomy 23:13–14 required sanitary habits that were not practised by the European armies until World War I. 'Further, there shall be an area for you outside the camp, where you may relieve yourself.' Separating the latrine from the camp and, most importantly, from the water supply was frequently not done even during the American Civil War. But separation alone was not sufficient. 'With your gear you shall have a spike [probably a small shovel], and when you have squatted you shall dig a hole with it to cover up your excrement.' These two simple practices would have done much to reduce the rate and spread of disease in Israelite armies.

Numbers 31:19–24 outlines procedures for dealing with those killed in battle. Anyone who has killed a man in battle or touched a corpse must remain outside the camp for seven days. While the origin of the corpse taboo may be religious, its practical effect was to reduce contagion by quarantining soldiers who had been exposed to blood, a common disease source.[143] Ancient battles often involved close combat where blood might easily splatter on the soldier.[144] This concern is also reflected in the need to purify any weapons and clothing that have been exposed to blood. Metal weapons ('whatever can stand fire') were required to be purified by fire. Other equipment, including booty, had to be washed before it could be brought into the camp.

As a result of Moses' reorganization, the Israelite army that marched out of Sinai 'on the twentieth day of the second month of the second year' since leaving Egypt was a far cry from the original *habiru* force. Nowhere is this more clearly revealed than in the Israelite order of march employed in the departure from Sinai. It is only after the Sinai encampment that the Exodus texts reveal an order of march or military organization. In Numbers 10:11–28, we see clearly the combat organization of the new Israelite national army. Figure 4 portrays the Israelite order of march.

The column is divided into four divisions, each led by a tribal levy and containing two additional tribal levies within it. Between the Judah Division and the Reuben Division are the clans of Gershon and Merari transporting the dismantled meeting tent, while the clan of Kohath carries the sacred objects for the dwelling, presumably the Ark of the Covenant as well, behind the Reuben Division. One is immediately struck by the fact that the division of the column into four sections, each divided into three sub-divisions, is the same general order of march found in the Egyptian army of the day.[145] When it is recalled that the military structure with which the Israelites were most familiar was the army of Egypt, it is not beyond reason that the Israelites might have adopted the Egyptian column of march order for their new army.

The combat arms order of the column can also be reconstructed by extrapolation from the military specialties attributed to each tribe in various places in the Bible. That tribes developed combat specialities seems probable. The Beni-Hasan mural dating from the 19th century BC depicts a semitic clan entering Egypt and being recorded by Pharaoh's officials. The mural depicts the full panoply

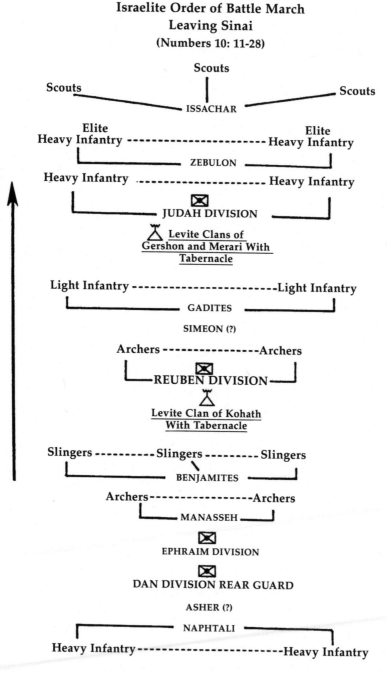

Figure 4. The Israelite Army at Sinai

of tribal arms: spear, sword, and bow. The metal smith's bellows strapped to the donkey suggest that the tribe had its own craftsmen and armourers.[146] Chaim Herzog and Mordechai Gichon in their *Battles of the Bible* suggest that the development of military specialities during and after the Exodus is almost certain.[147] Moreover, the Israelite experience as mercenaries in the armies of Egypt would also have acquainted them with the full range of Egyptian weapons. Military specialization, therefore, is not out of the question.

However, since the tribal basis of Israelite military organization was not instituted until the Sinai encampment, we may regard its further development as an Israelite innovation. A difficulty arises from the fact that the descriptions of tribal military specialities are not contained in the Exodus texts, but are found only in the later texts, making it somewhat uncertain as to whether these specialities existed during the Exodus as well. Given that so much of Israelite military structure and practice of the Exodus period survived well into the period of the monarchy, it is probably a reasonable assumption that the military capabilities of the different tribes did so as well. Still, we cannot be certain that this was the case.

The Israelite column that marched out of Sinai had the Judah Division at its head. Far to the front were the men of Issachar, whose special ability was 'to know how to interpret the signs of the times, to determine how Israel should act'.[148] These were the scouts who excelled at intelligence gathering and interpretation.[149] Behind them at the head of the column's main body were the men of Zebulon, elite heavy spear infantry who fought in phalanx, who 'were expert with all instruments of war...who could keep rank'.[150] Next in the column's van were the troops of Judah 'equipped with shield and spear' as regular heavy infantry protecting the disassembled tabernacle.[151] The tribes of Reuben, Gad and Simeon comprised the second division, an entire division of light troops capable of quick response in all directions. The Gadites were light infantry 'armed with spear and buckler...and were as swift as the gazelles upon the mountains'.[152] The troops of Simeon are mentioned only as 'valiant men', and were probably light infantry, as were the Reubenites, skilled with the bow.[153] The Ephraim Division was third in line and was comprised mostly of missile troops, archers (Manasseh) and archer/slingers, the Benjamites 'who gave support in battle; they were armed with the bow and could use both right and left hand to sling stones and shoot arrows with the bow'.[154] There is no description of the combat capability of the Ephraimites. The Dan Division made up the column's rearguard. Aside from knowing that the men of Asher were 'ready to man the battle line' (light or heavy infantry), there is no military capability given for Asher and Dan. The last place in the column was occupied by the men of Naphtali armed 'with shield and lance', that is, heavy infantry.[155]

It will not escape students of ancient armies that the distribution of combat capabilities by unit throughout the column, with the exception of chariots, is very similar to the combat order of march employed by the Egyptian army.[156] In a movement to contact, the Egyptian army deployed chariot scouts far forward of the main column. Next came the elite heavy infantry, the *nakhtu-aa*, literally 'the strong arm boys'.[157] As the column approached the enemy, light infantry and archers deployed through the front ranks and engaged at a distance with the bow. As the enemy closed, the light forces withdrew behind the heavy units or retired to the flanks to continue indirect or enfilade fire.[158] As with the Israelites, the Egyptian arm of decision, the fame of its excellent chariot corps notwithstanding, was its infantry. Once again, the Israelite experience in Pharaoh's army might have made itself evident in the design of the Israelite column of march at Sinai.

The encampment at Sinai was a momentous event in the history of the Israelites, for it was there, under Moses' command, that the Israelites formed a national army to replace the mercenary corps of the old *habiru* society. Israel was becoming a nation, and it instituted its first tribal levy to raise sufficient manpower for war, producing an army of 5–6,000 men. At Sinai, Moses instituted the first formal command structure, quasi-judicial in nature, staffed by officers who met strict ethical standards, and giving the world its first lesson in military ethics. Ceremonies were instituted to instill martial spirit in sometimes reluctant conscripts, as were regulations governing troop selection on psychiatric grounds, and camp hygiene. The Israelite army established a combat formation that permitted it to protect itself as it moved from one place to another. The previous Israelite experience as Egyptian mercenaries seems to have been reflected in some of these reforms, although to what extent is uncertain. Two additional Israelite military innovations, however, are almost certainly to have been influenced by their Egyptian experience: Moses' praetorian guard and the Desert Tabernacle.

Moses' Praetorian Guard

Moses' creation of a praetorian guard to protect him from the anger of the Israelites and their attempts to remove him raises the question of where he obtained the idea of a personal bodyguard to enforce his will on the often recalcitrant Israelites. Among the *habiru*, no such institution existed. The *habiru* military arm was small, ultimately democratic insofar as position depended on demonstrated military competence, and had no territorial or institutional base. After Sinai, however, Israelite society changed into a genuine tribal society with a semi-permanent military establishment supported by a quasi-judicial organizational structure around which to raise and organize a national army. Under these changed conditions, a praetorian guard might have appeared necessary, especially so if Moses anticipated resistance to the new institution of military conscription.

Elite military units serving as personal bodyguards to the kings of the Middle East were permanent elements of the military establishments of the major powers of the day. They were known in Egypt and elsewhere as 'troops of the feet', and were charged with protecting the king's person on and off the battlefield. If Moses had been raised in Pharaoh's court as the Bible suggests, he would have been familiar with the idea of a praetorian guard. It is also possible that some Israelite *habiru* may once have served in Pharaoh Akhenaten's personal guard.[159]

Moses recruited his bodyguard from among his own clansmen of the tribe of Levi. The Levites were singled out by Moses for special status in the Exodus texts. Unlike other tribes, the Levites were exempt from military conscription and were given no territorial status with lands of their own. The three Levite clans – Gershon, Kohath, and Merari – were given the task of guarding, dismantling, assembling, transporting, and attending the Desert Tabernacle, Moses' command tent where he communed with Yahweh. Numbers 3:12 makes it clear that the Levites were a clan apart, in service only to Moses and Yahweh: 'I hereby take the Levites from among the Israelites in place of all the first-born, the first issue of the womb among the Israelites: The Levites, therefore, are mine.'

Like true praetorians, the loyalty of Moses' bodyguard extended even to the use of violence against their kinsmen. That the Levites would do violence against their kinsmen is clear enough from the incident recorded in Exodus 32:26–29. The people had created a golden calf while Moses was away atop Mount Sinai. Upon his return, he saw the Israelites worshipping the idol and flew into a rage. Fearing that the

> people were out of control...Moses stood up in the gate of the camp and said, 'Whoever is for the Lord, come here!' And all the Levites rallied to him. He said to them... 'Each of you put sword on thigh, go back and forth from gate to gate throughout the camp, and slay brother, neighbour, and kin.' The Levites did as Moses had bidden; and some three thousand of the people fell that day.

Then, as if to assuage the conscience of the Levites who had just slaughtered their kinsmen, Moses made them swear an oath of loyalty to him. Moses said, 'Dedicate yourselves to the Lord – for each of you has been against son and brother – that He may bestow a blessing upon you today.'[160] Moses would use his praetorian guard again and again to do violence against Israelites, Moabites, and even his Midian relatives. Like all autocrats, once in power Moses created the mechanisms to remain in power.

It is interesting that Moses' praetorian guard did not survive him, perhaps because of other incidents like the one that took place at the foot of Mount Sinai. We hear of the Levites as armed police in four additional instances, but never again after Moses dies. Once Joshua assumes command of the Israelite army, the Levites are heard of only as religious guardians of the Ark, suggesting that they were disarmed and relegated to religious functions. There is nothing resembling a special military unit or palace guard again until the time of Saul and David. Perhaps the Israelite experience with the institution was unpleasant, as its activities under Moses' command strongly suggest. The Israelite praetorian guard formed at Sinai apparently did not survive the death of the man who created it.

The Command Tent

Exodus 25:8–9 tells us that Moses ordered the construction of a tabernacle where Yahweh could live, and Exodus 26–27 and 36–38 set forth in great detail how and from what materials the tent is to be made. This Tabernacle is described in more detail than any other structure in the Bible, including the Jerusalem Temple.[161] What is of great interest is that the Tabernacle is nearly an exact copy of the Egyptian war tent portrayed in the reliefs of the war camp of Ramses II at the Battle of Kadesh on the wall of the Great Hall at Abu Simbel.[162] This observation was first made by the famous Old Testament scholar Hugo Gressmann in 1913.[163] The parallels between the two camps are very strong and the similarity in dimensions and layout are striking. Ramses' camp forms a rectangular courtyard twice as long as it is wide, just as the Tabernacle is rectangular in shape and is one hundred cubits long and fifty cubits wide, the same ratio.[164] Ramses' camp is oriented east to west, with the entrance in the eastern wall just as in the Tabernacle. The orientation to the east is distinctly Egyptian in that the east is where the sun rises and where each day Pharaoh greets his father, the sun god. This greeting was expressed in the saying 'waking in life in the tent of Pharaoh'.[165] All Egyptian monumental architecture is oriented toward the east, and it is probable that the Jewish religious ritual of praying while facing east at the start of a new day or the ancient Christian practice of burying a corpse with its head to the east to greet the sun on resurrection day may have Egyptian origins as well.

The entrance to both Ramses' compound and the Tabernacle is in the middle of the eastern wall with a path leading to the 'reception tent' located in the middle of the walled-off compound. Pharaoh's tent is twice as long as it is wide, preserving the same ratio as the compound's outer walls. The 'reception tent' of the Tabernacle is also twice as long as its width, preserving the same ratio. In both cases the reception tent leads to a holy of holies that is square, not rectangular like the reception tent.[166] The sides of each square are equal to the width of the reception tent in both cases. Figure 4 portrays the layout and relative dimensions of each

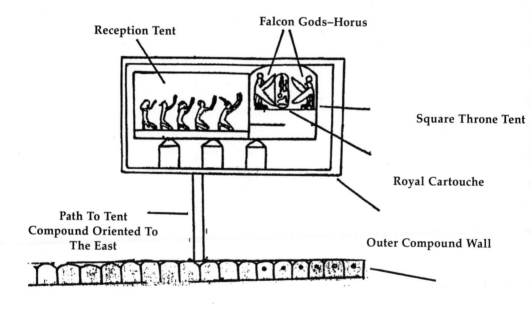

Figure 5. Abu Simbel Relief Portraying Ramses II's War Tent at the Battle of Kadesh

structure. In the Egyptian camp the square tent holds Pharaoh's golden throne, and it is from here that he holds his meetings with his generals or other important persons. The square tent of the Tabernacle is where the Ark of the Covenant is kept, and where Yahweh sits when he communicates with the Israelites.

What is equally impressive is the strong similarity of the interiors of both square tents, their respective holy of holies. The relief at Abu Simbel (Figure 5), shows Ramses' cartouche, the Egyptian symbol of the presence of the god that Ramses was regarded to be, flanked on either side by a representation of the falcon god, Horus. The wings of Horus cover Pharaoh's golden throne in a symbol of divine protection, similar to the description of the wings of the two cherubim that cover and protect Yahweh's golden throne in the Tabernacle. Exodus 25:18–22 describes it this way:

> Make two cherubim of gold – make them of hammered work – at the two ends of the cover [of the Ark of the Covenant] ... The cherubim shall have their wings spread out above, shielding the cover with their wings. They shall confront each other, the faces of the cherubim being turned toward the cover... There I will meet with you, and I will impart to you – from above the cover, from between the cherubim that are on top of the Ark of the Covenant – all that I will command you concerning the Israelite people.

It would appear that the holy of holies of Pharaoh and Yahweh are similar not only in design, but in function. For both, it is the place where God speaks to his people.

The strong similarity between the exterior and interior arrangements of the Desert Tabernacle and Ramses II's war tent is puzzling. Some scholars have suggested that the descriptions were taken from portrayals of Babylonian camps encountered by Israelite writers during the Babylonian Captivity. Recent archeological research has ruled this out, however, since evidence shows that Babylonian military camps were round or oblong, not rectangular.[167] But the dilemma remains only if the Israelites in Egypt are regarded as slaves, for as slaves they would have had no opportunity to examine or experience an Egyptian military camp. If the Israelite *habiru* were mercenaries in Pharaoh's army, then surely their officers would have been familiar with an Egyptian military camp. If so, when the Israelites first organized their national army at Sinai, Moses may have decided that it was time for him to have an appropriate command van as well, and ordered that one be constructed along the lines of the only model with which he was familiar, the Egyptian command tent.

Not only does the physical configuration of the Tabernacle conform to the Egyptian command tent, 'but it is also likely that Yahweh's portable tent originally had a military function similar to that of Ramses' camp'.[168] Egyptian and Israelite texts describe Yahweh and Pharaoh in similar terms, as divine warriors and field commanders. Exodus 15:3 refers to Yahweh as 'a man of war' and again as one 'who fights single-handedly for Israel'.[169] The identification of a divine pharaoh with military command is a common Egyptian artistic portrayal and literary theme, so that both Pharaoh and Yahweh are often portrayed as divine warriors. Like Pharaoh's war tent, the Tabernacle may have been regarded as a mobile military headquarters from which Yahweh, travelling with the Israelites, led his people to victory in Canaan.

This explanation solves only part of the puzzle. Service in Pharaoh's army by Israelite mercenaries would have made it possible for them to see his command tent and compound, but only from the outside. The similarities of Yahweh's and Pharaoh's inner chamber are too detailed not to have been designed by someone who had gained entrance to Pharaoh's inner sanctum. How would this have been possible? The answer may lie in the earlier speculation that some Israelite units may have served in a pharaoh's, perhaps Akhenaten's, praetorian guard, just as the Egyptian reliefs of Semitic special units at Akhetaten strongly suggest. The *habiru* praetorian guard would have protected the king's person around the clock and would have been familiar with the inside of Pharaoh's command tent where at least some of their guard stations would have been located. Or, having been raised in Pharaoh's court, Moses might have had opportunity to become familiar with the war tent. It may also help explain why Moses ordered the creation of his own praetorian guard.

From Kadesh to Canaan

Having spent much of their time at Sinai reorganizing, replenishing and training their new national army, the Israelites set out 'in the second year, on the 20th day of the second month' to return to Canaan prepared to fight their way in if necessary.[170] After a few day's march, they camped in the desert of Paran. In sound military fashion Moses prepared for the invasion by ordering a thorough reconnaissance of the objective. He assembled a task force of twelve men, one from each tribe, and placed Joshua in command. Moses instructed them to

> go up there into the Negeb and on into the hill country and see what kind of country it is. Are the people who dwell in it strong or weak, few or many? Is the country in which they dwell good or bad? Are the towns they lie in open or fortified? Is the soil rich or poor? Is it wooded or not? And take pains to bring back some of the fruit of the land.[171]

This is one of the earliest examples in military history of an intelligence brief listing all the important operational requirements of the enemy force about which one must have knowledge prior to battle. Moses ordered the reconnaissance task force to return within forty days. In the meantime, Moses moved the main body of the Israelites up to Kadesh-Barnea, where he planned to rendezvous with the task force upon its return from Canaan.

The news from the reconnaissance team was not good. The scouts reported a land of difficult terrain, inhabited by a fierce and strong people with large armies and fortified cities. The three main avenues of advance were blocked by powerful enemy armies and fortifications.[172] All of the scouts concurred in the report except Joshua and Caleb, who argued that bold action (and faith in God) could carry the day. Here we see the first hints of the self-confidence, courage, daring and risk that characterized the tactics of Joshua's later campaigns. Napoleon observed that the commander's instinct was the same as that of a professional gambler. Joshua was willing to risk it all in one bold campaign for Canaan. But Joshua was not yet in command. Moses concluded that the Israelite army was not yet ready for a full-scale campaign against the more militarily sophisticated Canaanite armies. If the earlier analysis concerning the loss rates the Israelites may have suffered on the march to Sinai is correct, it is probable that the Israelite army was still too small when compared to its adversaries in Canaan and, perhaps, comparatively under-equipped. There would be no attack on Canaan

Kadesh-Barnea was not a single place, but refers to the entire area of level valleys lying south of Canaan between Akaba and Beersheba. It is located some forty miles south-south west of Beersheba, and is the largest oasis in the Sinai. The area is several miles across, fifteen miles long, and encompasses sixty square miles in area. It is about a hundred miles from the border of Egypt.[173] Even today the area has sufficient water to nurture the soil which is several feet deep, and still provides the Arabs who till the land with rich harvests of grain when rainfall is sufficient.[174] The resources at Kadesh were sufficient to support our earlier estimate of an Israelite population of 20–25,000, but could not support the larger populations cited in the biblical text. And so the Israelites remained at Kadesh-Barnea for a long time, perhaps long enough for a new generation to reach military age and increase the size of the army.

Deuteronomy 2:14 tells us that it was thirty-eight years later when the Israelite army left Kadesh-Barnea, crossed the Wadi Zered, and entered the Transjordan, taking the eastern route toward Canaan. We are not told why the Israelites left Kadesh when they did. One possible reason is that the population had grown too large for the Kadesh's resources to sustain.[175] Apparently, the Canaanite forces encountered earlier remained sufficiently formidable to convince Moses to seek another route. The eastern route also had its risks and took the Israelites through hostile territory.

Moses' strategic goal was to reach Canaan. To accomplish this, Moses decided to fight only when he had to, employing negotiation when he could and taking circuitous routes of march to avoid battle. In attempting passage through Edom and Arad, the Israelite route was blocked by hostile armies. Except for what appear to have been minor skirmishes, Moses refused to offer battle, choosing instead to march around the two lands. In Moab he again adjusted his route of march to avoid battle.

But once Moses and the Israelites had crossed the Arnon River, the boundary between Moab and the land of the Ammonites, there was no avoiding a battle. With Moab to their rear, the harsh desert to their right and the Dead Sea blocking manoeuvre to the left, there was no choice but to fight. Moreover, the land of Ammon was the strategic platform from which Moses intended to launch the Israelite invasion of Canaan itself. The two armies met at Jahaz on the edge of the desert, and here the new Israelite army gained its first major triumph of arms. The Ammonite army was completely destroyed. As often happened in antiquity, the defeat of an opponent's army left the rest of the country open to conquest and occupation. The Israelites overran the entire area from the Arnon River in the south to the Jabbok River in the north, and east as far as the border with Canaan.

The Israelite army revealed an important new military capability during the Ammonite campaign. Not all of the towns surrendered without a fight and some of them had to be taken by storm. Deuteronomy 2:36 tells us of the Israelite storming of these towns: 'no city was too well fortified for us to whom the Lord had delivered them'. The text also distinguishes clearly between fortified towns and *bat*, 'daughter' towns, the smaller unfortified villages and settlements around them. The same distinction between fortified and unfortified settlements is found in Numbers 33:41 when describing the campaign in Gilead where 'we campaigned against the tent villages'. After their victory and occupation of Ammon, the Israelites attacked the kingdom of Gilead to the north. Once again we find the Israelite army subduing fortified towns. Deuteronomy 3:3–5 describes the victory over King Og at Edrei:

> We defeated him so completely that we left him no survivor. At that time we captured all his cities, none of them eluding our grasp, the whole region of Argob, the kingdom of Og in Bashan: sixty cities in all, to say nothing of the great number of unwalled towns. All the cities were fortified with high walls and gates and bars.

The textual evidence suggests that the Israelite commanders knew well enough the distinction between genuine fortifications, 'tent villages' and unfortified towns, and had developed the operational capability to subdue them all. Lacking any evidence of a siege capability, the Israelites must have taken these strong points by storm.

What evidence there is concerning the military capabilities of the armies of Moab, Edom, Ammon and Gilead suggests that the Israelite account of the battles is fundamentally accurate. It is likely that the old Canaanite cities of these areas had given way, sometime after 1300 BC, to the rise of what Gottwald calls 'national states', by which he means a conglomeration of peoples – Moabites, Ammonites, Edomites, etc. – much like the Israelites who moved into the area and, in the manner of the later Philistines, imposed their rule upon the Canaanites.[176] These kingdoms developed monarchies early on and had a strong central political organization. Much of the population lived in towns, some of them fortified.[177] The fortifications were probably originally built by Canaanites along traditional lines, which means that they were very substantial indeed. Their military organization was based upon a small standing army (like the later Philistines) imposed upon a tribal or lineage levy.[178] The armies were primarily infantry, although there is a letter showing that on one occasion an Ammonite king hired chariots from Mesopotamia. Since there is no mention of chariots in the biblical text, we may safely assume that the armies the Israelites defeated were infantry armies.

The textual and archaeological evidence suggests that Moses' new Israelite army that conquered the Transjordan had become a formidable fighting force. It fought well-organized and disciplined armies and defeated them all. At Jahaz, the terrain forced the battle to occur on an open plain. To fight in the open requires a highly disciplined army, one capable of maintaining formations and conducting tactical manoeuvre, directed by experienced commanders who could orchestrate the tactical employment of various types of units, heavy infantry, light infantry, archers and slingers. To have won at Jahaz, the Israelite army would have had to have been at least close to the size of its adversaries, otherwise it would have been suicide to stand in the open plain against an adversary that had greatly superior numbers. Given that we know the size of other armies of this period to be around 6–10,000 men, the earlier estimate of the Israelite army as having been between five and six thousand strong (before any increase at Kadesh-Barnea), might be generally correct. Finally, the Transjordan campaign provides the first evidence that the Israelite army was sufficiently powerful to carry a fortified town by storm.

It was by force of arms, then, that the Israelites captured the territory from the Arnon River to the foothills of Mount Hermon, comprising all the cities of the plateau and all of Gilead. While some Israelite elements remained in the north, the main body of Israelites settled in the plains of Moab, the lowlands to the northeast of the Dead Sea, between Jordan and the foothills below Mount Nebo. They remained there until another great general, Joshua, led them across the Jordan into Jericho in a military campaign that was to complete the return of the Israelites to Canaan.

It was a very different military force that crossed the Wadi Zered than had crossed the Reed Sea. As a consequence of considerable trial and experience, the military arm of the Israelite *habiru* had developed into a genuine national militia army. Its leadership had been transformed from a coterie of mercenaries into an officer corps drawn from among the people on the basis of competence and warrior spirit. Its military formations, hardly evident at all at the Reed Sea, had been transformed into those similar to those found in the army of Egypt. The same is probably true as to its mix of weaponry, although the sling never achieved the same importance in the army of Egypt as it did in the army of Israel.

All this seems to have been carried out under Moses' direction and command. That the Israelites and the authors and redactors of the Exodus texts came to regard such a great commander as somehow possessed of near-divinity is hardly surprising in light of the Egyptian belief that Pharaoh, their military commander, was also a god, a concept shared by other cultures and armies of the day. What is clear from the preceding analysis is that the Exodus texts reveal the beginning of an Israelite tradition of arms and, thus, a military history, evident before Joshua's campaign against Canaan began. And much of it is owed to Moses, the first great general of the Israelites.

The Death of Moses

There is very little historical information that can be extracted from the biblical texts regarding Moses' death. Moses died in the land of Moab, where the Israelites had settled and were preparing for the assault on Canaan. Moses was 'buried in the valley in the land of Moab over against Beth-por, and no man knoweth of his sepulchre unto this day'.[179] The biblical texts are absolutely clear that Moses was killed by Yahweh, who was still angry that Moses had brought water out of a rock at Meribah-kadesh by striking it with his rod instead of calling it forth with his voice as Yahweh had commanded. The story is clearly metaphorical, and has driven biblical scholars to distraction for decades.

What has disturbed biblical scholars and theologians alike is the central element of the metaphor: namely that Moses did not die a natural death, but was killed! A less metaphorical explanation might suggest that hardship and suffering, more than theological disputes or ritual offences, was what caused the many revolts and power struggles recorded in the biblical text. These events resulted in large scale killings of Israelites at Moses' command.

Moses may well have had cause to fear for his life. Moses complained to Yahweh on more than one occasion that the Israelites were trying to kill him, and not without good reason.[180] After returning from Sinai, Moses ordered the death of more than 3,000 Israelites for worshipping the idol. When Kohar led 'the princes of the congregation, the elect men of the assembly, men of renown' in a revolt challenging Moses' authority, Moses had all 250 of them killed.[181] At Shittim, Moses ordered the chieftains of the twelve Israelite tribes hanged for the offence of permitting their people to worship Baal. Taken together, there were hardly any members of the Israelite leadership left!

In addition, 'every one' of the Israelite men who had been fornicating with the 'daughters of Moab' was killed.[182] A plague struck the Israelites at the same time, killing 24,000 people. Moses' genocide against the Midianites so upset the military leadership that they refused to accept their share of the booty. Moses' actions may have created a climate of fear and anger in which no one, not even Joshua and the military commanders, any longer felt safe. Biblical tradition attributes the killing of Moses to Yahweh as punishment for what can only be described as a minor ritual offence. But it is at least conceivable that the casualties during the desert trek were so high, the suffering so great, and the dissatisfaction with Moses' brutal leadership so intense, that Moses may have been deposed, banished, or killed by the Israelites themselves.

Chapter 2

Buddha: The Soldier Pacifist

To understand Buddha's military life, one must first understand India, especially the martial context of the country's history and, specifically, the military history of the period during which Buddha lived. Because India is the birthplace of the pacifistic religion that Buddha founded, it is a common misconception, especially in the West, that India is and was historically a pacifistic and anti-militaristic state. Nothing could be further from the truth. From the collapse of the Harappa culture sometime early in the second millennium BC until modern times, Indian culture has been strongly characterized by frequent wars among rival domestic and foreign combatants. India possesses one of the most enduring military cultures in the world. Buddha was born and lived within the context of this military culture and his own military experiences strongly influenced the foundation and practice of the new religious movement he created.

Historical Background

Indian history in the ancient period began thousands of miles away from India itself, on the great steppe land that stretches from Poland to Central Asia. Around 2000 BC, this land was inhabited by a semi-pastoral, stock-breeding, warlike tribal people who, even at this early date, had tamed the horse and invented a chariot whose spoked wheels, light cart, and dual horse teams made the chariot far superior to the onager-drawn, solid-wheeled, wooden platform vehicles extant in Sumer during the same period.[1] Sometime in the early part of the second millennium, perhaps around 1700 BC, these Sanskrit-speaking people that history came to call Indo-Europeans or Aryans ('nobles' in Sanskrit), began to migrate westward, southward, and eastward probably under the pressure of desiccation of the land or overpopulation. Over several centuries, the Indo-Europeans moved into Europe proper, where they became the ancestors of modern European peoples, ie the Greeks, Romans, Balts, Celts and Germans. Map 2 shows the direction and ultimate European settlement of these peoples. Indo-European migrants also invaded Anatolia and the surrounding area, imposing themselves as a warrior aristocracy upon the natives. In Anatolia, the Aryan settlers became known to history as the Hittites. Further east, the Aryans settled among the Hurrians and became the Mitanni. Over several more centuries, Indo-European Aryan tribes moved further southeast, invading and settling Iran ('Iran' is a variant of 'Aryana', or 'land of the Aryans'), and what is now Afghanistan. Later, these Indo-European migrants settled in India.

Most of the population of India at this time was comprised of stone-age aboriginal peoples that the Aryans called *dasas*, referring to the dark colour of their skin. The word became the Aryan word for slave. The exception to the stone-age cultures was the relatively advanced Harappa culture of the Indus Valley, dating from circa 3000 BC. The Harappa civilization had been under pressure from the aboriginal peoples for more than a millennium and by the time of the Aryan invasions (circa 1500 BC) had been greatly weakened, and fell easily before the invaders. For the next five hundred years, beginning in the northwest of India, the Aryans spread throughout the Indian sub-continent, gradually displacing the original population and becoming the dominant culture. From this point forward, the culture of India was transformed into an Aryan culture, particularly in its warrior ethos and practices.

The Aryans were a Caucasian people, lighter skinned than the native Dravidians, and were physically taller, stronger and bigger boned. They were originally a pastoral people and counted their wealth in cows and horses. As stock breeders, their difference in

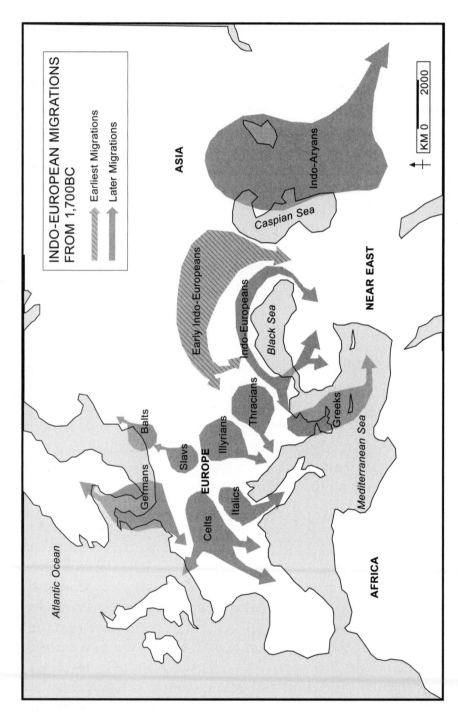

Map 2. Indo-European Migrations

body size, strength and endurance was probably the consequence of their diet of meat and milk in contrast to the Dravidian diet of mostly grains. The second century CE Roman historian, Tacitus, noted a similar physical difference between Romans and Gauls. Tacitus says the Gauls were 'eaters of meat and drinkers of milk', and were much taller (as much as 7 inches) and bigger-bodied than the Romans. The physical and racial characteristics of the Aryans are important in that these characteristics became the basis of the caste system around which the later Aryan society was organized.

The first images of Buddha reached the West in the eighteenth century. By then, however, Buddhism had spread throughout Asia, where Buddhist images had taken on the racial and ethnic characteristics of the different peoples of the region among whom the new religion had taken root. Indian portrayals often show Buddha as dark-skinned, for example, while those of other countries show him as oriental. In fact, Buddha was an Indo-Aryan Caucasian. Familiar Western portrayals of Buddha as doughy and overweight, an image intended to portray his passive character, are also misleading. The oldest texts describe him as at least six feet tall and of muscular build. One can obtain a more ethnically accurate image of Buddha by looking at a modern Afghan: tall, muscular, light-skinned, with dark hair and eyes, physical characteristics typical of the Indo-Aryan warriors from whom Buddha was descended. The Macedonian Greeks attributed these same traits to the Indo-Aryans they fought during Alexander's Indian campaign.[2]

Linguistic and genetic evidence suggests that the Aryan invaders swept over the Hindu Kush from Afghanistan into the Punjab in northern India during the Early Vedic Period (1500–900 BC).[3] Even today, upper-caste, lighter Indians can be distinguished from their lower-caste brethren by the presence of their Aryan genes.[4] The original Aryan invaders moved down the Indus River and eastward until blocked by the thick forest and jungle of the plain through which the Ganges River runs (the Gangetic Plain). The result was that most early Aryan settlements remained in the Punjab for several centuries. The discovery of iron from which weapons and

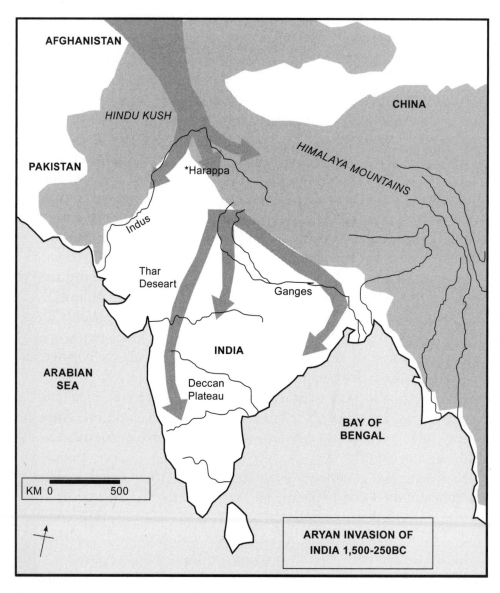

Map 3. Aryan Invasions and Settlement Routes

agricultural implements (the axe and iron plough) could be forged made it easier to clear the forests, with the result that in the Later Vedic Period (900–600 BC), the Aryan tribes began to push into the Gangetic Plain. To clear the thick jungle, they chopped down the vegetation and allowed it to dry. It was then set on fire to clear the underbrush and leave a coating of rich ash to fertilize the soil for planting. The Aryans thought these huge fires to clear the land were the gift of Agni, their fire god, and from earliest times the Aryans continued to worship a god of fire. The Aryan efforts to clear and occupy the land transformed the Gangetic Plain from a thick jungle into a fertile agricultural plain, well-watered by two rivers. It was here where rice was first cultivated in India.[5] The expansion into the Gangetic Plain and the introduction of iron agricultural implements allowed for the production of an agricultural surplus that gradually transformed the Aryans from a pastoral and quasi-nomadic people into one settled upon the land, living in towns and in clearly demarcated tribal territories. By the end of the 5th century BC, the population of India had grown to around fifty million.[6]

This period of war and conquest called the Epic Age (1200–700 BC) was the time of the *Rigveda*, the great collection of epic and heroic myths and tales chronicling the battles and settlement of the Aryans. The most famous of their epic poems is the *Mahabharata*. Composed as an oral poem like the *Iliad* and comprising 90,000 verses, the *Mahabharata* is the longest single poem in the world, and falls into the same category as the great Irish and Icelandic sagas telling the tale of a warrior people. The Aryans (also called Vedics) imposed their culture, gods, societal structure, martial values and military technique upon the original Indian population, completely transforming India into a martial culture.

Vedic-Aryan Society

Permanent settlement in a particular area eventually lent a geographical identity to a given tribe or group of tribes. This identity took concrete shape in the possession of the area occupied by the tribe. The area was usually named after the tribe and each tribe could trace its origins to some great warrior ancestor who founded it. The Vedic texts show these early tribal settlements, called *janas* meaning 'people' or 'tribe', living in a semi-nomadic state and fighting amongst themselves or with other tribes over land and animal herds. By the end of the Later Vedic Period, however, these tribes had coalesced into small territorial states called *janapadas* or 'footholds of the tribe'. The *janapadas* fell into two types: smaller ones comprised of a single tribe and larger ones comprised of a coalition of tribes. Smaller tribes tended to be ruled by a hereditary chief and are often referred to as 'republics' to distinguish them from the larger states ruled by monarchs. Buddha's tribe, the Sakyas, were a republic. All the *janapadas* were military states whose ruling elites were *kshatriya* or members of a professional warrior aristocracy and caste. In true Aryan warrior fashion, each *janapada* sought to conquer and dominate other *janapadas* to become a *mahajanapada* or 'a great realm', somewhat akin to the city-states of later Greece. The result of the unending struggle for power among the *mahajanapadas* was a period of constant war and slaughter that lasted for almost three centuries.

The Aryan-Vedic social order originally imposed upon the native Dravidians was tribal and ruled by a warrior aristocracy. Later, as the states grew larger and more complex, they developed a more sophisticated administrative and political structure under powerful monarchies, but retained their warrior aristocracies. The Vedic king was a warrior-chief whose skill at war and ancient bloodline provided legitimacy for his claim to rule. His first obligation was to protect the tribal kingdom (*rashtra*), so that preparation for and the conduct of war was a major characteristic of these states. At this early date, there was no concept of the king being divine, a belief that would develop over the next 500 years. The *rashtra* was comprised of tribes (*jana*), tribal units (*vish*), and villages (*grama*). The nucleus of the tribe was the family (*kula*) with the eldest male as its head (*kulapa*).[7] The warrior king was called the *raja*, a term closely related to the Latin *rex*. The king was assisted in governing by a council of elders (*sabha*) and other advisors like the *purohita* or chief priest and astrologer; the *senapati* or military commander (although it was the king who personally led the army into battle); and the charioteer, often the king's oldest military comrade who drove the king's chariot in battle.

Vedic society was originally divided into three classes: the military aristocracy, originally *rajanya*, but more commonly *kshatriya*; the priests or *brahmin*; and the more prosperous land owners and traders, the *vaishyas*. Later, native Indian agricultural cultivators and servile labourers, or *shudra*, comprised a fourth group. In Aryan belief, the duty of the *brahmin* was to study and teach, to sacrifice, to give and receive gifts. The Aryans cultivated the drug *soma*, which the *brahmin* priests used to enter an ecstatic trance wherein they heard the inspired Sanskrit texts known as the Vedas, the fundamental principles of the cosmos dictated by the gods.[8] It was the sacred duty of the *brahmin* priests to memorize and preserve these eternal truths to pass them to the next generation. The primary task of the *kshatriya* was to protect the people (the word means 'shield' or 'safe place'). The *kshatriya* constituted the military aristocracy responsible for the conduct of war and the staffing of government during times of peace. The warriors must also sacrifice and study but were required to learn only the first part of the sacred Vedas. The *vaishya*'s chief function was to till the earth, breed cattle, pursue trade and lend money; and the *sudra*'s duty was to serve the three higher classes.[9] These social classes were known collectively as *varnas*, the Sanskrit word for 'colours', a reference to the racial basis of each group's identity.

Early Aryan society showed no sign of the separateness of the caste system and all classes mixed with little difficulty. Presumably, some limited mobility was permitted within castes.[10] However, the Aryan conquerors erected early prohibitions against eating with and marrying the darker aboriginal peoples, most probably as a way of maintaining their status as rulers over the vast majority of indigenous peoples. The caste system became more rigid as time passed and became regarded as sacredly immutable. Any

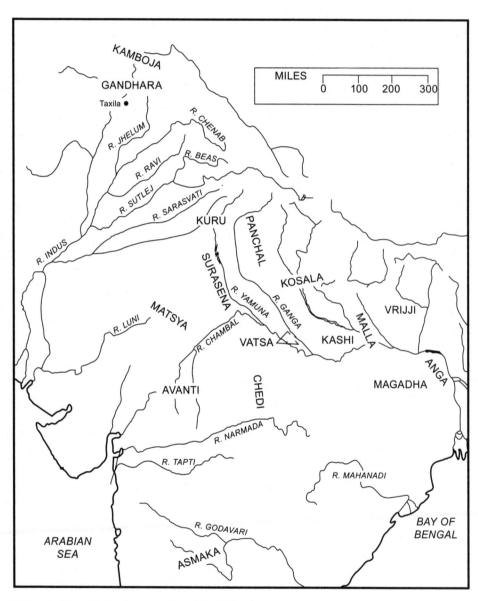

Map 4. The *Mahajanapadas*, 600 BC

upward mobility from one caste to another that might have once existed had long disappeared by the time Buddha was born. The earliest expressions of caste appear in the sacred Vedas, compiled sometime between 1500 and 1000 BC. Based on skin colour, these prohibitions gradually evolved into the Indian caste system still evident in modern India.[11]

The Vedic tribal social order lasted until circa 600 BC, when it gradually began to give way to larger, more stable societies of regional scope (*mahajanapadas*), even as it preserved its essential social and governing institutions within the new larger monarchies and republics. The Vedic social order persisted most strongly, however, in the few remaining *janapanda* republics, like the Sakyas from which Buddha came. By 600 BC, the many *janapandas* of northern India had coalesced into sixteen large states, all constantly at war with each other. Map 4 depicts these states and their locations relative to one another. The Aryan-Vedic martial tradition continued unabated, however.

Vedic Martial Tradition

As a consequence of the caste system and the occurrence of frequent wars, the warrior class was able to maintain its hold on power for the next millennium. The martial values of the Aryan-Vedics struck deep roots in Indian culture and persist into the modern era. War was not merely a means to an end but part of the warrior's *dharma* or his very reason for existing, and regarded as good for its own sake. Without war in which to demonstrate status and personal bravery, the Aryan *kshatriya* had no reason to live. In various texts, war is compared to a *yajna* or Vedic sacrifice and he who fights it enjoys the same benefits, ie the attainment of heaven.[12] In this sense, the Aryan *kshatriya* was akin to the Japanese *samurai*. In the Aryan tradition, war was the normal activity of the state, and as soon as a king gained power he was expected to begin to attack his neighbours. The king's primary task was always to prepare for and fight wars.

In the traditional Aryan view, war was essentially a large tournament fought for the honour and glory of the king and great warriors. A well-developed code of chivalrous conduct, unchanged from Vedic days, existed, even though it was mostly ignored once the states grew more complex and their armies larger. Nonetheless, cowardice in battle dishonoured the soldier and his lord, while bravery and fighting to the death were rewarded with immediate entry into heaven. A defeated king might even follow the ideal of *jauhar*, where the king, his family and closest advisors were burned to death in suicide in the innermost chambers of his great hall while his men fought to the end on the battlements.[13] The conduct of battle was governed by chivalrous ideals. A warrior fighting from a chariot could not strike at a soldier fighting on foot. A wounded soldier, one disarmed or who offered surrender could not be killed.[14] For the king the true reward of battle was honour, glory and the homage of the defeated king who, not surprisingly, immediately began plotting his revenge.[15]

This last point is important, for it explains much as to why the Vedic martial tradition persisted for as long as it did. In Aryan thinking there were three kinds of conquest: righteous conquest, conquest for greed and demonic conquest. The first, righteous conquest, involved defeating the rival king on the battlefield and then making him a vassal. Whatever booty was taken was minimal and the defeated king was permitted to continue to rule his own land as long as he paid homage to the superior king. Conquest for greed levied great burdens upon the defeated to provide money, materials or manpower to the victor. But once again the defeated king was permitted to remain in power and govern his state. The third type of conquest, demonic conquest, occurred when the enemy's lands were ravaged, the king deposed and his territory incorporated into the victor's realm, politically destroying the vanquished state.[16] From the time of the early Aryan-Vedics, the last two – greed and demonic conquest – were discouraged as being without moral standing as, one surmises, clearly befitted a warrior society wherein rival kings were members of the same aristocratic class and even ethnic identity, and often closely related by bonds of blood kinship. None of these limits, of course, applied in wars between Vedics and native Indians.

This system of warfare permitted the rival Aryan aristocracies to survive even military defeat and never wrought destruction of such a magnitude that would permit the destruction of the Vedic social order by the lower classes or indigenous peoples. As with the kings and aristocracies of absolutist Europe, who had more in common with one another than with the peoples they governed, war fought for glory was never permitted to destroy the system. For the system to change, both Europe and India would require someone whose martial values did not include a sense of societal limit, someone from outside the royal class and of low birth. In Europe this person was Napoleon. In India it was Chandragupta Maurya.

The martial tradition that encouraged warfare in early India prohibited warfare on such scale and of such scope that could effect a strategic decision that would permit a strong leader to unify the entire nation. Derived from the early conquests and cattle raids, the Vedic ideal of war was not unlike that found in the *Iliad*, with much the same results. Indian warfare finds its parallel in Greece, where the ideal of war as individual combatants seeking glory led to a social order (city-states) and military agency (citizen hoplites) that guaranteed constant warfare without ever permitting a strategic decision that would have allowed the social order to advance beyond tribal warfare. There was frequent war but no systemic change. It was Philip II of Macedon who eventually developed the military instrument to fight war on a scale that could effect a strategic decision. The result was the unification of Greece for the first time in its history and the emergence of a scale of warfare that could produce an empire. The same set of circumstances emerged in India and, interestingly, at about the same time as in Greece.

This type of limited warfare persisted until around 600 BC, when most of the smaller *janapandas* had been absorbed into the sixteen larger *mahajanapanda*s that quickly turned on one another in a two-centuries-long series of wars. These wars were fought with terrible ferocity that frequently aimed at the complete conquest and absorption of the enemy's territory, the enslavement of his population and even its extermination. In the war between Magadha and Kalinga, Osaka recorded that one hundred thousand people were killed, one hundred and fifty thousand captured, and 'many time that number wounded'.[17] The old Vedic limits on warfare were abandoned, replaced by a brutality and scope heretofore unknown in India, as the larger states brought larger populations, larger armies and more resources to their fight for survival or expansion. When the Magadhan emperor, Mahapadma Nanda, attacked a coalition of rival *janapandas* and tribes in mid-India, he exterminated all the *kshatriya* warriors of all the enemy armies and incorporated his enemies' territory into his realm. Nothing was ever heard of these states or tribes again. Buddha's people, the Sakyas, were also exterminated by the Kosalas, and nothing was ever heard of them again either.

Vedic Warfare

It is possible to obtain a sense of how Indian warfare changed by Buddha's time by examining the way it was conducted during the Vedic and post-Vedic periods. Our understanding of warfare in Vedic times is clouded by a lack of hard information. We are forced to deduce much of what we know from descriptions on a few reliefs and from the lines of the *Mahabharata* which, because it was written down long after the events portrayed in it, is not a reliable source. This aside, some approximation of the tribal warfare conducted by Aryan chiefs against the indigenous peoples and each other can be assembled.

As livestock herdsmen accustomed to gathering and driving their herds, the Aryans were superb horseman and charioteers. Although the horse was known to the Indus Harappa people, the animal was never employed as an instrument of war. The Aryan chariot provided such a great military advantage against a people barely out of the Stone Age that the newcomers must have quickly established their dominance on the plains of the Indus, driving the original peoples into the jungles and forests. The Aryan chariot was a light, two-man vehicle drawn by a two-horse team probably like the early Hurrian model of the same period. With its turning point forward of the wheels, it provided the vehicle with excellent stability and manoeuvrability. The chariot was used only by the warrior aristocracy, while the common members of the tribe (Aryan warfare was a tribal activity involving all social classes) fought on foot. The chariot warriors probably wore armour, perhaps leather jerkins or metal scale armour, but there is no evidence of the helmet until much later. The chariot warrior carried a lance, a short thrusting spear and javelin. The simple bamboo bow was used extensively in this period by foot soldiers, and may have been adopted from the local Indian model. When he used a bow, the chariot warrior most likely used the composite bow fashioned of animal horn.

Swords, axes, and slings were used by infantry as well. The early Aryans were a Bronze Age culture and were adept at fashioning bronze weapons. At the time of the Aryan invasion, the indigenous Dravidian peoples of India had only recently (the Harappa excepted) exited the Stone Age. Their only metal technology was copper. Iron did not make its appearance in India until around 1000 BC. We know little of Aryan tactics during this period, but on the plains at least it could not have been very much different from those of the Mitanni, whose tactics involved clashes of chariot-borne warriors in individual combats, as the rest of the scuffle raged around them, every man fighting for himself with no coordination with other combatants. At least this is the impression one receives from the epic literature of the time. Figure 6 depicts Ravana, the king of Ceylon and southern India, in full battle array, equipped with a fine selection of the weapons commonly employed by the Aryan tribes of the day.[19]

The chariot had originally been the spine of the Aryan armies. Over time, however, the chariot gave way to the war elephant and the warhorse as the primary mounts of the *kshatriya* warrior aristocracy. By the sixth century BC, armies contained cavalry contingents numbering in the thousands. In true Indo-Aryan fashion, the warhorse was held in almost mystical esteem, and the

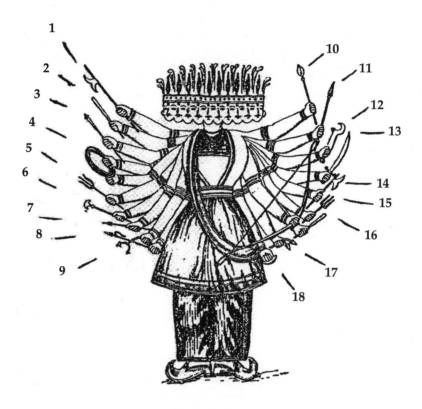

Figure 6. Ravana in Full Battle Array. (1) Dagger axe, (2) club, (3) mace, (4) lasso, (5) metal trident spear, (6) crescent axe, (7) cane arrow, (8) incendiary arrow, (9) unknown, (10) brownze leaf-point javelin, (11) iron-tipped spear, (12) sickle-sword, (13) sword, (14) battle-axe, (15) trident dagger, (16) club, (17) stimulum (?), (18) composite bow.

Rigveda endowed the animal with divinity. The chariot declined as a true implement of war probably circa 650 BC, although some Indian state armies seemed to have retained it, if only in small numbers, until the third century BC. The Chinese pilgrim, Hiuen Tsan, wrote of his travels in India in which he described the Indian army as having chariots. He noted that 'the army is composed of foot, horse, chariot, and elephant soldiers...The chariot in which an officer sits is drawn by four horses, whilst infantry guard it on both sides.[20]

This description is not of a war chariot but a field command vehicle in which the officer sits while guarded by infantry. During a later visit the same Chinese author wrote again of the Indian army, this time omitting completely any mention of the chariot, suggesting that the chariot as a fighting vehicle was fast disappearing from the ranks.[21] In 493 BC, during the sixteen-year war between Ajatashatru of Magadha and the Vrijis, two new weapons appeared for the first time on the Indian battlefield. One of these, the *mahashilakantaka*, was a large catapult for hurling heavy stone shot, and the other, the *rathamushala*, was a two-horse, spoked-wheel chariot with scythe blades attached to the hubs, designed to be driven through infantry formations.[22]

Both these weapons were likely the result of increased Persian influence as a consequence of Persian imperial incursions into the northwest of India. Barely fifty years earlier in 530 BC), Cyrus the Great, the Achaemenid emperor of Persia, had crossed the Hindu Kush and extracted tribute from the tribes of the northwest region, the prelude to a much larger incursion to come. Darius I added northwest India to the Achaemenid empire and Herodotus reports that Indian troops equipped with reed bows, cane arrows, iron-tipped spears and chariots, fought in the Persian army against the Greeks in the wars of 486–465 BC.[23] In any event, there is no further mention of these chariots in his narrative of these campaigns.

About a century and a half later, in the army of Chandragupta Maurya (321–297 BC), there is mention of cavalry, foot and elephants, but no chariots. At the Battle of the Hydaspes in 326 BC Porus put 4,000 cavalry and 200 war elephants in the field, along with his 30,000 foot, but deployed only 300 chariots, all of these the four-horse variety carrying six men each to transport infantry into battle.[24] As in the Near East, the chariot probably gave way to cavalry in India because of the greater ability of the horse to traverse and manoeuvre over difficult terrain. But there was another reason for replacing the chariot. One role of the chariot, especially against tribal or otherwise primitive armies, was to deliver shock. And nothing could quite deliver shock like an elephant.

As early as the eighth century BC, the elephant was mentioned in Indian literature as the *mrigahastin* or 'the beast with a hand', a description that suggests the animal was still a wild beast and not yet domesticated. It was probably not until the sixth century BC or so that the animal was tamed, and probably another fifty years before it made its appearance on the Indian battlefield. The first mention of the elephant as an instrument of war appears in the account of one Sung Yun, a Chinese traveller who visited the kingdom of the Hunas in the early 6th century BC. His report speaks of fighting elephants with swords fastened to their trunks that produced great carnage. But there is no other mention of this practice elsewhere. The report of another Chinese traveller noted earlier, Hiuen Tsan, of about the same time makes mention of

> war elephants covered with a coat of mail [probably scale armour], and his tusks are pointed with sharp barbs [*metal tips*]. On him rides the commander in chief who has a soldier on each side to manage the elephant.

By the end of the sixth century BC, the elephant had replaced the chariot as a major combat arm in Indian armies.[25] The Indian elephant was much larger than the African forest cousin used by the Seleucid Greeks and Carthaginian armies three centuries later. The Indian elephant is 10 to 11 feet high at the shoulders and carried tusks averaging more than 6 feet in length. They were trained and cared for with great reverence by their *mahouts* or handlers, who rode them into battle. Their great bulk made them an excellent instrument for shock and they were often employed in the van of the army, using their great strength to break enemy ranks or smash palisades, gates and other defences. They could even be employed next to one another in a line, like a living bridge over which troops walked to cross a stream or river. Elephants were often equipped with leather, textile, or scale armour to protect against arrows and pikes. They were usually employed with a basic combat load of the *mahout* and three other soldiers equipped with composite bows, javelins and a long spear to ward off any attackers.[26]

Like modern tanks, elephants in the Indian tactical scheme of things were rarely deployed alone and were usually accompanied by a small infantry contingent whose task it was to protect the animal from attack by enemy infantry. The animals were trained diligently for war. Porus' elephants at the battle of the Hydaspes retained their discipline in the face of massed Macedonian infantry advancing with long pikes pointed at the animals' eyes. Calmly, the animals retreated one step at a time, retaining formation and composure as they went. In other cases, however, they simply broke and ran, stampeding over everything in their way. No matter how great the number of instances where the animal panicked or otherwise proved useless, Indian commanders continued to place great faith in the war elephant, often to their regret. Centuries later, the Muslim rulers of India placed the same heavy reliance upon them only to be equally disappointed.

The Mauryan Empire (321–120 BC)

By the beginning of the fifth century BC, regional monarchies had become the dominant form of socio-political life in northern India. Far larger, richer, and more populated than any of the old tribal fiefdoms of the Vedic age, these states battled each other for predominance for more than 200 years. During Buddha's lifetime, four states – Magadha, Kashi, Kosala, and Vrijis – continually and violently struggled with one another for control of the Gangetic plain. These struggles witnessed the conquest and often total extermination of what was left of the smaller *janapanda* states, including the Sakyas. Around 550 BC, Bimbisara, king of Magadha, succeeded in bringing the small republic of Anga under his control. In 493 BC, seven years before Buddha's death, Bimbisara was murdered by his son, Ajatashatru, who assumed control of Magadha. In 493 BC, Ajatashatru attacked and conquered the Vrijis state. Ajatashatru died in 461 BC and was followed by five kings, all of whom gained the throne by parricide.[27] In 413 BC a usurper, Mahapadma Nanda, came to the Magadha throne and established a short-lived dynasty. In the space of fifty years, however, the Nandas proved themselves powerful and capable kings who expanded Magadha control and

Map 5. Indian States, 500 BC

made the first attempt at an Indian empire in the north in which all rivals were reduced to vassalage or annihilated. In 321 BC the Nandas were overthrown by another usurper, Chandragupta Maurya, who established the first and last genuine Indian empire of any significant size. It lasted less than two hundred years.

There is a legend concerning Chandragupta Maurya that as a young man he travelled to Taxila in the north where he met Alexander the Great, who had conquered the city and made it his base of operations for his invasion of India. As a result of this meeting, Chandragupta resolved to become a powerful prince. Seven years later, at the age of twenty-five, Chandragupta defeated the last Nanda king of Magadha and usurped the throne. A second legend has it that at his side was a powerful *brahmin*, Kautilya, who guided the young prince in matters of statecraft. Kautilya is supposedly the author of one of the most important works on statecraft produced in India, the *Arthasastra* or Treatise on Polity. Like a combination of Machiavelli's *The Prince* and Plato's *Republic*, the *Arthasastra* is both a theoretical and practical dissertation on how to organize a state and its army, and how to employ both successfully in foreign policy. It provides us with a good deal of our information on the political and military organization of the Mauryan imperial state.

Chandragupta moved quickly against the Greek governors and allies that Alexander left behind, reducing them by force of arms. He then extended his control to both the Indus and Ganges plains, and further northward into Afghanistan. His empire comprised the largest territory ever controlled by an Indian monarch. In 303 BC, the Seleucid Greeks under Seleucus Nikator attempted to invade India once again, but were rebuffed by Chandragupta's army in a series of battles, and eventually withdrew. In 297 BC, as legend has it, Chandragupta relinquished his throne, became a Jain monk and slowly starved himself to death. His son, Bindusara assumed the throne. Known to the Greeks as Amitrochates because of his title, *amitraghata* (destroyer of foes), Bindusara continued his father's policy of armed conquest, bringing all of the sub-continent under the Mauryan empire except for the Kalinga state on the east coast. Bindusara's son, Ashoka, came to the throne in 272 BC and immediately attacked Kalinga, bringing it within the imperial realm. The imperial idea had become a reality in India for the first time in its history. Ashoka ruled for thirty-seven years. After his death, decline set in almost immediately and by 180 BC the empire began to collapse.

Chandragupta governed a true monarchical imperial state. The king ruled with the help of a small body of elder statesmen, the *mantri-parisad*, that functioned as advisors. This privy council is said to have been as small as seven members or as large as thirty-seven, and included an inner core of very powerful advisors. These included the great councillor or *mantrin*, the *purohita* or chief priest, the treasurer or *sannidhatr*, the chief tax collector, *samahatr*, the minister of military affairs, *sandhivigrahika*, the *senapati* or chief military advisor or general, and the chief secretary or *mahaksapatalika*. Below this council the state was governed on a day-to-day basis through powerful individuals called superintendents, who oversaw various government departments. Although every effort was made by Chandragupta and his successors to select competent people to fill government positions, in a very short time these offices became virtually hereditary and, over time, the quality of government officials declined.[28]

The Indian imperial state never developed a permanent bureaucratic system staffed by officials selected for merit and competence. As a consequence, the administrative system of imperial India never rose above the competence expected of a group of the king's personal retainers. The military system itself was controlled by high ranking civilian superintendents who oversaw the operations of state armouries where all military equipment and weapons were manufactured, as well as supply depots, cavalry, elephants, chariots and infantry, including provisions, training and general combat readiness. According to Megasthenes, the Seleucid ambassador to Ashoka's court, the imperial army was run by a committee of thirty superintendents while each branch or department (infantry, cavalry, elephants, chariots, navy, commissariat, etc) was run by a committee of five men. It is likely that these committees reported directly to the chief military man, the *senapati*, who then reported to the king. It is interesting to note that despite the increased bureaucratization of the military under the Mauryas, the old martial ideals survived unchanged, and it was still the common practice for the kings themselves to take the field with the army, sometimes in the vanguard.[29]

The Mauryan Army

There were six types of troops in the Mauryan imperial army: the *kshatriya* or troops of the hereditary warrior class who formed the spine of the professional army; mercenaries and freebooters hired as individuals seeking military adventure; troops provided by corporations or guilds; troops supplied by subordinate allies; deserters from the enemy; and wild forest and hill tribesmen used in much the same manner as the French and British used Native American tribes in their wars in North America. The troops of the corporations are little understood and may have been units maintained by guilds to guard their caravan routes and trade stations. Similar units were later found in the armies of Medieval Europe. Or it might simply have been that certain occupations were required to provide troop levies in times of war, perhaps in much the same manner as certain occupations provided membership regiments to the European armies of World War I. The imperial armies, then, were not conscript armies. In Vedic times, war fighting had been the responsibility of all members of the tribe. But the development of the caste system prevented the various classes from associating even in war, thus removing the largest manpower pool, the lowest caste, from military service. By the time of the Mauryas, whatever sort of conscription had once existed earlier had disappeared and the large imperial armies were professional armies of warrior aristocrats and other professionals fed, equipped, trained, paid, and otherwise maintained at great cost to the state.

The Mauryan army was quite large. Classical sources (Pliny) state that the size of the army of the last Nanda king was 200,000 infantry, 20,000 cavalry, 2,000 chariots, and 3,000 elephants before it was overwhelmed by Chandragupta's force of 600,000 infantry, 30,000 cavalry, and 9,000 elephants.[30] When Alexander confronted Porus on the banks of the Hydaspes, he faced an army of 30,000 foot, 4,000 cavalry, 300 chariots, and 200 war elephants, an army of considerable size to be deployed by a minor king of a minor state in the Jhelum region.[31] Less than a year later, Alexander confronted the army of the Malavas state, another minor regional entity, and faced a force of 80,000 well-equipped infantry, 10,000 cavalry, and 800 chariots.[32] Even accounting for the exaggeration common in ancient accounts, it is by no means unlikely that these armies were this large. The population of India during this period was somewhere between 120,000,000 to 180,000,000 people. Even excluding the lower social orders, the Mauryan empire possessed an enormous manpower pool. Moreover, India was rich in gold and metals and the skills to produce weapons in great quantities in state armouries. The Gangetic Plain and other areas further north were excellent for breeding cavalry mounts in large numbers, and India's agricultural production was more than adequate to feed the armies. Whatever the true size of the imperial armies, they are all recorded as smaller than those said to have existed during the later Medieval and Muslim periods of Indian history.

The tactical organization of the Mauryan army may have been influenced somewhat by the Chinese innovation of combining several combat arms within a single tactical unit, and training it to fight together as a unit and employ their arms in concert. Indian armies of this period had within them a basic unit called the *patti*, a mixed platoon comprised of one elephant carrying three archers or spearman and a *mahout*, three cavalrymen armed with javelins, round buckler and spear and five infantry soldiers armed with shield and broadsword or bow. Three of these fifteen-man *patti* formed a *vsenamukha* or company. Three of these formed together comprised a *gulma* or battalion. Units were added in multiples of three forming an *aksauhini* or army comprised of 21,870 *patti*. Sources also speak of military units formed around multiples of ten, and there were no doubt units of single arms that could be employed individually or in concert with other arms. The *Arthasastra* mentions a unit called the *samavyuha* or battle array that was about the size of a Roman legion (5,000 men). This unit was comprised of five sub-units joined together, each sub-unit containing 45 chariots, 45 elephants, 225 cavalry and 675 infantrymen each. It goes without saying that managing such units in battle requires a high degree of tactical sophistication.

The military equipment of the Mauryan imperial army was essentially the same has it had been for the previous 500 years and a relatively complete portrayal of personal weaponry can be found in Figure 2 shown earlier. The Indian bamboo bow was between 5 and 6 feet long, and fired a long cane arrow with a metal or bone tip. Nearchus, the Greek chronicler who accompanied Alexander into India, noted that the Indian bowman had to rest the bow on the ground and steady it with his left foot in order to draw it fully. At the Hydaspes, the battle took place over muddy ground which prevented the archers from steadying their bows in this manner, rendering them useless. The composite bow or *sarnga* was also used, but probably far less so and not by cavalry. When Alexander's cavalry at the Hydaspes attacked the Indian cavalry, the Indian cavalry took heavy losses and had no means of returning fire. It is unlikely that the Indian cavalry ever became proficient with the bow, relying completely upon lance and javelin, the weapons of light cavalry. If the Mauryan army possessed heavy cavalry, they appear to have done so in small numbers. Infantry carried a long narrow shield made of raw oxhide stretched over a wooden or wicker frame that protected almost the entire body, unlike the small round buckler carried by the cavalry. Armed with thrusting spear, bow, and javelin, the infantry tended mostly to be of the light variety. Heavy infantry carried the *nistrimsa* or long two-handed slashing sword, while others were armed with iron maces, dagger-axes, battle axes and clubs. A special long lance, the *tomara*, was carried by soldiers mounted on the backs of elephants and used to counter any enemy infantry that had fought its way through the elephant's infantry screen to attack the animal itself. What evidence we have suggests that from Vedic times until the coming of the Greeks, only slight use was made of body armour and most of that was of the leather or textile variety. With Alexander's invasion, however, the use of metal, lamellar, and linen laminate armour became more widespread, as did the use of scale armour for horses and elephants. The helmet did not come into wide use until well into the Common Era. For most of the ancient period, the soldier relied upon the thick folds of his cloth turban to protect his head.[33]

By the Mauryan period the Indians possessed most of the ancient world's siege and artillery equipment including catapults, ballistas, battering rams and other siege engines. A distinguishing characteristic of Indian siege and artillery practice was a heavy reliance upon incendiary devices, such as fire arrows, pitch pots and fireballs. From time immemorial, the Aryans had worshipped the fire god, Agni, who they called the Destroyer of Fortifications. There was even a manual instructing how to equip birds and monkeys with the ability to carry fire inside buildings and on to rooftops. This was not surprising in a country whose military fortifications and buildings were made mostly of wood. Megasthenes described the fortifications of the Mauryan capital as comprised of a 'mighty wooden wall with 570 towers and 64 gates'.[34] Most cities and towns were surrounded by wooden palisades, and the supporting structures of gates were mostly wood as well. Fire was such a constant threat to Indian towns that thousands of water containers and buckets were required to be kept full of water and placed outside of dwellings at all times to extinguish fires. All citizens were required by law to assist in fighting fires. It was even required that people sleep in the room nearest the street exit to escape fire more easily and to be quickly available to help in fighting them. So serious was the concern for fire that the punishment for arson was death by burning alive!

While the *Arthasastra* offers much advice on how to prepare for battle, there is nothing on the tactics which shaped the conduct of the battle itself. We may be relatively certain, however, that an army of such size and complexity as the Mauryan imperial army with its thousands of attendants, merchants, family members, elephants, horses etc, would hardly have been able to move quickly. The *Arthasastra* declares that a good army can march two *yojanas* a day and that a bad army can only manage one. This amounts to a rate of march for an effective army of about ten miles a day, considerably below what the armies of the Near East could manage during the same period. It is likely that the Mauryan army followed the age-old practice from Vedic times of agreeing with the enemy as to the location of a battlefield in advance. Under these conditions, surprise was likely to have been a rare event.

A detailed tactical description of an Indian army in battle comes to us from the Roman historian Arrian's description of the Battle of the Hydaspes between Porus and Alexander.[35] We might examine that battle somewhat speculatively in an effort to deduce what tactical capabilities might have characterized Indian armies of the imperial period. Porus had deployed his army in a line awaiting Alexander's attack. A line of elephants ran across the entire front with infantry deployed behind it. Chariot units and cavalry anchored the wings. One can infer from this deployment that Porus expected Alexander to attack the centre of his line with his infantry. In response, Porus might then unleash his elephants against the phalanx, break it and then attack the shattered infantry with one or both of his cavalry wings, following up with his infantry all along the line. Porus' deployment lacked flexibility. Alexander arrived on the battlefield without his infantry, who were still struggling to catch up after a long march. Porus might well have attacked Alexander then or even while his infantry was arriving and still in column of march. Porus did neither.

Alexander began the battle with a strong cavalry attack against Porus' left wing. Outnumbered, Porus showed tactical manoeuvre by ordering elements of his cavalry on his right wing to redeploy to his left by riding behind the battle line. This they accomplished, stopping Alexander's attack in its tracks. Alexander now ordered fresh cavalry units into the attack, ordering them to extend to Porus' left and ride around the flank and turn it. With an excellent tactical eye, Porus ordered his left wing to break contact, form in order of march and extend further to the left to stop the envelopment. This was an excellent but risky response. Alexander's cavalry now stopped their advance around the flank, turned inward and struck Porus' left wing in the middle of its redeployment. At the same time, Macedonian cavalry which had followed Porus' right wing cavalry behind the battle line arrived behind the redeploying left wing, striking it from behind. It was at this point that Porus's army demonstrated its discipline and training. Under attack from two directions, Porus ordered the cavalry wing to deploy back to back and engage the Macedonians from two directions. Once more Alexander's brilliant manoeuvre had been stymied by Porus' excellent tactical response.

Alexander now ordered his infantry phalanx into the attack. They moved slowly toward the Indian centre with *sarissae* (pikes) extended. This pinned the elephant line in place, making it impossible for Porus to bring his infantry, deployed behind the elephant line, into action. The elephants kept their discipline and retreated step by step before the Macedonian pikes. Pushed back against the infantry, the elephants were vulnerable to attack by Thracian javelinmen and the Agrianian swordsmen who proceeded to decimate the elephant line. Gradually the Macedonian infantry began to encircle the Indian army. On the left flank, the Indian cavalry found its spirit and made one more attack only to have it repulsed. Alexander's cavalry now pressed the Indian cavalry back upon the infantry and elephants into one great mass. The Macedonian infantry pressed against the mass 'with great slaughter'. For eight hours the armies fought hand-to-hand. Much to the credit of the Indian army, it fought on and never lost its discipline.

This summary of the Battle of the Hydaspes reveals an Indian army that was every bit as tactically sophisticated as any army anywhere during this period. It was an army capable of integrating combined arms into a tactical whole and very capable of tactical flexibility after it was engaged. Moving thousands of cavalrymen across the entire battlefront in response to an attack on the opposite wing is no easy manoeuvre. Even more impressive was the ability of Porus' cavalry to engage the enemy attack from two directions at once after itself being struck from the rear. These are the tactical characteristics of a well-trained professional army. Even the war elephants revealed a high degree of training. Under attack from the *sarissae* and swords of the Macedonian infantry, the animals did not break. They held their ground backing up slowly and in formation. Even when there was nowhere to go, the elephants stood their ground. If we remind ourselves that Porus was but a minor king as Indian kings went, we are led to the conclusion that the level of tactical sophistication of the imperial army of a few years later surely equalled that of Porus' army, and in all probability even surpassed it. If so, it is a fair conclusion that the Indian armies of the imperial period were no less accomplished than any other army of the period, including the large and complex armies that characterized the previous period of Buddha's lifetime.

Buddha's World

Buddha was born in 563 and died in 483 BC at about the age of eighty.[36] The foregoing analysis ought to make clear that Buddha lived in a time when war and its attendant suffering were frequent occurrences. The evidence is clear that Buddha witnessed, experienced, and participated in this violent world, and it is a reasonable assumption that these events shaped his life. During Buddha's lifetime, Indian society was changing under the impact of these frequent wars and most of the smaller republics, and even the few remaining 'larger realms', were taken over in one way or another by the four major states vying for control of the Gangetic Plain. A new economic order based on trade, transport, and iron agricultural technologies was taking hold, and the old rural way of life and its independent villages were giving way to the rise of new cities, increased urbanization and stronger political establishments capable of exercising increased control over their populations.[37] These forces gave rise to a new merchant class and independent guilds that sought a share of political power, a development that led to serious challenges to traditional Aryan values and religious practices. The old Aryan social, economic and religious order of things that had existed for more than a thousand years was slipping away, and with it the security and meaning that it had bestowed on India's people for so long.

The impending breakdown of the old order during Buddha's lifetime contributed strongly to a persistent feeling of general insecurity and a starkly pessimistic outlook on the world, perspectives that became widely held throughout this period.[38] For many, including Buddha himself, life seemed full of endless pain filled with *dukkha*, a word meaning 'suffering', or a life that is 'awry' or out of control.[39] One consequence of the pessimism of the age was the emergence of an asceticism that represented a withdrawal from the material world. This rejection was accompanied by a search for an inner state of mind or philosophy that promised relief from worldly suffering and insecurity. Mystics and preachers of all kinds roamed throughout the Gangetic Plain, all advocating some form of mental discipline and ascetic practice that would bring relief from human suffering and offer the means to some sort of psychic salvation.

These wandering ascetics presented a direct challenge to the traditional *brahmin* religious establishment, calling into question as they did the legitimacy of the traditional practices of animal sacrifice and other religious rituals that emphasized the values and obligations of the individual to the community. The mystics preached a freedom that could only be attained by the individual alone, outside the community. Indeed, the promised freedom required the renunciation of the very community that supported the *brahmin*. Not surprisingly, the *brahmin*, and later the *kshatriya*, came to violently oppose these new movements as corrosive to the established order. Once Buddha's reputation as an ascetic teacher began to grow, at least three and possibly four attempts were made on his life for precisely this reason.

It is easy to forget how fragile ancient societies were to traumatic events like war. In Buddha's lifetime, the frequent comings and goings of large armies through an area often wreaked havoc on the life of the locals, their families, farms, livestock, houses, wells etc. Ancient battles killed thousands at a time and wounded many more who later succumbed to their wounds. Disease caused by the presence of armies in one place for an extended period killed more soldiers than enemy action, often spreading to devastate local towns and villages. Armies ate their way across the land to and from the battlefield, leaving famine in their wake. These conditions occurred frequently during Buddha's lifetime and it is hardly surprising that many people lost their mental balance and whole sections of the country succumbed to a general feeling of alienation from the material world in which they lived.

Antiquity was full of madness resulting from external trauma to its populations, and no less so in India than, say, in ancient Palestine during the Roman occupation.[40] There were no means of identifying or treating the traumatized and they wandered aimlessly throughout the countryside. Some of these victims became the wandering ascetics of Buddha's time, offering new religious creeds as the way to inner peace or salvation. Modern wars have proved no less efficient in generating madness among the populations that endured it. During and after the American civil war (1860–1865), the countryside was littered with the wandering insane.[41] After World War II, thousands of the mentally disturbed wandered aimlessly over Russia for more than two decades before the Soviet government was able to address their madness, if only rudimentarily.[42] Similar conditions obtained in Western Europe. Just as in India during Buddha's time, many of the mentally unstable turned to new cults and marginal creeds to achieve relief from their mental torment.

In Buddha's day, the general malaise that afflicted Indians manifested itself in the emergence of asceticism as a primary characteristic of the new creeds offered by wandering Messianists. Why this should have been so remains puzzling, for the Aryan view of life offers no hint of asceticism. Aryan religion emphasized the desire to live a long life, conquer women, slay enemies, sire many sons, acquire large lands and cow herds, obtain substantial riches and otherwise enjoy life to the fullest. There is only a marginal hint of asceticsm in Aryan religion and that pertains only to a small number of *brahmin* priests who seemed to have incorporated minor ascetic rituals, like fasting, ritual washing etc, as spiritual preparation into some of the sacrifices.[43] Ascetic practices were in most ways opposed to the central Vedic ideas of religion and the achievements of the good life.[44]

Still, asceticism came to play a central role in classical Hinduism, as well as in Buddhism and Jainism, the two other religions that arose on Indian soil. One can to some degree trace the gradual evolution of various ascetic practices in Hinduism and Jainism, but in neither were these practices central and widespread among the Indian populace. Rather, they were contained mostly to a small number of priests and ascetics for whom religious practice was a full-time occupation. The emergence of asceticism in Buddhism, by contrast, did not evolve gradually but emerged fully developed as doctrine and practice during Buddha's lifetime. Moreover, asceticism in Buddhism is not fundamentally ritualistic, that is, not subordinate to or submerged in some other more important religious practice. Instead, asceticism in Buddhism is fundamental to the everyday practice of its followers and is not, therefore, limited to a formal priesthood as in Jainism and Hinduism. In both these senses, then, Buddhist asceticism is quite different from the practice found in the other Indian religions. This, of course, raises the question of why Buddha made ascetic practice central to his new creed. To inquire as to the source of Buddha's asceticism leads us to an examination of his life and the events and experiences that shaped his view of the world in which he lived.

Buddha's Life

The ancient accounts of Buddha's early life tell the story of a child born to a powerful Indian king named Suddhodana. It was prophesied upon his birth that the boy, named Siddhartha Gautama, would someday become either a great king or a great teacher. To prevent Gautama from giving up the pleasures of this world and becoming a teacher, Suddhodana raised his son in great luxury, preventing him from witnessing the evils of the world. One day Siddhartha ventured beyond the palace grounds with his charioteer, where he came upon an old man, a sick man and a dying man. He was shocked by the realization that he, too, might suffer their fate and resolved to become an ascetic and discover how he might escape the cycle of perpetual rebirth that Indians believed to be the central affliction of humanity. At 29, Siddhartha left his wife and child, slipped past the palace guards and began a life of wandering and contemplation that lasted until his death at age 80. His teachings were written down centuries later and became the scriptures of the Buddhist religion.

This tale was first encountered by Marco Polo, but written texts of the account did not reach the West until late in the eighteenth century.[45] Nonetheless, the story remains the generally accepted account of Buddha's early life to this day. It is, as we shall see, largely inaccurate and fails to account for the historical and sociological circumstances of the time and place in which Buddha lived. In addition, the Pali Canon presents an entirely different picture.

Siddhartha Gautama (563–483 BC), known to history as the Buddha or 'the enlightened one', was born in the Indo-Aryan Sakya republic in the foothills of the Himalayas, north of the Ganges River in the province of northeast India known today as Bengal. Buddha himself described the Sakyas (origin: 'mighty oaks') as 'the noblest people' and its capital, Kapila-vatthu, as 'the most grand and luxuriant city' in the land.[46] The land of the Sakyas lay along the foothills of the Himalayas, upon a stretch of open fertile plain measuring some 50 miles from east to west and 40 miles southward from the mountain foothills.[47] Although the republics were smaller than the new *mahajanapada* states, they were not insignificant military powers. Some texts record that the Sakyas comprised 160,000 families during Buddha's lifetime. More modern sources suggest the country comprised some 80,000 families, and at least half a million people, counting men, women, and children.[48]

The Sakya capital at Kapila-vastu on the banks of the Rhoni River (modern Kohana) was surrounded by seven defensive walls. It was the location of a famous school of archery for training bowmen. Other towns in the country were also fortified. The country was about the size of the American state of Rhode Island. Besides having to contend with the predations of Kosala and Magadha, each of which sought to control the Gangetic Plain, the Sakyas were surrounded by other states that were often hostile. As with the *mahajanapada* states of India at this time, war was an almost constant occurrence for the Sakyas. Their location on the open plain made them vulnerable to frequent attacks from their neighbours. The powerful state of Kosala bordered the Sakya lands on the south and west and the Koliya republic bordered it on the east. Conflicts between the Sakyas and these powerful and aggressive border states were frequent and of long standing.

As we have seen, the Aryan republics (*samghas*) of Buddha's day were tribal kingdoms (*rashtra*) governed by an oligarchy of nobles (*sabha*) and led by a warrior chief. The *rashtra* was comprised of tribes (*jana*), sub-tribes (*vish*) and villages (*grama*). The nucleus of the tribe was the family (*kula*), with the oldest male as its head (*kulapa*).[49] Perhaps as a consequence of its small size, somewhat isolated location and having to deal with constant military threats, Sakya society was closer to the traditional organization of the earlier Aryan warrior tribes than to the more complex social organization of the newly emerged *mahajanapanda* states.[50] Although Buddha's father is portrayed in the texts as a mighty king living in great luxury, more likely he was a warrior chief or *raja*. Although the office had originally depended upon consent of the nobles, by Buddha's day the position of chief had become hereditary.[51] All able-bodied men were trained for war and were led in battle by the professional *kshatriya* warrior caste. At a maximum effort, the Sakyas could probably raise an army of 100,000 men.[52] The *raja* personally commanded the army in battle.

Buddha, then, was the son of the *raja* of the Sakyas, a warrior people 'of great heroes' as Buddha himself described them. According to the Aryan rule of primogeniture, as the oldest son of the chief Buddha was expected to succeed his father.[53] The texts tell us that like all *kshatriya* men, Buddha was trained from a very young age to be a soldier. At age 3, the male child's hair was shaved, leaving only a topknot (*cudakarma*), the symbol of a warrior, and he was taught the alphabet and numbers. Both events were initiated by ceremony.[54] By 6 years of age, he entered the formal educational and military training programme that lasted until he was 16. The curriculum included courses in logic, politics and economics. *Kshatriya* also studied the ancient Vedic religious texts, but were only required to memorize the first lines of the *vedas*. For over a decade, the young Buddha was subjected to a rigorous curriculum of studies and military training that required proficiency in the Aryan weapons of war, including handling the chariot, warhorse and elephant.[55]

The weapons curriculum was called the *Dhanur Veda*. Buddha's instructors were professional tutors and military subjects were taught by combat-hardened veterans. Instruction was personalized and students lived in the homes of their instructors for the duration of the specific course of study. Special tutors called *sutas* recited the *Itihasas* to the student at fixed times during each day. The *Itihasas* were the historical accounts of the exploits of the great Sakya warriors and battles of the past. Great stress was placed upon accustoming the student to discipline, hardship, and endurance.[56]

At age 11, the young warrior underwent the great rite of *upanayana*, a 'second birth', whereby the boy was recognized as a full member of his class. This rite was very ancient indeed, having its origins in a time before the Aryans invaded India. The youth was dressed in the clothing of an ascetic and carried a staff in his hand. It was now that the *yajnopavita* or sacred thread was hung over his right shoulder and under his left arm. He was expected to wear this thread continuously for the rest of his life.[57]

As befits a warrior people, the Aryans believed that luxury weakened the spirit required of a soldier. Before being consecrated as a knight at 16 years old, the young soldier was required to demonstrate his competence with weapons. If he passed the test, he was given the special costume of the *kshatriya* warrior fashioned of dyed flax cloth and a girdle of *munja* grass adorned with pieces of iron.[58] As a consecrated warrior, Buddha was now allowed to participate in war and enjoy the privilege of rendering and receiving the military salute. He was also allowed to marry, although only within his caste, a requirement enforced by the Aryans to keep themselves separate and racially distinct from the conquered peoples.

The texts are clear that Buddha went through the *kshatriya* ceremony of becoming a warrior. Moreover, when Buddha was sixteen, his father announced that his son would become his heir apparent. The accounts tell us that the assembled nobles required Buddha, as a potential heir, to demonstrate his martial prowess by a display of weapons drill to prove that he would make a competent commander in battle. Buddha was required to demonstrate competence in the 'twelve tests', including proficiency with the bow, sword, spear, lasso, iron-dart, club, battle-axe, thrown iron discus and trident. Also included were fencing, swimming, wrestling, hand-to-hand combat, horsemanship and shooting the bow from a moving chariot. The texts tell us that Buddha passed the tests with excellent performance and that the nobles were satisfied that he was capable of leading them in war. Only then did his father name Buddha as his heir. A short time later, Buddha married his cousin. Buddha was now a *kshatriya* warrior and as heir apparent took his seat in the 500-member tribal assembly (*sangh*).

The discipline and rules of the *kshatriya* warrior governed Buddha's entire existence including, as we shall see, exposure to war, until he was 29 years old. The ancient law texts are clear that a warrior was forbidden to give up the military life and take up a life of asceticism, as Buddha later did after leaving his father's court at the age of 29. The texts note that even when he left his palace on his war horse, Kanthaka, he was carrying his broad sword and his hair was still worn in the warrior's top-knot, both visible signs of Buddha's warrior status and training. As a member of the *kshatriya* caste, Buddha was forbidden to pursue any other profession except that of the soldier.[59] Military life was an all-consuming profession for the Indo-Aryans. The *Samyutta* scripture tells us that, 'for the *kshatriya* there is no other rule but to fight', and the *Adi Parva* that 'among men, the highest duties are those performed by the *kshatriya*'. The Aryan gods were warrior gods, like Indra, who helped the warrior in battle, and Agni the fire-god, loved for the blessing of fire with which to destroy enemy strongholds. The entire weight of Indo-Aryan religious sanction and social conditioning required warriors to fight. Being born warriors and prohibited from taking up other professions, the *kshatriya* were impatient of peace. It was this 'psychological barrenness of peace' that led to many wars in India's ancient history.[60] War was a fundamental function of the Aryan state and waging it was the primary responsibility of the *kshatriya* caste.

The code of the *kshatriya* required that the soldier die gloriously in battle, for only then could he attain salvation (*moksha*) and enter paradise (*swarg*), freeing him from the cycle of rebirth and suffering. Cowardice was punished by death. Offenders were stoned or beaten to death, or wrapped in grass and set on fire. Senior officers who showed a lack of resolve were required to dress in a woman's clothes until the public disgrace drove them to suicide. To live long enough to die in bed was a sin. Many warriors, of course, did die in bed. Under these circumstances, the dying warrior was laid upon a bed of *kusa* grass and his body cut with a sword as special prayers were said over him. The dying warrior was permitted to achieve heaven through this ritual.[61] After a battle, the dead were gathered and cremated in a huge funeral pyre. The wives of the dead climbed upon the pyre and were burnt with the corpses of their men. This custom, called *sati* by the Indians, was still being practised in India until the British (who called it *suttee*) put an end to it in the colonial era.[62]

Against this background, some key elements of the accepted story of Buddha's early life can be questioned. First, it is clear that the story of Buddha being raised in luxury by his warrior chief father cannot be true. The *kshatriya* regarded luxury as a sin. If Buddha had been raised in this manner, he would never have been able to become a warrior, which, of course, would have made it impossible for him to succeed his father. Second, it is also clear that as the oldest son of a *kshatriya* aristocratic family and the son of an Aryan chief, Buddha must have been trained from childhood as a soldier, as all Aryan males of his caste were and as the texts tell us he was. He would have had no real choice in the matter. Third, had he failed to meet the warrior standard, he would have been relegated to a life of obscurity and never anointed as his father's heir, nor would the *sangh* have permitted it. Fourth, during Buddha's life northeast India was wracked by frequent wars. While Buddha was still alive, the Sakya republic was attacked and its entire population massacred and we hear no more of the people which produced the greatest of the Indians. Under these circumstances, it is unlikely that the Sakyas had abandoned their warrior traditions and practices, as Armstrong has suggested, at a time when they were very much needed.

While we have only partial accounts of Buddha's activities from age 16, when he became a warrior knight, until he left home at 29, it is all but certain that Buddha experienced the trial of war as a soldier in the Sakya army. India produced no historian comparable to Thucydides, Xenophon or Herodotus as chroniclers of the wars of the Indian ancient period, so that Buddha's war experience can only be inferred from limited evidence. However, it is inconceivable that the son of an Aryan warrior chief and heir apparent would not have accompanied his father into battle. If Buddha had refused to fight, he would have disgraced his father, his family, his clan and his people and would have been expelled from his tribe and forced into exile. As noted, the Aryans usually punished cowardice with execution or, in other cases, with social ostracism that pressured the accused to commit suicide. There is no reason to believe that Buddha did not behave in the manner expected of a *kshatriya* warrior, including going to war, before he left his father's house.

We have only fragmentary evidence regarding the Sakya wars that occurred during Buddha's lifetime in which he would have taken part. There seems to have been some sort of revolt of the smaller tribal republics in which the Sakyas, Koliyas, Moriyas and Mallas broke free of the influence of the larger Kosalan state.[63] These early events caused an almost continuous state of simmering conflict between the Sakyas and the Kosalans that persisted on and off until the Kosalans finally defeated and exterminated the Sakyas decades later, while Buddha was still alive. Second, when Buddha was 24 and a member of the Sakya *sangh*, a conflict broke out between the Sakyas and the neighbouring Koliyas over irrigation rights to water from the Rohini River that formed the boundary between the two states. A series of skirmishes were fought over the next four years until, when Buddha was 28, a major battle took place in which both sides suffered significant casualties.[64] Although tradition holds that Buddha refused to support the Sakya declaration of war that followed the battle and, indeed, refused to accompany the army to battle, there is no reason to believe that he had refused to take part in the earlier skirmishes.[65]

Another series of wars between Kosalas and Sakyas occurred after Buddha had begun his wanderings. These wars throw the brutal nature of the conflicts between these two states into sharp relief. The Kosala king, Vidudabha, attacked the Sakyas in an effort to incorporate their territory into his larger kingdom. The war seems to have lasted for years, with the Kosalan army launching three major campaigns against the Sakya, each time being badly beaten.[66] The text records that the Kosalan commanders were concerned that if the war continued, 'there will not be left a soul living amongst us'.[67] The fourth campaign finally brought victory, but only after a great battle in which the Sakyas agreed to sue for peace. On the advice of the *sangh*, the gates to the city were thrown open, permitting the Kosalan army to enter. Immediately the Kosalas began to kill the population:

the king Vidudabha slew all the Sakyas, beginning with babes at the breast, and with their heart's blood did he wash the bench on which he [Buddha] had sat in the Sakyan assembly.[68]

The cost of victory had been high, however, and the losses taken against the Sakya had so weakened the Kosalas that shortly after the war they were attacked by the kingdom of Magadha, their king slain and the territory incorporated into the expanding Magadhan empire.

If it is reasonable to conclude that Buddha experienced war during his young life, we are left to explain why he abandoned his wife, his young son, his family, his clan and his father's court to embrace the life of a wandering ascetic (*parivraja*). Whatever caused Buddha to do this must have been some sort of traumatic event. The story that he was shocked by his first encounter with a sick man, an old man and a dying man is hardly credible, though it may contain a kernel of truth. Another tradition suggests the reason Buddha left his life behind at the age of twenty-nine was his abhorrence of war. The tradition holds that when the *sangh* voted to go to war against the Koliyas, Buddha refused to accept the majority vote and vowed he would not take part in the fighting. The tradition records him as saying, 'I shall not join your army and I shall not take part in the war.'[69] Buddha was very clear that it was the evils of war that prompted his action saying, 'Dharma, as I understand it, consists in recognizing that enmity does not disappear by enmity. It can be conquered only by love.'[70] This was serious business indeed and Buddha could have been executed. Perhaps because he was the son of the chief, the *sangh* agreed to his going into exile.[71]

What both versions of Buddha's actions have in common is that both are rooted in strong feelings of personal despair. Karen Armstrong suggests as much when she notes that 'when he decided to leave home, Gotama [Buddha], one might think, appeared to have lost his ability to live with the unpalatable facts of life and to have fallen prey to a profound depression'.[72] She notes that when Buddha looked at human life, 'he could see only a grim cycle of suffering, which began with the trauma of birth and proceeded inexorably to aging, illness death, sorrow, and corruption'.[73] For some reason, life had become meaningless for the young Buddha, and he was consumed by a sense of helplessness, obsessed with the finality of life, and felt a profound terror and alienation from the world.[74] He found no comfort in his family, wife or even his newborn son, whom he named Rahula, which means 'fetter'. It was as if he felt that the child would be but another burden.

While not impossible, deep and prolonged depression like that displayed by Buddha in the twenty-ninth year of his life is not usually the result of a single short-term event. Thus, the claim that Buddha's depression was the result of suddenly becoming aware that people grow old and die is hardly credible, especially so for a soldier. A more likely cause of such profound depression is *prolonged* exposure to stressful and disturbing events, such as those a soldier is likely to have encountered on the battlefield. A more likely explanation for Buddha's deep depression, and his resulting flight from the extant circumstances of his life that forced his exposure to war, is that his experiences on the battlefield may have rendered him a psychological casualty. In this regard, it is interesting that the familiar tradition explaining Buddha's departure attributes his actions precisely to a desire to avoid being sent to war again. Buddha surely knew that if he remained with his tribe and as the son of the Sakya warrior chief, he would have had little choice but to return to the battlefield.

Dynamics of Psychiatric Collapse in War

There is no good reason to believe that soldiers in ancient times were any less fearful of dying or being maimed than today's soldiers. Whether in ancient or modern times, exposure to the stress of war is likely to seriously affect one's sanity and ability to function normally in society.[75] It is, then, not unlikely that Buddha's exposure to violence and slaughter might have seriously affected his mental condition.

The stresses of war impose terrible burdens on the physiology and psychology of most human beings. Humans are equipped with the normal physiological mechanisms of any animal that prepare the body to deal with and survive under stress. Under stress, the body automatically reacts. The soldier's blood pressure rises; the heart beats rapidly; the body begins to sweat; muscles tense increasing short-term strength; the mind races and the endocrine system activates all the biological mechanisms that contribute to increased sensory awareness. Once the soldier perceives danger, few have any control over the onset of these physical reactions. Only when the danger has passed does the body's biological system gradually return to normal.

What happens when the perception of danger is of longer duration? It is not only direct perceptions of death and mutilation on the battlefield that induce stress. The military environment itself is a sensory universe of stressors: the sight of the dead or mutilated bodies; loss of comrades; the screams of the wounded; the sounds of the dying; the odour of decayed flesh; the guilt that comes with killing or having survived when others were killed, are but a few things that cause a soldier stress. Other physical factors such as inadequate nutrition, hunger, thirst, dehydration, heat, cold, wet weather, minor injuries caused by poor equipment (blisters from poorly fitting boots and packs, etc.), lack of sleep; fatigue from marching, carrying weapons, tents etc; and the anticipation of battle, all work to increase the stress on the soldier's physiology.[76] Even after the battle, the body will maintain itself in a high state of physiological tension for a considerable period. If the stress is prolonged, say a few days, the biological systems that sustain the physiology of stress will remain aroused and unable to return to normal. A soldier in this state will eventually collapse from nervous exhaustion.[77]

The mind can also affect the physiological operations of the body. Psychosomatic illnesses, conditions of genuine physical debilitation brought on by affective mental states in which the mind is able to produce physical ailments, are common when soldiers are subjected to prolonged stress. Conversion reactions characterized by hysterical blindness, paralysis and surdo-mutism (the inability to speak) are extreme forms of such illnesses found among soldiers exposed to intense combat. Memory loss, depression, lack of energy, inability to comprehend orders, palpitations, muscle tremors, uncontrolled urination and defecation are also common, but less extreme, examples of stress reactions.

Even under the most trying of circumstances, soldiers must continue to believe that they will somehow survive or they will collapse. The desire to survive is so deeply embedded in our genetics and evolutionary experience as to be self-evident. When confronted with the face of death from which there seems no escape, few soldiers can retain their sanity. The onset of a soldier's mental debilitation can be rapid or gradual. When the onset is rapid, the condition is referred to as 'battle shock'; when it is gradual, it is called 'combat fatigue'. In general, about fifty per cent of all psychiatric casualties develop debilitating symptoms in less than five days' exposure to military action.

There is no getting used to combat. Exposure to war often takes a reasonably normal and sane individual and, sometimes in a matter of hours, transforms him into a completely different human being. Since World War I, military psychiatrists have defined the major psychiatric conditions that soldiers suffer most frequently in war. These are fatigue cases, confusional states, conversion hysteria, anxiety states and character disorders. Given human nature and its physiology as a constant, there is no reason to expect that soldiers in the armies of antiquity did not suffer the same conditions.

A soldier suffering from fatigue is mentally and physically exhausted; his autonomic biological systems, after repeated periods of hyperactivity maintaining his physiology at a heightened state, have collapsed. Physical exhaustion begins to erode his mental strength. Fatigue is 'prodromal', that is to say it sets the stage for further and more complete collapse that is inevitable if the soldier is not given prolonged rest. To reduce the tension, the soldier will abuse drugs and alcohol and become overly irritable. The soldier becomes prone to emotional outbursts, such as crying fits, anxiety, paranoia and fits of rage and violence. If not given sufficient respite from the perceived dangers, the fatigued soldier will develop deeper psychiatric symptoms.

A fatigued soldier can quickly shift into a confusional state marked by a general psychotic dissociation from reality. Unable to deal with the danger, the soldier mentally removes himself from it. Confusional states often involve delirium of some sort and are likely to engender schizophrenic states of dissociation. Frequently, manic-depressive psychosis develops in which wild swings of mood and activity are evident. The degree of affliction in confusional states ranges from the profoundly neurotic to the overtly psychotic.

Conversion hysteria is one of the most pronounced and dramatic manifestations of battle shock, and is among the most common psychiatric conditions brought on by the stress of war. Torn between his fears and his socially derived values of duty, courage and honour, the soldier 'resolves' the tension by 'converting' his fears into some somatic symptom severe enough to incapacitate himself and gain relief from the terror he feels. The physical symptoms allow the soldier to gain relief with a 'legitimate' physical condition, thus preserving his self-respect and that of his peers. Conversion hysteria can occur traumatically in response to a specific incident or in post-traumatic situations, especially if the soldier fears he will be forced to return to the dangerous environment his symptoms have permitted him to escape. Whenever conversion hysteria occurs, it is the mind that produces the physical symptoms of debilitation. Conversion hysteria can involve massive or partial dissociative states. *Massive dissociation* manifests itself in fugue states, an inability to know where one is or to function at all. It is often accompanied by a dreamlike wandering with complete disregard for evident dangers. Very often a soldier in a fugue state is totally or partially amnesic, blocking out parts of his past and present memory from his consciousness. The psychosis can also take the form of twilight states, repeated passing in and out of consciousness, sometimes accompanied by severe and uncontrollable tremors. Hysteria can degenerate into convulsive attacks in which the soldier rolls into a foetal position and begins to shake violently. At the most extreme, dissociation can manifest itself in catatonia.

Among the most common afflictions associated with *partial dissociation* are hysterical paralysis, deafness, blindness and surdo-mutism in which the mind forces the body to become incapacitated. Soldiers suffering from partial dissociative hysterical states can also undergo acute sensory disturbances, including somatic pain in which parts of the body feel numb or paralyzed, or chest pain simulating the symptoms of a heart attack.

Soldiers suffering from combat shock often endure severe anxiety states characterized by weakness and tenseness that cannot be relieved by sleep or rest. When the soldier is able to sleep, he is often awakened by nightmares associated with battle experiences. The soldier becomes obsessed with death and fear. If the anxiety state persists, the soldier will develop phobic conditions, an extreme fear of some object. Anxiety can make itself felt in a range of severe somatic neuroses, such as effort syndrome, an abnormal physiological reaction to effort. It is accompanied frequently by shortness of breath, weakness, precordial pain, blurred vision, vasomotor abnormalities, and fainting. Another reaction is emotional hypertension in which the soldier's blood pressure rises dramatically, with all the accompanying symptoms of weakness, sweating, nervousness etc.

The foregoing analysis of the symptoms of acute and gradual psychiatric collapse in war by no means exhausts the psychiatric manifestations that emerge among soldiers subjected to prolonged battle stress. The human mind has shown itself infinitely capable of bringing about any number of combinations of symptoms and then forcing them deep into the soldier's psyche, changing his personality, sometimes forever. War can exact a terrible cost on human emotions, and it is a cost that every soldier will eventually pay if exposed to the horrors of the battlefield long enough.

The fear of death and maiming that so clearly affect modern soldiers was no less evident in antiquity, in some instances even more so. For example, my earlier study of casualty rates in fourteen ancient battles in the Bronze and Iron ages suggests that a defeated army in antiquity, on average, would suffer 37.7 per cent of its combat force killed and another 35.4 per cent wounded.[78] Seven out of ten soldiers who took the field could expect to be killed or wounded. The victorious army suffered much fewer losses, with only 5.5 per cent killed and 6.0 per cent wounded. Comparative figures for American armies in all wars from the Civil War to the Korean War were 17.7 per cent killed and 46.1 per cent wounded.[79] Thus, the chances of a soldier being killed or wounded in antiquity were much greater than in modern times, suggesting that the levels of stress engendered by the fear of being killed or maimed were at least the same, if not greater, in ancient as in modern battles.

There was another factor, however, that suggests that the stress suffered by ancient soldiers was considerably greater. All the killing in ancient battles was done with muscle-powered weapons inflicted upon the victim at close range, so that the slayer directly witnessed the fate of the slain, a fate he caused with his own hands. Studies have shown that the strength and duration of the psychological impact of killing at close range is much greater than killing at a distance. Soldiers that have killed 'at knife range' are more likely to suffer psychiatric symptoms of stronger intensity and for longer duration than soldiers who killed at more distant ranges, where the victims were seen only as a fleeting image in the distance.[80] The greater distance permits the modern soldier to believe he has never really killed anyone, or at least, probably did not, because he never saw the results of his actions up close. Soldiers in ancient battles could sustain no such illusion. The gory business of close killing (blood, screams, torn flesh, terror in the victim's eyes etc) was immediately evident to the killer and the impact of these visions upon the killer's psyche was likely to be very strong.

When trying to assess the stress endured by the ancient soldier, it is important to recall that stress in a military environment arises from other factors besides close combat. The basic physical conditions of life in an army on the march or garrisoning a hostile country are, by themselves, sufficient to cause psychiatric breakdown. If we compare the rates of PTSD in the American army across three wars, Vietnam, Iraq and Afghanistan, it becomes clear that military life is very stressful indeed. Of soldiers in these three wars *who experienced direct combat*, only 12.5 per cent (on average) reported symptoms of PTSD. In Vietnam, 54 per cent of the soldiers reporting PTSD symptoms *had not been in combat at all*; similarly, 45 per cent of soldiers in Iraq/Afghanistan reporting symptoms had no combat exposure.[81] It is a remarkable testament to the general stress of war that more men suffered psychiatric symptoms from being in the war zone (area of operations) than from exposure to combat!

A similar finding emerges when suicides for veterans of Afghanistan and Iraq are examined: 30 per cent committed suicide while deployed overseas and 35 per cent after returning from deployment. But 35 per cent of suicides were committed by soldiers who had never been deployed to a war zone, much less experienced combat.[82] The armies of antiquity had very short 'tails', that is logistics and supply trains, and every soldier was expected to take his place in battle when the time came. In modern armies, only a small percentage, 10 to 15 per cent, of the total deployed force is likely to actually be exposed to combat. Even so, for a substantial number of soldiers, the general stress of military life, even without exposure to battle, is enough to cause them to develop psychiatric symptoms and become debilitated. There is no reason to believe that this was not so in antiquity.

Was Buddha a Psychiatric Casualty?

The accounts of Buddha's wanderings for the six years after he left home reveal a soldier suffering from symptoms that a modern psychiatrist would associate with post-traumatic stress disorder (PTSD). Victims of PTSD often first reveal symptoms by disrupting the traditional social ties to which they are most closely bound, often by abandoning their wives and children and ending social contact with parents and friends. Buddha's abandonment of his wife, new born child, extended family, clan and tribe clearly fit this pattern.

Among the most dramatic of Buddha's actions was his repudiation of his identity as a *kshatriya* warrior, perhaps realizing that being a warrior was at the root of his difficulties. Immediately upon leaving the palace, Buddha cut off the top-knot of his hair, a distinguishing mark of his warrior caste status, and threw away the uniform that identified him as a soldier. It may have been Buddha's war experiences that also led him to renounce the warrior caste in general into which he had been born. The central ethical claim of the *kshatriya* was that he protected the society, and his selfless service and glorious death in battle gained him salvation and paradise. Buddha rejected this claim in the *Samyutta,* when he admonished a soldier that death in battle did not bring the soldier salvation at all. Instead, he asserted that the soldier would be reborn as an animal or suffer the purgatory of yet another life, directly challenging the moral legitimacy of the warrior class. Buddha also forbade soldiers to join the monastery.

Others forbidden to join were criminals, slaves, and lepers. Placing *kshatriya* warriors in the company of the outcasts of Aryan society demonstrates Buddha's strong rejection of his own caste. Monastic rules also forbade monks from visiting an army that had marched out of its camp preparing to fight. A monk could visit a military camp if he had good reason, but could stay no longer than three days. Monks were also forbidden to attend mock combats or military reviews. Along with the well-known Buddhist pacifism and rejection of war per se, Buddha rejected the very notion of the warrior class as possessing any moral legitimacy. Simply by virtue of being a soldier, the soldier violated many of the basic ethical principles of Buddhism. As if to make his point more strongly, Buddha donned the saffron robe worn by condemned criminals on their way to execution. This 'identification with the damned' speaks strongly to what may have been Buddha's sense of guilt, either for having survived when others had died (survivor guilt) or for having killed other human beings.

Buddha left the palace with no particular plan, at least as far as we know. He found his way into a forest where he wandered, sometimes with others, sometimes alone. This aimlessness is also characteristic of PTSD sufferers, often leading to homelessness. Buddha was homeless during this time and slept outdoors, as modern sufferers of PTSD often do. Victims of PTSD often engage in self-destructive behaviours like alcohol or drug abuse, cutting and extreme sexual behaviour. During this time in the forest, Buddha inflicted what the texts call 'tortures' upon himself, including going without food until he looked like a skeleton. He rarely ate (lack of appetite), and one text says he was so thin that his stomach touched his spine, suggesting anorexia, yet another condition often endured by victims of PTSD.

He remained silent for long periods, often falling into deep trances and extreme disorientation, what psychiatrists would today call fugue states. Buddha also suffered from night terrors, disturbing dreams about battles with demons, which plagued him for the rest of his life. The texts tell us that Buddha often had dreams about Mara, 'the Lord of the world, the god of sin, greed, and death', who confronted him, sometimes violently, 'following him like an ever present shadow', trying to tempt him in a moment of weakness.[83] We are told that these dreams never went away and that long after Buddha had attained supreme enlightenment he was ever on guard against the appearance of Mara.

After six years of this penitent existence, Buddha encountered a young girl who brought him a bowl of milk and rice. He came to the realization that his life of self-inflicted suffering was not the way to achieve nirvana and relief from the birth-death-rebirth cycle. He renounced asceticism for what he called 'the middle path', left the forest and began a new life as a wandering teacher. Buddha went on to live a long life, travelling throughout the Gangetic Plain (still the location of many skirmishes and battles) and southern Nepal, attracting converts and establishing schools and monasteries to support the new faith. Such extensive activity speaks to his likely recovery from post-traumatic or combat stress disorder, or whatever psychological disturbance prompted him to renounce his former life. We are told that he returned to his village after he had gained a modicum of fame for his teaching, and was welcomed by his family and tribe. It is worth noting, however, that his founding of a new religious practice complete with initiation rites, theology, monastic rules and institutions, is not without its modern equivalent. Soldiers recovering from severe trauma often turn to some form of religiosity as part of their redemption from suffering and return to normal life.[84]

An interesting aspect of post-traumatic stress is the tendency of its recovering victims to retain a strong, often emotional, attachment to elements of their former lives, even though these elements are associated with the circumstances that surrounded the trauma that caused the onset of their stress-related condition. It is not uncommon, for instance, for soldiers to feel strong attachments to their comrades left behind, to being part of something larger than themselves, to miss the sense of importance conveyed by rank and authority etc. In some cases, this attachment is so strong that wounded soldiers affirm their willingness to return to the very lives that produced their injuries or psychiatric collapse.

Despite his condemnation of war and prohibition against serving soldiers entering the monastic orders, Buddha's teachings and the Pali Canon continued to praise the military and its practices as important for monks to emulate in their search for nirvana. If all the militarily relevant passages of the Pali Canon were to be gathered into a separate volume it would be 500 pages long.[85] Many of the positive references to military life and discipline come from the *Jataka*. This is important since the *Jataka* are the main sources from which the Buddhist laity receive instruction.[86] There is, then, an exaggerated importance of the military in the *Jataka* in teaching the Theravada point of view (Theravada Buddhism's reliance upon the Pali Canon makes it the oldest and most original version of Buddhist history/doctrine). Buddha himself often compared the struggle to reach nirvana with the difficulties faced by the soldier in war, and the *Jataka* contains many apocryphal stories of Buddha's participation in battles. Even elements of the monastic organization followed the military model. For example, the title for the second-in-command and director of monastic training was the *senapati*, the same title as the secular king's chief military advisor and field commander. Perhaps it was Buddha's military training and status as a *kshatriya* that so shaped his personality that even when it led to the often terrible experiences of war, he could not, once he recovered from his psychological condition, bring himself to completely abandon his former life. The result is the paradox of a religion strongly rooted in the condemnation of war that encourages its members to acquire and follow many of the habits and practices of soldiers.

Buddha's Death

It may have been Buddha's public rejection of the moral legitimacy of the *kshatriya* that led to the attempts on his life. As Buddhism gained popularity, it was said that many soldiers joined the movement, although not as monks. Buddha's pacifist teaching may have been seen as a threat to the fighting *élan* of the warrior class, as well as to the caste system itself, which he also rejected. Sometime after 491 BC, tradition holds that several attempts were made to kill Buddha. The texts imply that it was Buddha's cousin and second-in-command, Devadatta, who conspired with King Ajatashatru of Maghada to carry out the plot. Devadatta first tried to remove Buddha as head of the movement. When this failed, Devadatta is said to have made three attempts on the Buddha's life.[87] All failed and Devadatta tried to create a schism in the movement. When this failed, he broke away from the movement and started his own order. If the popularity of Buddhism was indeed eroding the moral status and martial spirit of the warrior caste, then Vidudabha, a parricide who came to the throne of Kosala by murdering his father and was engaged in a protracted war at the time, could have had reason to neutralize Buddha and may have been the instigator of these attacks.

As it was, Buddha died in 483 BC, at about the age of 80. The circumstances of his death remain somewhat suspicious, however, and Buddhist tradition suggests that murder cannot be entirely ruled out. Buddha visited the town of Kushingara and took to sleeping in a grove. A blacksmith named Chunda came to him and offered to feed him. This in itself was not unusual since monks routinely received food from people who offered it to gain merit. The texts tell us that Buddha ate the meal at Chunda's house and immediately became violently ill and died.[88] The suddenness with which he was stricken and succumbed suggests the possibility of poisoning. If Buddha was poisoned, the most likely suspect again was Vidudabha.

Modern medical analysis, however, suggests that Buddha may have died from mesenteric infarction, a condition accompanied by acute abdominal pain and the passage of blood, symptoms attributed to Buddha in the Pali Canon and commonly found among the elderly. Mesenteric infarction is caused by an obstruction of the blood vessels of the mesentery, that part of the intestinal wall that binds the intestinal tract to the abdominal cavity, and results in a laceration of the intestinal wall.[89] The condition causes massive blood loss and is usually lethal. If the modern medical analysis is correct, Buddha died a natural death from old age.

As with Moses and Muhammad, we are forced to glimpse the life of Buddha through the dark and clouded glass of time, where reliable material sources are generally lacking or only partially extant. The task of discovery is not made easier by the tendency of Buddha's followers to express the relevant information about the subject in mythic and even supernatural terms. It is still possible, if somewhat speculative, to examine the ancient accounts of Buddha's life while interpreting them within the context of the known history and sociology of the times and reach reasonable conclusions about what the facts may be. On this basis, it seems likely that the usually accepted story of Buddha's life is questionable on a number of key points that are at least worthy of reconsideration if we are ever to understand the man who created one of the world's great religions.

Chapter 3

Muhammad: The Warrior Prophet

To think of Muhammad as a military man will come as something of a new experience to many. And yet Muhammad was truly a great general. In the space of a single decade he fought eight major battles, led eighteen raids, and planned thirty-eight military operations where others were in command, but operating under his orders and strategic direction. He was wounded twice, suffered defeats, and twice had his positions overrun by superior forces before rallying his troops to victory. But Muhammad was more than a great field general and tactician. He was also a military theorist, organizational reformer, strategic thinker, operational level combat commander, political-military leader, heroic soldier, revolutionary, inventor of the theory of insurgency and history's first successful practitioner. Muhammad had no military training before actually commanding an army in the field. Orphaned as a child, he had no opportunity to learn military skills at the hands of an Arab father, the usual means of acquiring military training among the Arabs in his day. Yet, Muhammad became an excellent field commander and tactician, and an even more astute political and military strategist.

The Land of Arabia

The Arabs call their land *Jazirat al-Arab*, the 'island of the Arabs', and it is indeed an island surrounded on three sides by water and by sand on the fourth. The land is harsh and until modern times, when armies could take advantage of motorized transport, history knew of no invader who had succeeded in penetrating the country's sandy barriers to establish a permanent presence in the land. The ground is comprised of a single uniform bloc of ancient rock called the Arabian Shield, and is made up mostly of desert and steppe. The climate is uniformly hot, dry and harsh, receiving only 6 inches of rain per year. There are no permanent rivers anywhere in Arabia.

Arabia is divided into four geographical regions. The first is the Hijaz comprised of the western highlands that parallel the coast of the Red Sea. The mountains themselves reach as high as 4,000 feet and separate the narrow coastal plain from the steppe land of the interior, making the mountains a formidable obstacle to military passage. Running sometimes along the coast and sometimes on the interior side of the mountains is the famous Arabian spice road, the route connecting the ports at the southern tip of the peninsula with the road to the north and the Byzantine border provinces, including Palestine and Egypt. Ships from India and Africa unloaded their cargoes in these ports, were transferred to camel caravan trains and carried northward to Mecca, the commercial centre located halfway between the ports and the markets further to the north. This road was the commercial lifeline of Mecca and the entire westernmost part of the country. Muhammad spent most of his life in the Hijaz.

The second geographic zone is the interior, largely stony sandy wastes and desert. The Rub' al-Khali (Empty Quarter) is a vast desert in the south that has large sand dunes sometimes reaching more than 100 feet high and running on for miles at a stretch. In the centre of Arabia are the Nafud and Dahna deserts that constitute formidable barriers to west-east travel. In the north lies the great Syrian Desert and the smaller wastes of Hisma and Hamad. The routes used by the Meccan caravan trains skirted these desolate areas. It was impossible for man or beast to attempt a crossing and survive. The third zone lies far to the east and comprises the hot and humid eastern coastal lands of the Persian Gulf where agriculture is possible due to abundant ground water. Far to the south is Yemen, the fourth zone, the famous land of antiquity from which the prized aromatic plants that produced frankincense and myrrh were found.

Yemen is a land of towering mountains, fertile valleys and coastal plains. The monsoon rains make the ground fertile and well-suited to agriculture. The population of Yemen was mostly settled rather than nomadic.

During Muhammad's time, five-sixths of the population of Arabia were Bedouin and permanent settlements were few.[1] Ptolemy, writing in his *Geography* sometime around 150 CE, listed only 218 settlements in Arabia, and more than 150 of these were small villages. Only six 'cities' were listed and all of these were in the Yemen, where the land was sufficiently fertile to sustain large populations.[2] Most of these 'cities' were relatively small in both area and population and only two were surrounded by walls of mud-brick and stone. One might reasonably guess that the size of these cities was around 2,000 souls.[3] The language of Arabia itself reflects the lack of urbanization, for there is no word for 'city' in classical Arabic.

In a few places ground water seeps to the surface forming a fetid, swamp-like area called an oasis. Most of the oases in the Hijaz are located north of Medina, itself the largest oasis in the region. The second largest oasis in the Hijaz is only 10 square miles in area. Although malaria is endemic, the oases are valuable for their water supply and their ability to sustain substantial agriculture. Agriculture was probably introduced to the area sometime around the first century CE, most probably by the Jewish tribes. The origins of the Jewish tribes in al Hijaz are obscure. By Muhammad's time, the Jewish tribes of the area were indistinguishable from the Arab tribes in structure, ethos and behaviour. Only their religious observance distinguished them from other Arab clans.

In the harsh land of the Hijaz only the Bedouin was truly at home. Those who lived in the oases or the few towns often had to hire Bedouin guides to travel from one place to another or hire them as caravan guards to ensure a safe journey. The heat, trackless roads, lack of food, scarcity of water and the general discomfort of life in the desert, while problematic during times of peace, became the allies of the Bedouin in times of war. His daily ration of dates, camel milk and water would bring any other army to its knees in a few days but the Bedouin could subsist on this diet forever. Living on dates, water and the camels that carried them, Arab armies were far more mobile than those of their adversaries. During the first battles of the Arab conquests, their armies chose battlefields that were close to the desert so that in the event of a defeat they could retreat into the desert where the enemy could not follow.

The Bedouin nomads of the Hijaz moved with their flocks on a regular basis, searching for pasture and water for their animals. These Arab nomads practised a form of enclosed nomadism, that is, movement in a regular pattern that brought them close to settlements and towns where they could trade or purchase goods with the few meagre resources they possessed. The relationship between nomads and the settled populations was genuinely symbiotic in that neither could survive without the products of the other. The grain and dates that were staples of the nomad diets were obtained in the oases where they grew; saddles, weapons, cloth and other goods were manufactured in the towns. In return, the nomad provided the town dweller with goats, sheep and camels, as well as the materials from which tents and blankets might be woven.

Most Bedouin were desperately poor and were almost always on the brink of malnutrition. In times of drought or starvation, it was not an uncommon practice to bury their female babies alive in order to free up resources for the surviving adults. Moreover, spending long days watching animals graze made for stultifying boredom. It is not surprising that the *ghazw* or raid became a way of Bedouin life.

Raiding the camps and flocks of other Bedouin, or the outskirts of the towns where the horses and camels were usually set to grazing, served two important functions. First, it provided a needed form of social stimulation, the only way in which the Bedouin could practise the manly virtues of the warrior. For the most part these raids were more a rough sport than real conflicts. Pitched battles were usually avoided and casualties few. Sometimes they resulted in individual combats between chiefs but even these rarely resulted in death. The second function of the raid was to act as a form of redistribution of wealth, a source of goods that would otherwise be unattainable by some Bedouin families. In a poor country like Arabia, where malnutrition was endemic, raiding was often the only way a man could improve his lot in life. Finally, the competition for water and grazing often caused skirmishes between Bedouin clans. In difficult climatic times these skirmishes could become very bloody indeed, since to be defeated meant to be driven from the water and grass and risked the destruction of the flocks. Still, it is hard to escape the impression that raiding was more a social enterprise than either a military or economic one. Arabs often explain raiding in the following terms: 'Our business is to make raids on the enemy, on our neighbour, and on our brother, in case we find nobody to raid but our brother.'[4]

The basis of Bedouin society was the clan. Every tent represented a family; an encampment of tents was a *hayy*. The members of a *hayy* comprised a *qawm* or clan. A number of clans related by blood and kin formed a *qabilah* or tribe. All members of the same clan considered themselves as of one blood and submitted to the authority of a single chief called a *sheikh*, whose power to command was limited by the fact that all males in the tribe were considered equals who might reasonably disagree and even resist the *sheikh* in important matters. As an Arab proverb put it, 'a man's clan are his claws'. Loyalty to one's clan was unconditional. Anyone committing a crime inside the clan was either banished or killed by the clan members themselves. The murder of a clan member by someone outside the clan required all males to avenge the crime in any manner possible, the usual rules of chivalry and combat being ignored in favour of treachery and ambush. This was the *asabiyah* or blood loyalty that rendered anyone outside the clan devoid of any moral standing that might place limits on revenge. During Muhammad's day the clan was the centre of the Arab's moral universe. Only members of the clan had any claim to ethical treatment, and even this bound only fellow members of the clan. Those outside the clan lacked any moral standing and were treated accordingly.

The Arabs of Muhammad's time lived in a harsh society in a harsh land. There were few laws and no institutions to afford justice or restrain violence. Only the blood feud and its threat of retaliation against a wrongdoer provided a rough balance of power to limit violence. Blood feuds were not to be taken lightly, since the feud did not end until the wrongdoer was dead or some member of his tribe had been killed as compensation. Later, it became a common practice to limit the feud by paying the blood wit (*diya*), financial compensation usually in the form of a number of camels, to the person or clan against whom the wrong had been committed. This aside, anyone outside the clan remained without moral standing. When Muhammad divided the ethical world between believers and unbelievers in which the latter might rightly be enslaved or even killed by the former, he was only extending the practice of the blood feud to religion. The religious community of believers, to which absolute loyalty was owed and outside of which there were no obligations, replaced the old clan community of blood and kin.

Muhammad the Man

Muhammad was born on 20 August 570 in Mecca. The original inhabitants of Mecca were the Jerhum tribe who, according to legend, were related to the Amalekites of the Old Testament. At some point the Khuzza tribe, migrating north from Yemen, drove the original occupants from the town and took up residence there. About a century before Muhammad's birth, the Quraish tribe, led by one Qusai, drove the Khuzza from Mecca and settled his people there. The Khuzza had not lived in houses, but in tents surrounded by shallow walls to break the wind and wind-driven sand. Qusai is said to have convinced his people to give up their previous bedouin ways and to build houses. These houses were little more than hovels made from rough stones held in place with mud mortar and roofed with palm logs or brushwood that offered some protection from the sun. Some of the tribe lived in the town while other clans, the Quraish of the Hollow, lived outside its confines. Muhammad was a member of the Quraish residing in Mecca. By the time of Muhammad's birth, Mecca's location as a stopping and transfer point for the north-south trade route between the coastal ports and Gaza had led to the growth of a merchant class. Mecca became a semi-urban society comprised of groups of traders and artisans. While the Quraish tribe dominated Mecca's affairs, they were not the only ones whose interests had to be considered.

Mecca lay 48 miles inland from the Red Sea in a barren rock valley 600 yards wide and 1.5 miles long, squeezed among stony mountains. It is described in the Qur'an as 'unfit for cultivation'.[5] The name of the town in Arabic was originally Makkah, derived from the ancient Sabean word, *mukuraba*, meaning 'sanctuary'.[6] From time immemorial, Mecca had possessed a shrine (the Ka'bah) where Arabs had come to worship the idols kept there. For at least a century before Muhammad's birth, the main idol worshiped in Mecca was Hubal. Other towns and settlements had their own shrines and idols. Most Arabs remained idol worshipers until their conversion to Islam.

Once a year, Arabs came from all over Arabia to worship at the Ka'bah in Mecca. Providing services to these pilgrims was a lucrative business, and the Quraish profited handsomely. The pilgrimage itself lasted only three days. But in the weeks before the pilgrimage a number of trading fairs grew up around Mecca that offered rich commercial opportunities to Meccan merchants. There was a large sacred territory, the *haram*, that surrounded the Ka'bah and within which fighting and the carrying of arms was prohibited. By Muhammad's time, Mecca had established itself as one of the important commercial and religious centres in Arabia, and the Quraish controlled the Ka'bah and much of the city's commerce.

One Abdul Muttalib (b. circa 497) was the grandfather of Muhammad. He was the head of the Hashim clan and in charge of the wells around the Ka'bah that provided water to the pilgrims. As a clan chief, he was a man of considerable influence. Abdul Muttalib had five sons, one of which, Abdullah, was Muhammad's father. Abdullah died in 570, leaving his wife pregnant. The child she was carrying was Muhammad, who was born in August that year. It was the custom among Arab town dwellers to place their new babies in the care of a wet nurse of a Bedouin tribe to care for the child as its foster mother. The child mortality rate from disease and malnutrition in Arab settlements was horrendously high, and it was believed that sending the child into the healthier environment of the desert increased the child's chances of survival.

Because Muhammad had no father, it was difficult to find a wet-nurse willing to take him. Muhammad was eventually accepted by a woman of the Beni Saad tribe living outside Mecca. Muhammad spent two years with his foster mother before being returned to his mother in Mecca, where he lived with her for four years until she died. Muhammad was 6 years old when he was orphaned. His grandfather took him in, and he was looked after by a slave girl in his grandfather's household. When Muhammad was 8, his grandfather died, and he was placed in the charge of his uncle, Abu Talib, the new head of the Hashim clan.

The fortunes of the Hashim clan were in decline and Muhammad continued to live in poverty. As an orphan, he had no one to protect him, to educate him or supply him with money and contacts to make his way in business. Muhammad sometimes worked as a shepherd and spent considerable time alone. He became a fixture around the Ka'bah where he sometimes helped provide water to the pilgrims and other worshipers. When Muhammad was about 14, a tribal war broke out between the Quraish and the Hawazin that lasted for five years. In one of the earliest battles of this war, Muhammad went along with his uncles where he retrieved arrows that could be shot back at the enemy.

As far as the texts tell us, this was Muhammad's only military experience prior to commanding his own troops in the later war with the Quraish. Military training was provided to Arab males by their fathers or uncles as a matter of course and the fact that Muhammad received no military training is curious. All the more so since one of his uncles, Hamza, was already a renowned warrior when Muhammad was a boy. Perhaps because Muhammad was a quiet boy who kept to himself, spending long hours tending flocks or at the Ka'bah, his uncles may have concluded that he lacked the necessary aptitude for fighting. If so, they could hardly have been more mistaken.

Over the next decade Muhammad tried his hand at commerce with no noticeable success. He did, however, acquire a reputation for honesty, and may have acquired the nickname 'the trustworthy', but we cannot be certain of this.[7] When he was 25, his uncle secured a place for him in a caravan to Syria. His reputation for honesty served him well, and he was made responsible for selling some of the goods as well as the purchase of some return goods. The caravan belonged to a rich widow of the Quraish tribe named Khadijah. The death rate among Arab men from disease, injury and blood feuds left Mecca with a considerable number of widows, among them a few who had property and considerable wealth.[8] Khadijah was one of these. Khadijah's assignment of her caravan to Muhammad was apparently a testament to his merchant skill and honesty.

Upon Muhammad's return to Mecca, Khadijah proposed marriage. Muhammad was 25. Khadijah was already twice widowed, and said to have been about 40 years old, but may have been somewhat younger, since she bore him several children, four girls and two boys, although some sources (Seyyid Hossein Nasr) say Muhammad had only one son.[9] The marriage provided Muhammad with considerable commercial opportunities and he succeeded very well. More important was his relationship with Khadijah. She became his true love and confidante. He trusted her in all things and she supported him when he began to have his revelations. It was Khadijah's cousin, Waraqah, a Christian, who also supported Muhammad on Khadijah's word that his revelatory experiences were the signs of a genuine prophet. Muhammad loved Khadijah until the day she died and, while she lived, Muhammad never loved another woman.

The next fifteen years, 595 to 610, are the 'hidden years' in which the texts are mostly silent about Muhammad's life. He seems to have had a modestly successful business career and as an organizer of large caravans he gained experience as both an administrator and logistician. Muhammad must have travelled with the caravans several times and the texts tell us of his encounters with Christian monks living in caves along the caravan route. It was during this period that Muhammad's infant son or sons died. He adopted his cousin, Ali, the son of his uncle, Abu Talib, who had once looked after him. Muhammad also took in Zayd, a Christian slave boy given to him by his wife's nephew. Both Ali and Zayd looked upon Muhammad as their father and were among his earliest converts.

Sometime during this time Muhammad developed the habit of going off by himself to meditate, often taking refuge in a cave for days at a time. It is noteworthy that other Arabs would not have found Muhammad's habit an unusual occurrence. Even the idolaters of Mecca sometimes turned to this form of desert asceticism. In Arabic the practice is known as *tahannuth* and was something like a modern retreat, a temporary withdrawal from worldly affairs for the purpose of religious meditation.[10] Tradition holds that Muhammad's grandfather, Abdul Muttalib, was in the habit of spending the entire month of Ramadan each year in a cave in the mountains around Mecca.[11] It is not unreasonable that the old man may have introduced the young Muhammad to the practice. It may have been no more than coincidence, however, that Muhammad experienced his first revelation while living in a cave during the month of Ramadan.

Muhammad continued his practice of retreating into the desert throughout his life. Aisha, whom he married after the death of his beloved Khadijah in 619, recalled that 'solitude became dear to him and he would go to a cave on Mount Hira to engage in meditation there for a number of nights, before returning home for a short time to procure provisions for another stay'.[12] It was during one of these retreats, during Ramadan in 610, that Muhammad experienced his first revelation. Muhammad interpreted these revelatory experiences as instructions from God and they continued for the rest of his life. He would repeat the instructions to his followers who memorized them and/or wrote them down.[13] Sometime later they were collected in what became known as the Qur'an. The Qur'an and its moral instructions became the foundation for the new religion of Islam.

It is interesting to examine the physical circumstances that Muhammad himself described as accompanying the onset and duration of his revelations insofar as they indicate an identifiable medical condition that may have accompanied the revelations. Only two of his revelations, his first call to God's service and the revelation in which he recounted journeying from Mecca to Jerusalem in a single night where he met Moses and Jesus, seem to have been visual experiences. All other revelations which came to him throughout his life seem to have been completely auditory and did not include any visual components.[14] When Muhammad was asked to describe his revelatory experience, he said 'Sometimes it cometh unto me like the reverberations of a bell, and that is the hardest upon me; the reverberations abate when I am aware of their message. And sometimes the Angel taketh the form of a man and speaketh unto me, and I am aware of what he saith.'[15] Whenever a revelation was imminent, Muhammad was gripped by a feeling of pain. Even on cold days he would sweat profusely.[16] Ibn Ishaq records that the prophet knew when a revelation was about to occur. He would lie down and cover himself with a cloak or blanket. He would perspire profusely. At the end of the event Muhammad sat up and repeated the message he had been given. In only a few instances did the revelation come upon him when he was riding or at a public gathering.[17]

The symptoms recorded as accompanying Muhammad's revelations seem strongly similar to those associated with recurrent malaria, a disease whose episodes are often accompanied by vivid visual and auditory hallucinations. Often the first onset of the disease is 'acute', that is, its symptoms are greatly exaggerated and the fever very high. Ibn Ishaq in describing the first attacks of 'the fever' that afflicted Muhammad's followers when they arrived in Medina seems to describe an acute onset. He tells us that:

> When the Apostle came to Medina it was the most fever infested land on earth, and his companions suffered severely from it...they were delirious and out of their minds with a high temperature.[18]

Malarial infection does not confer "immunity" from other outbreaks, but does confer a resistance to the disease, so that follow-on episodes are usually not as severe as the first onset. And so it was that while Muhammad's followers arrived in Medina from Mecca and immediately contracted malaria, Ibn Ishaq tells us 'God kept it from his Apostle'.[19] This suggests that Muhammad may have already contracted the disease and was resistant to, though not immune from, further outbreaks.

Mecca is a hot and dry place where malaria was not endemic. If Muhammad had malaria, it is unlikely that he first contracted the disease there. Malaria thrived in places like Medina and other swampy, humid, and fetid oases throughout Arabia. Medina had a reputation among caravaneers as a place where fever was endemic and they sometimes by-passed the town to avoid contracting it. As a caravan organizer, Muhammad would likely have stopped at any number of oases during his journeys where he might have been exposed to and contracted malaria. Moreover, the symptoms that accompanied Muhammad's later revelations are not those of an acute onset but of an episodic recurrence. None of this, of course, is to bring into question the legitimacy of Muhammad's claim that his revelations were of divine origin. It is only to say that Muhammad's own descriptions of his revelations suggest they were accompanied by symptoms usually associated with malaria.[20]

After his first revelation Muhammad had no further revelations for three years. Then a second revelation commanded him to preach the message of Allah. Muhammad's ministry lasted from 610 to his death in 632, with the public phase beginning in 613. Although some Meccans first thought Muhammad mad, most had no difficulty with his preaching until he began to denounce their worship of idols. This denunciation of idol worship at the Ka'bah generated much ill-will since the Ka'bah was the object of the annual pilgrimage to Mecca and the trade fairs that brought considerable income to the city. The most objectionable of all Muhammad's pronouncements, however, was his claim that all those who had not become Muslims before their deaths were suffering in hell. To claim that non-Muslims were in hell was a direct attack on the memory and reputation of one's ancestors. In a society which revered ancestors whose exploits preserved in oral accounts established the ideals of virtuous behaviour, Muhammad's condemnation was a grievous insult to Arab honour, one that could result in a blood feud. Muhammad was treading on dangerous ground and the opposition to him in Mecca grew stronger.

For the next six years Muhammad and his few followers were the objects of ridicule and persecution. Conversions to Islam cut across tribal and familial lines, with the result that Muslim converts were sometimes persecuted by their own kin. The most severe persecutions were suffered by the converts who came from the lower social classes, slaves, widows, orphans and the poor, who had no families or clans to protect them. Ibn Ishaq tells us:

> The Quraish showed their enmity to all those who followed the Apostle; every clan which contained Muslims attacked them, imprisoning them, and beating them, allowing them no food or drink, and exposing them to the burning heat of Mecca, so as to seduce them from their religion.[21]

Muhammad never forgot the persecution inflicted upon his early followers, and when the time came he took his revenge.

In 619 Muhammad's beloved Khadijah died. Abu Talib, Muhammad's uncle, clan chief and Muhammad's protector in Mecca, died shortly afterwards. Muhammad was now alone with no clan relatives to protect him from violence. The Meccans continued their ridicule and harassment, but stopped short of violence directed against Muhammad himself. It was clear, however, that life was becoming dangerous in Mecca and that sooner or later someone would try to kill him. To avert this fate, Muhammad journeyed to Ta'if, a small trading town 50 miles east of Mecca, to see if their chiefs might permit him and his followers to emigrate to the town. Met with ridicule and rejection, Muhammad returned to Mecca even more afraid for his life. Desperate for someone to protect him, he approached three clan chiefs in Mecca to ask for their protection. Two refused, but one, al-Mut'im bin 'Adiy, chief of the Nofal clan of the Quraish, agreed to take Muhammad under his protection.[22] The next day he and his sons appeared under arms in the public square of the Ka'bah to announce that Muhammad was under their protection.[23]

Even with al-Mut'im's protection, Muhammad was still in danger if he continued to preach among the Meccans, who regarded his preaching as both insulting to their family lineages and dangerous to their commercial interests. Muhammad ceased his efforts in Mecca and began to preach to the pilgrims and traders who came to the trade fairs and encamped on the town's outskirts. In 620 Muhammad preached to a group of seven pilgrims from the oasis of Yathrib (Medina). The next year these seven returned bringing with them five more to hear his message. Muhammad met with the group in a little valley in the mountains outside Mecca at a place known to the locals as Aqaba. Here the pilgrims from Yathrib were converted to Islam. Along with a number of moral maxims that they agreed to obey, the new converts pledged to obey Muhammad and recognized him as the Messenger of God. In the history of Islam this pledge is called the First Pledge of Aqaba. However, the pilgrims did not undertake any obligation to take up arms in defence of Islam or to use force to protect Muhammad himself.

The following year, 621, a larger group of pilgrims from Medina, seventy-three men and two women, arrived and met with Muhammad at Aqaba and converted to Islam. This is called the Second Pledge of Aqaba, and it is a very important event in the history of Islam. Unlike the first pledge, the converts swore an oath to protect Muhammad as they would their own family members, with force if necessary. The leader of the group, Al-Bara, swore that 'we will protect you as we protect our women. We give our allegiance and we are men of war possessing arms which have been passed from father to son.'[24] Muhammad replied, 'I am of you and you are of me. I will war against them that war against you and be at peace with those at peace with you.'[25] The pledge at Aqaba was a traditional Arab oath of obligation requiring mutual armed assistance. But Muhammad promised the new converts, known now as the *Ansar* or Helpers, something which no traditional clan chief could have offered: everlasting life in paradise.

The group of pilgrims seems to have come from the Kazrai clan of Medina. By these pledges, Muhammad gained two things. First, he expanded his influence to a clan beyond Mecca and his own Quraish tribe. Here was the embryonic beginning of what became the *ummah*, the new community of believers whose loyalties transcended the old clan and kin loyalties, but retained the moral exclusiveness of the blood feud. Second, Muhammad gained the protection of a clan living in Medina. Their guarantee of protection made it possible for Muhammad and his followers to emigrate to a less hostile place where they would be safe from persecution.

Before the Second Pledge of Aqaba, Muhammad's instructions received through his revelations had commanded him only to call men to God. Shortly after the Second Pledge, Muhammad received another revelation that granted permission for him and his followers to fight and shed blood. Ibn Ishaq tells us that the first permission for Muslims to fight appears in *sura* 22, verses 39–42 of the Qur'an which says:

> Permission to fight is given to those who are being killed unjustly and God is well able to give victory. Also to those who have been unjustly turned out of their country, merely because they said, 'God is our Lord.' Had God not used some men to resist others, the wicked would before now have demolished the cloisters, the churches, and the places of prayer and worship where the name of God is constantly remembered would have been destroyed. Assuredly God will help those who help Him. God is Almighty.[26]

The passage seems to justify violence only in self-defence.

According to Ibn Ishaq, the resort to violence was expanded by a later revelation when he tells us:

> Then God sent down to him [Muhammad]: 'Fight them so
> that there be no more seduction,' that is, until no believer
> is seduced from his religion. 'And the religion is God's,'
> that is, 'until God alone is worshipped.'[27]

The second and later revelation seems to justify violence beyond
self-defence to include preemptory force to prevent someone from
being 'seduced' from God's correct path. The significance of these
passages for the military historian is that Muhammad seems to
have anticipated the need for violence in order for his ministry to
survive.

Muhammad must have been a man of some physical strength,
which he demonstrated through his enjoyment of wrestling and
swimming and, on more than one occasion, by throwing his
opponents to the ground when they angered him. Martin Lings
has put together a convincing physical description of the man
from the extant original sources.

> He was of medium stature, inclined to slimness, with
> a large head, broad shoulders, and the rest of his body
> perfectly proportioned. His hair and beard were thick
> and black, not altogether straight but slightly curled. His
> hair reached midway between the lobes of his ears and
> his shoulders, and his beard was of a length to match.
> He had a noble breadth of forehead and the ovals of his
> large eyes were wide, with exceptionally long lashes
> and extensive brows, slightly arched but not joined.
> In most of the early descriptions his eyes are said to
> have been black, but according to one or two of these
> earliest sources they were brown or even light brown.
> His nose was aquiline and his mouth was wide and
> finely shaped, a comeliness always visible for although
> he let his beard grow, he never allowed the hair of his
> moustache to protrude over his upper lip. His skin was
> white, but tanned by the sun.[28]

Muhammad was handsome by any Arab standard of manliness and beauty, and women found him very attractive. Until he was 50, Muhammad had only one wife, his beloved Khadijah. After her death at 62, he had twelve others. He had six children by his first wife, but no children by the twelve who followed, although all were still of child-bearing age. He did, however, father a son with Mariya, an Egyptian Coptic Christian concubine given him as a gift, but who never became his wife.[29] Nearly all of Muhammad's later wives were widows. Perhaps he preferred the company of mature women to young girls; perhaps these older women reminded him of his own mother who died when he was 6.

Muhammad must have been a very psychologically complex person. Whatever glimpses into his psychology may be gained from historical accounts must be regarded as fraught with error. The preeminent scholar W. Montgomery Watt, drawing on Ibn Ishaq's notes, offers the following description of Muhammad's general psychological disposition.

> He was given to sadness, and there were long periods of silence when he was deep in thought; yet he never rested but was always busy with something...He never spoke unnecessarily. What he said was always to the point, and sufficient to make his meaning clear. He spoke rapidly. Over his feelings he had firm control....His time was carefully apportioned according to the various demands on him. In his dealings with people he was above all tactful. He could be severe at times.[30]

Although capable of ferocious anger, Muhammad seems to have generally been a calm man open to suggestions, who regularly sought the advice of others that he often accepted. There is no evidence that his followers were afraid to approach him and offer advice. Although he seems to have possessed an innate gift for things military, he often sought the advice of his more experienced officers before a military operation. He was democratic in the typical manner of Arab clan chiefs and remained accessible to his followers to the end. He was kind to the poor, widows and orphans, greatly loved by his followers and, later, even by some of his former enemies.

There is no doubt that Muhammad believed sincerely and deeply in his having been called by God and in his mission to spread the new faith. Yet, he remained psychologically balanced. He always knew the difference between his own thoughts and those he had received from his revelations. When, for example, he was arranging his troops before the Battle of Badr, one of his officers thought the disposition a mistake. He asked Muhammad if he was giving his men instructions he had received from God, or were they just his own ideas. Muhammad replied that the instructions were only his ideas. The officer suggested that the dispositions be changed for sound military reasons and Muhammad agreed. Although the *hadith* and oral traditions of Islam are full of accounts of Muhamamd performing miracles, Muhammad himself never claimed to be able to do so, and was well aware of his own mortality. This sense of balance was also reflected in his condemnation of religious asceticism which he had once witnessed among Christian monks living in the desert. In this regard, he remarked, 'God has not ordered us to destroy ourselves.'[31] He was scrupulously clean, perhaps even compulsively so, and often remarked how the presence of food adhering to a man's moustache disgusted him. He disliked strong smells, and would not eat anything flavoured with onions or garlic.[32]

None of these dispositions completely overcame Muhammad's fierce sense of rectitude, anger and violence which he could display when he thought it necessary. Like Moses, Christ, and Akhenaten of Egypt, Muhammad was 'a god-intoxicated man'.[33] He was also a man of physical courage and never seems to have feared death. Ibn Ishaq records an incident in which one Umar bin al-Khattab, one of the chief persecutors of the Muslims in Mecca, came to see Muhammad. He was armed with his sword and the Apostle's bodyguards feared that Umar might attempt to kill Muhammad. Muhammad ordered his bodyguards to stand aside and let Umar enter the house.

The Apostle gave the word and he was let in. The Apostle rose and met him in the room, seized him round the girdle or by the middle of his cloak, and dragged him along violently, saying, 'What has brought you, son of Khattab, for by God I do not think you will cease your persecution until God brings calamity upon you.'[34]

To attack an armed man who is openly your enemy with your bare hands requires a degree of fearlessness that most do not possess. But Muhammad was an Arab chief and courage was a required trait, especially in a warrior of God.

Muhammad's sense of divine purpose led him to regard violence as an acceptable means to achieve God's ends. This tendency revealed itself early, during the period when his few followers were being persecuted by the Quraish in Mecca. One day Muhammad was spending some time at the *Ka'bah* when he was approached by a small group of men who began to insult and harass him. After enduring their taunts and threats for some time, Muhammad turned to them and said, 'Will you listen to me O Quraish? By Him who holds my life in his hands, I will bring you slaughter.'[35]

For a man of such rectitude, Muhammad seems to have possessed an acute sensitivity to personal ridicule. He hated poets and song-singers who were the primary means of spreading political propaganda and unkind portrayals of the enemies of the people that had hired them. In a society where honour meant as much as life, a man's reputation was sacred. Hiring a poet to travel about and ridicule a man was serious business indeed. At the same time, the poet was a respected member of Arab society and usually not subject to violence, although the person who hired the poet was. But Muhammad seems to have had a deep loathing for poets per se. Ibn Ishaq tells us that when Muhammad experienced his first revelation he was extremely frightened. Muhammad thought he might be possessed or, worse, a poet! 'Now none of God's creatures are more hateful to me than an ecstatic poet or a man possessed.' Muhammad was so frightened by what was happening to him that he said, 'I will go to the top of the mountain and throw myself down that I may kill myself and gain rest.'[36] Muhammad's hatred of poets was almost irrational in its intensity. As a poor orphan, Muhammad must have been regularly subject to insults and taunts by others, and it is possible that his hatred of poets was rooted in this early childhood experience.

Muhammad gave permission for his Meccan followers, the *muhajirun* or Emigrants, to emigrate to Medina shortly after the Second Pledge of Aqaba. Muhammad and a few of his closest followers remained in Mecca waiting for their opportunity to leave. Some Meccan hotheads gathered and formulated a plot to kill him in his bed. Legend has it that Muhammad was warned by the angel Gabriel not to sleep in his bed that night and escaped harm. Muhammad and one of his followers hid in a cave near Mecca for three days while the Meccans searched for them. The Meccans soon lost interest, and Muhammad left Mecca and made his way safely to Medina. Ibn Ishaq tells us that 'the Apostle on that day (when he arrived in Medina) was 53 years of age, that being thirteen years after God called him.'[37] Muhammad's journey to Medina is known to the Arabs as the *Hijra*, and marks the Year 1 on the Arab calendar from which all subsequent historical events have since been measured.

The Guerilla Leader

Seven months after arriving in Medina, Muhammad undertook his first military operation by attacking the Meccan caravans. With his own people destitute, Muhammad turned to the old Arab practice of raiding to solve the problem of his followers' poverty. Muhammad must have known that any attack on the Meccan caravans would be but the opening skirmish in a long campaign in which the Meccans would try to kill him and exterminate his followers. Muhammad's attack on his own kinsmen would have been unthinkable in pre-Islamic times as an atrocity of the worst kind. There was no greater sin among Arabs than to abandon or abuse one's own kin. It is no wonder, then, that Muhammad claimed a divine imperative (sura 22:39–40) to justify his actions. For the next eleven years, Muhammad conducted war against the Meccans and every other tribe that opposed him and his new religion.

Muhammad was too good a strategic thinker not to have been aware of these realities. And yet, he went ahead with his plans to challenge the Meccans. There may be two reasons why Muhammad did so. First and foremost, Muhammad was a 'god-intoxicated man', a true believer in himself as God's Messenger tasked by Allah to spread the doctrine of Islam to the unbelievers. Muhammad's revelations had condoned the use of violence to accomplish the task that God had set for him. If the struggle was ordained by God, then its successful outcome must also be ordained. Like later revolutionaries who believed in the 'inevitable forces of history' to guide their actions, Muhammad relied upon his personal relationship with God to guide his. He declared war on the Meccan idolaters because it was God's wish that he do so. The attacks on the Meccan caravans were the first strike in a larger strategy of conquest and destruction of his enemies.

The rectitude and certainty that often accompany such thinking sometimes have more common roots. In this case the insults and taunts Muhammad had suffered as an orphaned child in Mecca and the cruel, sometimes fatal, persecution laid upon his early followers by the Meccans, as well as his own ridicule at their hands, might easily have permitted a psychology of personal revenge to influence Muhammad's thinking. Both influences, a deep belief in God's will and a searing hatred for his tormenters, may have combined and led Muhammad to believe he was capable of overcoming the strategic realities that would obviously attend a war with the Meccans. Only someone who believed that victory was inevitable would have begun such a war.

Although his reforms and military achievements give him much in common with the greatest generals in history, Muhammad was not a conventional field general. He was, instead, a new type of warrior, one never before seen in antiquity. Muhammad was first and foremost a revolutionary, a fiery religious guerrilla leader who created and led the first genuine national insurgency in antiquity that is comprehensible in modern terms, a fact not lost on the *jihadis* of the present day who often cite the Qur'an and Muhammad's use of violence as justification for their own. Unlike more conventional generals, Muhammad's goal was not the defeat of a foreign enemy or invader, but the replacement of the existing Arabian social order with a new one based upon a radically different ideological view of the world.

To achieve his revolutionary goals, Muhammad utilized all the means recognized by modern analysts as characteristic of and necessary to a successful insurgency. Although Muhammad began his struggle for a new order with a small guerrilla cadre capable of undertaking only limited hit-and-run raids, by the time he was ready to attack Mecca a decade later that small guerrilla force had grown into a large conventional armed force with integrated cavalry and infantry units capable of conducting large-scale combat operations. It was this conventional military instrument that Muhammad's successors used to forge a great empire. It was the first truly national military force in Arab history.

Beginning with a small band of believers, Muhammad undertook a guerrilla war in which he waged a campaign of ambushes and raids to erode the economic and political base of his enemy's power. He introduced new social programmes and a politico-religious ideology that attracted others to his cause, expanding his base of military manpower and making it possible to recruit and deploy larger military forces. After years of guerrilla war, Muhammad finally defeated his enemies by drawing them into a series of set-piece battles, eventually capturing Mecca itself. Supporting the military effort was the political dimension of the insurgency that used political alliances to deprive his enemy of a source of military manpower and to erode their popular base of support. Political manoeuvre and negotiation, intelligence, propaganda and the judicious use of terror and assassination were employed to wage a psychological warfare campaign against those potential sources of opposition that could not yet be won over by calculations of self-interest or ideology.

Muhammad's rise to power was a textbook example of a successful insurgency, indeed the first such example in antiquity of which I am aware. Modern insurgents like Mao Tse Tung, Ho Chi Minh, Jomo Kenyatta, Fidel Castro and, perhaps, George Washington would easily have recognized Muhammad's strategy and methods in their own revolutionary struggles. The West has been accustomed to thinking of the Arab conquests which followed Muhammad in purely *conventional* military terms. But the armies that achieved those conquests did not exist in Arabia before Muhammad. It was Muhammad's successful *unconventional* guerrilla operations, his successful insurgency, that brought those armies into existence. Thus the later Arab conquests, as regards both strategic concept and the new armies as instruments of military method, were the consequences of Muhammad's prior military success as the leader of an insurgency.

This aspect of Muhammad's military life as a guerrilla insurgent is likely to strike the reader as curious and, as such, is worth exploring in some detail. If the means and methods used by modern military analysts to characterize insurgency warfare are employed as categories of analysis, it is clear that Muhammad's campaign to spread Islam throughout Arabia fulfilled each of the analytical criteria.

The first requirement for an insurgency to succeed is a determined leader whose followers regard him as special in some way and worthy of their following him. In Muhammad's case, his charismatic personality was enhanced by his deeply held belief that he was indeed God's Messenger, and that to follow Muhammad was to obey the dictates of God himself. Insurgencies also require a messianic ideology, one that espouses a coherent creed or plan to replace the existing social, political and economic order, which is seen as unjust, with a new order that is better, more just or ordained by history or even God himself. Muhammad used the new religious creed of Islam to challenge central traditional Arab social institutions and values as oppressive and unholy and worthy of replacement. To this end, he created the *ummah* or community of believers, God's community on earth, to serve as a messianic replacement for the clans and tribes that were the basis of traditional Arab society. One of Muhammad's most important achievements was the establishment of new social institutions that greatly altered and in some cases completely replaced those of the old Arab social order.

Successful insurgencies also require a disciplined cadre of true believers to do the work of organizing and recruiting new members. Muhammad's revolutionary cadre consisted of the small group of original converts he attracted in Mecca and took with him to Medina. These were the *muhajirun* or Emigrants. The first converts among the clans of Medina, the *ansar* or Helpers, also filled the ranks of the cadre. Within this revolutionary cadre was an inner circle of talented men, some of them much later converts. Some, like Abdullah Ibn Ubay and Khalid al-Walid, were experienced field commanders and provided a much-needed source of military expertise. Muhammad's inner circle advised him and saw to it that his directives were carried out. Not surprisingly some of his advisors came to hold key positions during the Prophet's lifetime and fought among themselves for power after his death.

Once Muhammad had created his cadre of revolutionaries, he established a base from which to undertake military operations against his adversaries. These operations initially took the form of ambushes and raids aimed at isolating Mecca, the enemy's main city, and other trading towns that opposed him. Only one in six Arabs lived in a city or town at this time; the others resided in the 'countryside' or desert, living as enclosed pastoral nomads.[38]

Muhammad chose Medina as his base of operations. Medina was strategically located in that it was a short distance from the main caravan route from Mecca to Syria that constituted the economic lifeline of Mecca and other oases and towns that depended upon the caravan trade for their economic survival. Medina was also sufficiently distant from Mecca to permit Muhammad a relatively free hand in his efforts to convert the Bedouin clans living along the caravan route. Muhammad understood that conversions and political alliances with the Bedouin, not military engagements with the Meccans, were the keys to success.

Insurgencies require an armed force and the manpower to sustain them. It was from the original small cadre of guerrillas that the larger conventional army could be grown, the force that would ultimately permit the insurgency to engage its enemies in set-piece battles when the time and political conditions were right. Muhammad may have been the first commander in history to understand and implement the doctrine that General Vo Nguyen Giap of North Vietnam later referred to as 'people's war, people's army'.[39] Muhammad established the idea among his followers that God had commandeered all Muslims' purposes and property for His efforts, and that all Muslims had a responsibility to fight for the faith. Everyone, men, women and even children, had an obligation for military service in defence of the faith and the *ummah* that was the community of God's chosen people on earth. If this is not properly understood, then it will be difficult to grasp that it was the attraction of the ideology of Islam more than anything else that attracted the manpower that permitted Muhammad's small revolutionary cadre to grow into a conventional armed force capable of large-scale engagements.

The growth of Muhammad's insurgent army is evident from the following figures. At the Battle of Badr (624) Muhammad could only put 314 men in the field. Two years later at Second Badr (626), 1,500 Muslims took the field. Two years after that (628) at Kheibar, the Muslim army had grown to 2,000 combatants. When Muhammad mounted his assault on Mecca (630) he did so with 10,000 men. And at the Battle of Hunayn a few months later the army numbered 12,000 men. Some sources record that Muhammad's expedition to Tabuk later the same year was comprised of 30,000 men and 10,000 cavalry, but this is probably an exaggeration.[40] What is evident from the figures, however, is that Muhammad's insurgency grew very quickly in terms of its ability to recruit military manpower.

Like all insurgent armies, Muhammad's forces initially acquired weapons and supplies by stripping them from prisoners and the

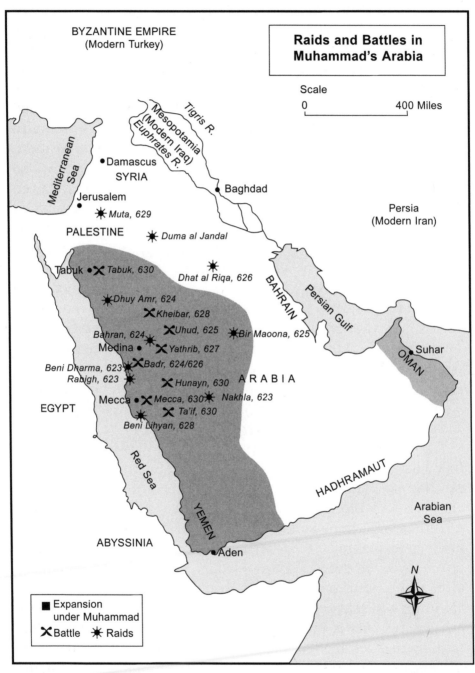

Map 6. Raids and Battles in Muhammad's Arabia

enemy dead. Weapons, helmets and armour were expensive items in relatively impoverished Arabia, and the early Muslim converts, drawn mostly from among the poor, orphaned, widowed, and otherwise socially marginal, could ill afford them. At the Battle of Badr, the first major engagement with an enemy army, the dead were stripped of their swords and other military equipment, establishing a practice that became common. Muhammad also established the practice of requiring prisoners to provide weapons and equipment instead of money to purchase their freedom. One prisoner taken at Badr was an arms merchant and was required to provide the insurgents with a thousand spears as the price of his freedom.[41] In the early days at Medina, Muhammad purchased what arms he could from one of the Jewish tribes in the city that were armourers. Later, when he drove this tribe from the city, he was careful to require that they leave behind their metal working tools, so that the Muslims could now manufacture weapons for themselves. Muhammad was eventually able to supply weapons, helmets, shields and armour to an army of 10,000 for his march on Mecca.

Muhammad's ability to obtain sufficient weapons and equipment had another important advantage. Many of the insurgency's converts came from the poorest elements of the Bedouin clans, people too impoverished to afford weapons and armour. Muhammad supplied these converts with expensive military equipment, immediately raising their status within the clan and guaranteeing their loyalty to him, if not always to the creed of Islam. In negotiations with Bedouin chiefs, Muhammad often made them gifts of expensive weaponry. Several pagan clans were won over to Muhammad's insurgency in this manner, although they did not convert to Islam. Horses and camels were equally important military assets, for without them raids and the conduct of operations over distances were not possible. Muhammad obtained his animals in much the same manner as he did his weapons and with equal success. At Badr the insurgents had only two horses. Six years later at Hunayn, Muhammad's cavalry squadrons numbered 800 horses and cavalrymen.[42]

An insurgency must also be able to sustain the popular base that supports the fighting elements. To accomplish this, Muhammad changed the ancient customs regarding the sharing of booty taken in raids. The chief of a clan or tribe traditionally took one quarter of the booty for himself. Muhammad decreed that he receive only one fifth, and even this he took not for himself but in the name of the *ummah*. Under the old ways, individuals kept whatever booty they had captured. Muhammad required that all booty be turned in to the common pool where it was shared equally among all combatants who had participated in the raid. Most importantly, Muhammad established that the first claimants on the booty that had been taken in the name of the *ummah* were the poor and the widows and orphans of the soldiers killed in battle. He also used the promise of a larger share of booty to strike alliances with Bedouin clans, some of whom remained both loyal and pagan to the end, fighting for loot instead of the faith. Muhammad's later military successes against towns, oases, and caravans provided an important source of wealth to supply the insurgent popular base with the necessities of life.

The leader of an insurgency must take great care to guard his power from challenges, including those that come from within the movement itself. Muhammad had many enemies and he was always on guard against an attempt upon his life. Like other insurgent leaders, Muhammad surrounded himself with a loyal group of men who would act as his bodyguard and carry out his orders without question. Muhammad created the *suffah* precisely for this purpose. The *suffah* was comprised of a small cadre who lived in the mosque next to Muhammad's house. They were recruited from among the most pious, enthusiastic, and fanatical followers, and were generally from impoverished backgrounds with no other way to make a living. The members of the *suffah* spent their time studying Islam and leading a life of spiritual avocation. They were devoted to Muhammad and served not only as his life guard but as a secret police that could be called upon at a moment's notice to carry out whatever task

Muhammad set for them. These tasks included assassination and terror.

No insurgency can survive without an effective intelligence apparatus, and the Muslim insurgency was no exception. As early as when Muhammad left Mecca, he left behind a trusted agent, his uncle Abbas, who continued to send him reports on the situation there. Abbas served as an agent-in-place for more than a decade, until Mecca itself fell to Muhammad. In the beginning, Muhammad's operations suffered from a lack of tactical intelligence. His followers were mostly townspeople and had no experience in desert travel. On some of the early operations Muhammad had to hire Bedouin guides to show him the way to where he wanted to go. As the insurgency grew, however, Muhammad's intelligence service became more organized and sophisticated, using agents-in-place, commercial spies, debriefing of prisoners, combat patrols, and reconnaissance in force as methods of intelligence collection.

Muhammad himself seems to have possessed a detailed knowledge of clan loyalties and politics within the insurgency's area of operations, and used this knowledge to good effect when negotiating alliances with the Bedouin. Muhammad often conducted an advance reconnaissance of the battlefields upon which he fought, and only once in ten years of military operations was he taken by surprise. In most cases Muhammad's intelligence service was able to provide him with sufficient information as to the enemy's location and intentions in advance of any military engagement. We have no knowledge of how Muhammad's intelligence service was organized or where it was located. That it was part of the *suffah*, however, seems a reasonable guess.

Insurgencies succeed or fail to the degree that they are able to win the allegiance of the great numbers of the uncommitted to support the insurgency's goals. Muhammad understood the role of propaganda in the struggle for the minds of the uncommitted and went to great lengths to make his message public and widely known. In an Arab society that was largely illiterate, the poet served as the major conveyor of political propaganda. Muhammad hired the best poets money could buy to sing his praises and denigrate his opponents. He publicly issued proclamations regarding the revelations he received as the Messenger of God, and remained always in public view to keep the vision of the new order and the promise of a heavenly paradise constantly before his followers and those he hoped to convert. He sent 'missionaries' to other clans and tribes to instruct the pagans in the new faith. Muhammad understood that the conflict was between the existing social order with its manifest injustices and his vision of the future and he surpassed his adversaries in spreading his vision to win the struggle for the hearts and minds of the Arab population.

The use of terror seems to be an indispensable element of a successful insurgency and no less so in Muhammad's case. Muhammad used terror in two basic ways. First, to keep discipline among his followers by making public examples of traitors or backsliders. It is sometimes forgotten that in Muhammad's day the penalty for apostasy in Islam was death. Muhammad also ordered the assassination of some of his political enemies, including poets and singers who had publicly ridiculed him. Never one to forget a slight, when his armies marched into Mecca Muhammad's *suffah* set about hunting down a list of old enemies marked for execution.

Muhammad also used terror to strike fear into the minds of his enemies on a large scale. In the case of the Jewish tribes of Medina, Muhammad ordered the death of the entire Beni Qaynuqa tribe and the selling of their women and children into slavery, before being talked out of it by the chief of one of his allies. On another occasion, again against a Jewish tribe in Medina, he ordered all the tribe's adult males, some 900, beheaded in a city square, the women and children sold into slavery and their property distributed among his Muslim followers. Shortly after the conquest of Mecca, Muhammad declared 'war to the knife' against all those who remained idolaters, instructing his followers to kill any pagans they encountered on the spot! Such public displays of ruthlessness and brutality, as with all insurgencies, strengthened Muhammad's hand when dealing with opponents and allies.

When examined against the criteria used by modern analysts to characterize an insurgency, Muhammad's military campaign to establish Islam in Arabia seems to qualify in all respects. Nothing in this conclusion detracts from the substance and value of Islam as a religion, any more than the history of the Israelite military campaign to conquer Canaan detracts from the substance and value of Judaism. Over time the violent origins of all religions are forgotten and only the faith itself remains. The result often is that the founders of the creeds come to be remembered as untinged by the violence of the historical record.

The New Moral Basis of War

Being a brave warrior had always been a central virtue in the Arab ideal of what constituted a good man. This warrior ethos was expressed in the Arabic terms *muruah* and *ird*. *Ird* is understood as honour and was closely tied to the obligations to avenge any wrong done to a man personally, to any others to whom he had extended his protection, or to his clan. *Muruah* literally means virility or manhood. While hospitality, generosity, and protection of the weak were all important Arab virtues, no virtue was held in higher regard than a man's courage in war.[43]

An Arab injured or insulted was not expected to forego revenge, but to extract either blood or compensatory payment. Failure to do so exposed him to charges of weakness, contempt and dishonour, perceptions that exposed him to further insult and attack. The notion that one ought to forego revenge, or that revenge itself was unethical per se, is an idea that comes mostly from Christianity. The Arab view of revenge was more like that of the ancient Greeks, where it was the duty of a good man 'to be sweet to friends and bitter to enemies; honourable to the first and terrible to the latter'.[44] One's honour, backed by the readiness to resort to individual combat in its defence or to redress a wrong was the central military virtue of Arab men. Every male was given military training in weapons and combat from an early age and instructed in the moral code of the warrior. This code of military prowess in defence of one's honour was passed to the West during the Arab wars with the Franks and later became part of the chivalric code of the Medieval Christian knight.[45]

The Arab emphasis upon warrior virtues sometimes led to the misperception that Arabia was a bloodthirsty land where war and conflict were endemic, and that the brutality sometimes shown by the armies of the Arab conquest was but a natural extension of these violent conditions. This is an erroneous view, probably the result of Western propaganda generated by almost 400 years of war during which Western armies fought the armies of Islam. Any reasonable examination of the conduct of Western and Arab armies during the Crusades would likely conclude that the brutality of the Western armies was by any measure at least equal to that of their Arab adversaries and, perhaps, even more brutal. Richard the Lionheart, to take but one example, routinely slaughtered Muslim prisoners, women, and children and had the unnerving habit of riding around with the decaying severed heads of Arab victims tied to his saddle. Saladin, the great Muslim general, was appalled at the behaviour of the Christian knights after Richard killed 2,200 Muslim prisoners at Acre.[46] The truth is that Arabia before Muhammad's time was neither a land torn by warfare nor populated by warriors accustomed to killing one another on the slightest pretext.

The Arab warrior's courage and honour were most commonly demonstrated by his performance in the *ghazw* or raid, in which a group of Bedouin would attack another clan to steal their flocks, camels or women. This was not 'war' in any real sense of the word since the object of the raid was to steal and not kill. The raid usually ended quickly enough once the alarm was sounded and the warriors rushed to protect their flocks. Often the two sides would merely shout obscenities at one another. Given the distances over which Arab Bedouin roamed, these raids were usually infrequent, involved only a few men on each side, and the shedding of blood, to say nothing of actual killing, was rare. Given the terrain of the desert and the general scarcity of goods to be had by even a successful raid, these Arab 'wars' were more entertainment and rough sport than genuine combat. They were not unlike the 'wars' fought by Native Americans in which the objective was to steal the enemy's horses, goods and women.

In those instances where Arab clans actually fought one another in some numbers, neither the term 'war' nor 'army' would be appropriate. If by 'armies' one means some form of standing organization with a formal command structure that fought as a unit and was capable of tactical application, there were no armies as such. Arab 'armies' were collections of individual warriors fighting for their own honour and opportunity to acquire loot. They were not unlike the gatherings of warrior knights that comprised the armies of Medieval Europe. Arab clan battles were usually fought on some agreed upon ground. Both sides formed up on the open field. Rival champions sallied forth and challenged the champions of the other side to individual combat. Often the death of a chief or even a few lesser men was sufficient to call off the fight, with the side suffering these casualties withdrawing from the field without being pursued. The formal nature of Arab battles was also evident in the practice of taking the clan women along to play instruments and sing songs encouraging their men to fight. Occasionally, of course, things got out of hand and a general melee might result that lasted until one side had had enough and withdrew. In most cases, however, casualties were likely to be light.

The Arab 'wars' of the pre-Islamic period never lasted very long and were never fought for what we would call today strategic objectives, that is, the enslavement or destruction of a rival tribe or the occupation of their lands which, in any case, would have been meaningless in a nomadic society where the value of the land shifted with the climate. Arab wars were primitive by the standards of warfare practised at the time by almost any society outside Arabia itself, and were so in terms of scale, tactics, logistics, and level of casualties. These 'battles' were tactical engagements only. There were no larger purposes to war other than to demonstrate honour and courage. No attempt was made to achieve strategic victory. Arab wars of the pre-Islamic period were highly ritualized and symbolic affairs, and lacked any ideological, religious, ethnic or strategic dimension.

The Arab reputation for bloody warfare even in the pre-Islamic period stems from the confusion of Arab warfare per se with the conduct associated with, and morally permitted in, those occasions when two clans engaged in a blood feud. A person killed or done serious harm or insult by a member of another clan had to be avenged by a member of the tribe to which the harm was done. It must be remembered that in Arabia before Muhammad there were no state or civic institutions, law, police forces or courts to protect the weak or render justice for harm suffered. The Arab relied solely upon his kin, clan and tribe to protect him. Thus, the old Arab proverb that 'a man's clan are his claws'.

The clans were democratic in that all members enjoyed the protection of its members. The strong protected the weak and once separated from the clan or tribe the individual was at great risk indeed. If the blood feud did not exist, there would have been no mechanism to bring even a rough justice to the Arabs' world. The weak or helpless would have been easily killed or enslaved. The blood feud acted as a check against this behaviour by entitling any kin or clan member of the victim to strike down the killer or any member of the killer's family.

The blood feud ended when the victim's family agreed to accept financial compensation for its loss, often paid in camels or other goods. If no agreement could be concluded, the feud went on forever if need be until the perpetrator himself was killed. In this way, a rough justice was brought to Arab conflicts in the absence of any other social institution to protect the weak. The blood feud was a deadly serious affair. It put everyone on both sides at risk, and could go on for a very long time, sometimes even generations. One had to think long and hard before killing a man, since the consequences could be deadly for everyone involved.

In Arab warfare *other than the blood feud*, then, there were rules of chivalry in which one's opponent possessed equal moral standing and worth. A warrior did not slay the wounded or kill cruelly or unnecessarily. The long Arab tradition of ransoming prisoners also limited the killing as the victorious warrior had much to gain by treating the wounded well and keeping them alive to be sold back for ransom. The result of these values was that Arab warfare in the pre-Islamic era was limited in scope, scale, frequency, and brutality.

The blood feud, by contrast, knew no such rules or limitations. No restrictions were placed upon how and when a man might be killed; in his sleep, by treachery, poison, or betrayal. In a blood feud, no moral standing was granted one's enemy, and torture, cruelty and brutality were often the result. Even under these conditions, the blood feud was aimed at the individual wrongdoer. There was no thought of attempting to kill the whole clan or even large segments of it, an attempt that would certainly have created a new blood feud with the former victims and aggressors trading places. The blood feud aimed at the proportional response of 'an eye for an eye', and not at a disproportionate response to a wrong.

Had the moral basis of Arab warfare remained unchanged, it is unlikely that Arabia would ever have produced the large, disciplined and highly motivated armies that it did in the Islamic era, with the consequence that the Islamic conquest of much of the ancient world would probably never have occurred. It was Muhammad who changed the traditional moral basis of Arab warfare, removing the traditional restraints on killing and bringing to Arabia a truly modern method and moral perception of war.

Unlike the old clan warriors, Muslim warriors were not primarily motivated by clan rivalries or the desire for loot, although both surely played a role. Muhammad's objective was to destroy the old Arab social order based on clan and kin and replace it with a new type of society, the *ummah*, comprised of a community of believers. The model for the new community was not the clan per se, but the clan as it operated when engaged in a blood feud. Any rules of ethical behaviour applied only to the community of believers;

those outside the *ummah* were held to possess no moral standing and could be killed or enslaved without moral consequences. In the community of believers, Muslim warriors fought because God had commanded them to do so or had delegated them to fight and destroy His enemies. Whereas the blood feud had proposed a life taken for a life lost, Muhammad redefined moral killing as a life taken for political purposes.

The idea of exterminating an entire town or a tribe was beyond the imagination of the blood feud. Under Muhammad, it became a common practice. Even murder became acceptable under the new rules, providing the victim was either a non-believer or an enemy of the faith. Murder had, of course, occurred in Arabia before Muhammad, but not for ideological, religious or other reasons of state. Assassination and massacre were not the usual tools of Arab political conflict. The difference between the traditional Arab view of killing and the new Islamic view is clear insofar as in all the accounts of the Prophet's life there is no mention of anyone else besides Muhammad sending someone to murder anyone.[47] On the other hand, 'Muhammad had at his disposal a number of fanatical young henchmen who were virtually prepared to strike down any opposition whenever necessary.'[48]

The new moral basis of war led to a more violent form of warfare – political ideological warfare – conducted on a larger scale with ever increasing casualties and consuming far more innocents than traditional Arab warfare had consumed. At times, war attempted and achieved the wholesale destruction of rival clans and tribes, as it did when Muhammad destroyed one of the Jewish tribes of Medina to a man. It was Muhammad who introduced the connection between tactics and strategy to Arab warfare; the connection between the use of violence as a means to the achievement of larger political/religious objectives. Muhammad sought nothing less than the subordination of the traditional clan-based society that Arabs had known since time immemorial and its replacement with a new society based on religious belief in which the moral relationship of the individual to the tribe and clan changed radically. These strategic objectives dictated the violent tactics used by Muhammad's insurgency and then adopted by the armies of the Arab conquest after his death.

Muhammad's adoption of the code of the blood feud as the basis of the new morality of war was a momentous decision that justified the use of violence against non-believers on a scale and frequency that had never before been seen in Arab warfare or social life. It also cast Islam as inhumane in its conduct of war, something the enemies of Islam in the West were quick to capitalize upon to portray Muslims as bloodthirsty barbarians. But Muhammad's adoption of the code of the blood feud becomes understandable when we realize that he never saw himself as a conventional general commanding a conventional army. Muhammad was first and foremost a religious revolutionary, the commander of an insurgency that had yet to create a military force that could bring his new social order into being. The old rules of war had to be changed because they were ineffective in achieving the revolutionary goals that Muhammad had set for himself. If he was to achieve his end of creating a new society governed by new ethical precepts, then a new military mechanism was required, one that served his strategic ends by expanding its repertoire of military capabilities. This required a complete change in the traditional values that had governed Arab warfare.

Military Reformer

One of Muhammad's more remarkable military accomplishments was his revolution in the manner in which Arabs for generations had fought wars, transforming Arab armies into genuine instruments of large-scale combat operations capable of achieving strategic objectives instead of small-scale, clan, tribal or personal objectives. In doing so, he created both the means and historical circumstances which transformed the fragmented Arab clans into a genuine national entity conscious of its own unique identity. Under these conditions, Arab military brilliance thrived, with the result that the greatest commanders of the early Arab conquests were selected and developed by Muhammad. Had Muhammad not brought about this revolution in Arab military capabilities, it is possible that Islam might not have survived in Arabia nor been capable of establishing the Muslim Empire.

Within a year of Muhammad's death (632), many of the clans that had sworn allegiance to Islam recanted, resulting in the War of the Apostates. It was the military brilliance of Muhammad's generals and the superior combat capabilities of his new army that made it possible for Islam to defeat the apostates and force them back into the religious fold. These same generals commanded the new Arab armies that made possible the Arab conquests of Persia and Byzantium. The old Arab way of war would have had no chance to win against the armies of either of these empires. In this sense, Muhammad's military revolution was an event that shook the ancient world, and changed history by creating the means that made the Arab conquests possible.

Muhammad's successful transformation of Arab warfare marks him as one of the great military reformers of all time. Muhammad stands in good company with those whose military reforms made possible the creation of empires by their successors. Kamose of Egypt led the fight against the Hyksos occupiers, reforming the Egyptian army and making it possible for Thutmose III to create the Egyptian empire of the New Kingdom. Philip II of Macedon completely changed the manner of Classical Greek warfare, forging a military instrument with which he united all Greece and which his son, Alexander the Great, used to create the empire of the Hellenes. The reforms of Augustus Caesar created the professional Roman army, making possible the expansion of the Roman Empire to its greatest geographical extent. And it was Muhammad who reformed Arab warfare and fashioned the military instrument his successors used to establish the great Empire of Islam.[49]

Social Composition: Muhammad changed the social composition of Arab armies from a collection of clans, tribes and blood kin loyal only to themselves into a national army loyal to a national social entity called the *ummah*, or community of believers in Allah. The *ummah* was not a nation or a state in the modern sense, but a body of religious believers under the unified command and governance of Muhammad. It was a locus of loyalty that transcended the clans and tribes and permitted Muhammad to forge a common identity, national in scope, among the Arabs for the first time in their history. It was leadership of this national entity that Muhammad claimed, not of any clan or tribe.

Loyalty to the *ummah* permitted the national army to unify the two traditional Arab combat arms of infantry and cavalry into a genuine combined arms force. Historically, Bedouin and town dweller had viewed one another with considerable suspicion, each living a very different way of life and fighting very different types of battles. Arab infantry had traditionally been drawn from the people living in the towns, settlements and oases of Arabia. While the larger towns often had a sufficient number of wealthy men who could afford horses, these cavalry units were generally small and ineffective. Arab cavalry was traditionally drawn from Bedouin clans whose nomadic warriors excelled at speed, surprise attack and elusive retreat, skills honed to a fine edge over generations of raiding.[50]

These different kinds of soldiers came from different socio-economic backgrounds and each possessed only limited experience in fighting alongside the other. Bound by clan loyalties and living in settlements, Arab infantry was steadfast and cohesive, and could usually be relied upon to hold its ground, especially in the defence. The infantry constituted the core of Muhammad's army throughout his life and remained so in the armies of the Arab conquest. Arab cavalry, on the other hand, was unreliable in a fight against infantry, often breaking off the fight to escape damage to their precious mounts or make off with whatever booty they had seized. Bedouin cavalry was, however, proficient at the surprise attack, protecting the flanks and pursuing ill-disciplined infantry. Each arm lacked the strengths of the other.

Muhammad was the first commander of an Arab army to successfully join both combat arms into a national army and to use them in concert in battle. This was more than a mere technical reform. The ability to combine both combat arms was the result of Muhammad's creation of a new type of community that made it possible to submerge the clan and blood loyalties of traditional Arab society into the larger religious community of believers, and combine the two primary elements of traditional Arab society, town dwellers and Bedouin tribes, into a single Arab national identity. The change in the social composition of Arab armies under Muhammad was preceded by a change in the social composition of Arab society.

Unity of Command: Arab military contingents before Muhammad fought under the command of their own clan or tribal leaders, sometimes assembled in coalition with other clans or tribes. While the authority of these clan chiefs was recognized by their own clan, every clan chief considered himself the equal of any other, with the result that there was no overall commander whose authority could compel the obedience or tactical direction of the army as a whole. Clan warriors fought for their own interests, often only for loot, and did not feel obligated to pursue the larger objectives of the army as a whole. They often failed to report to the battlefield, arrived late or simply left the fight once they had captured sufficient loot. Warriors and horses were precious and clan leaders often resisted any higher tactical direction that might place their men and animals in danger. Under these conditions, Arab battles often resembled little more than disorganized brawls lasting but a short time and producing no decisive outcome.

To correct these deficiencies Muhammad established a unified command for his armies. Command of the army was centred in the hands of Muhammad himself. Within the *ummah* there was no distinction between the citizen and the soldier, at least if the battle was considered defensive. All members of the community had an obligation to defend the clan and participate in its battles. The community of believers was truly a nation-in-arms, and all believers followed the commands of Muhammad, God's

Messenger. As commander-in-chief, Muhammad established the principle of unified command by appointing a single commander with overall authority to carry out military operations. Sometimes a second-in-command was appointed as well. Muhammad often commanded his troops in the field himself. All other commanders were appointed by him and operated under his authority.

As Muslims, all members of the army were equally bound by the same laws, and all clan members and their chiefs were subject to the same discipline and punishments as all Muslims. When operating with clans who were not Muslims, Muhammad always extracted an honour oath from their chiefs to obey his orders during the battle. The establishment of a unified military command gave Muhammad's armies greater reliability in planning and in battle. Unified command also permitted a greater degree of coordination among the various combat elements of the army and the use of more sophisticated tactical designs that could be implemented with more certainty, thereby greatly increasing the army's combat power. For the first time, Arab forces became an instrument of their commander's tactical will.

After Muhammad's death and during the Riddah (War of the Apostates) or civil war, Muhammad's successor, Abu Bakr, replaced many of the old generals who had fought under Muhammad with new officers selected mostly from among the experienced generals of Mecca. Unity of command extended not only to the strategic level, but to the operational and tactical levels as well. The fact that the old commanders could be replaced and the troops, tribes, and clans under them would obey Meccan commanders who, after all, had been their former enemies, is testimony to Muhammad's success in establishing unity of command as a major institutional reform in Arab armies.

Combat Unit Cohesion: The moral basis of traditional Arab warfare placed an emphasis on the courageous performance of individual warriors in battle. While every warrior recognized that he was part of a larger kin group, Arab warfare placed no emphasis on the ability of the clan to fight as a unit. The Arab warrior fought for his own honour and social prestige within the kin group, not for the clan per se. One consequence was that Arab armies and the clan units within them did not usually reflect a high degree of combat unit cohesion, the ability of the group to remain intact and fight together under the stress of battle.

Muhammad's armies, by contrast, were highly cohesive. These armies usually held together even when they fought outnumbered or were overrun. Muhammad did not just strengthen the blood and kin ties of the traditional Arab clan. He went far beyond that in creating the *ummah* as a higher locus of the soldier's loyalty that transcended the clan. It is important to remember that many of Muhammad's early converts had left their families and clans to follow the Prophet. It was a common occurrence to find members of the same clan, family, and even fathers and sons fighting on opposite sides during Muhammad's early battles. Religion turned out to be a greater source of unit cohesion than blood and clan ties, the obligations of faith replacing and overriding the obligations of tradition and even family. Muhammad's soldiers quickly gained a reputation for their discipline and ferocity in battle, soldiers who cared for each other as brothers which, under the precepts of Islam, they were.

Motivation: Muhammad's armies demonstrated a higher degree of military motivation than traditional Arab armies. Being a good warrior had always been the central core of Arab values. Muhammad raised the status of the warrior to an even greater degree. It was a common saying among Muslims that 'the soldier is not only the noblest and most pleasing profession in the sight of Allah, but also the most profitable.'[51] Muhammad's soldiers were always guaranteed a share in the booty. Instead of the usual quarter, Muhammad himself took one fifth of the booty in the name of the *ummah*, leaving more booty to be distributed among the soldiers. Under these arrangements, Muhammad's soldiers were actually paid better than Persian or Byzantine soldiers.[52]

But better pay was only a small part of the motivation of the soldiers of Islam. The idea of a soldier motivated by religion in the certainty that he was doing God's work on earth seems to have been one of Muhammad's most important military innovations. There were, of course, Christian soldiers who must have felt that they were doing their religious duty even when they attacked their fellow Christians as heretics. But no army before Muhammad ever placed religion at the centre of military motivation and defined the soldier primarily as an instrument of God's will on earth. The soldiers of Islam were usually extremely religious and saw themselves as fighting under God's instructions. The result, often still seen in Islamic societies, was a soldier who enjoyed much higher social status and respect than soldiers in armies of the West.

A central part of the motivation of the Islamic soldier was the teaching of his faith that death was not something to be feared, but to be sought. Muhammad's pronouncement that those killed in battle would be welcomed immediately into a paradise of pleasure and eternal life because they died fulfilling the command of God was a powerful inducement to perform well on the field of battle. To die fighting in defence of the faith (*jihad*) was to become a martyr. Life itself was subordinate to the needs of the faith; to die a martyr was to fulfill God's will.

Muslim soldiers killed in battle were accorded the highest respect on the Arab scale of values. While those who died in battle had been traditionally celebrated as examples of courage and selflessness, it was never suggested that death was to be welcomed or even required to be a good soldier. Muhammad's religious pronouncements changed the traditional Arab view of military sacrifice and produced a far more dedicated soldier than Arab armies had ever witnessed before. The respect for the soldier killed in defence of the faith is reflected in the Muslim belief that, unlike other Muslims who must endure the 'torment of the grave' after death while awaiting resurrection day to enter paradise, the soldier killed in battle enters paradise immediately.[53]

Strategic War: Arab warfare prior to Muhammad's reforms involved clans and tribes fighting for honour or loot. No commander aimed at the enslavement or extermination of the enemy, nor the occupation of its lands. Arab warfare was war at the tactical level, nothing more. There was no sense of strategic war in which long-term, grand scale strategic objectives were sought and toward which the tactical application of force was directed. Muhammad was the first to introduce the notion of war for strategic goals to the Arabs.

Muhammad's ultimate goal, the transformation of Arab society through the spread of a new religion, was strategic in concept. His application of force and violence, whether unconventional or conventional, was always directed at the strategic goal. Although Muhammad began as an insurgent, he was always Clausewitzian in his thinking in that the use of force was seen not as an end in itself, but as a tactical means to the achievement of strategic objectives. Muhammad was the first Arab commander to use military force within a strategic context. Had he not introduced this new way of thinking to Arab warfare, the use of later Arab armies to forge a world empire would not only have been impossible; it would have been unthinkable.

Once war was harnessed to strategic objectives it became possible to expand its application to introduce tactical dimensions that were completely new to traditional Arab warfare. Muhammad used his armies in completely new ways. He attacked tribes, towns, and garrisons before they could form hostile coalitions; he isolated his enemy by severing their economic lifelines and disrupting their lines of communication; Muhammad was a master at political negotiation, forming alliances with pagan tribes when it served his interests; and laid siege to cities and towns. Muhammad also introduced the new dimension of psychological warfare, employing terror and even massacre as means to weaken the will of his enemies. Various texts mention Muhammad's use of catapults (*manjaniq*) and movable covered cars (*dabbabah*) in siege warfare.[54] Most likely, these siege devices were acquired in Yemen, where Persian garrisons had been located on and off over the centuries. Muhammad seems to have been the first Arab commander to use them in the north. Where once Arab warfare had been a completely tactical affair, Muhammad's introduction of strategic war permitted the use of tactics in the proper manner, as means to greater strategic ends. War, after all, is never an end in itself. It is, as Clausewitz reminds us, always a method, never a goal.

Experienced Combat Officer Corps: As an orphan, Muhammad lacked even the most rudimentary military training provided by an Arab father. Probably to compensate for this deficiency, he surrounded himself with other men who were experienced warriors. He constantly asked questions of these more experienced soldiers and frequently took their advice. He frequently appointed the best warriors of his former enemies to positions of command once they had converted to Islam. As commander-in-chief, Muhammad sought to identify and develop good officers wherever he found them. Young men were appointed to carry out small-scale raids in order to give them combat experience. He sometimes selected an officer from a town to command a Bedouin raid in order to broaden his experience in the use of cavalry.[55] Muhammad always selected his military commanders on the basis of their proven experience and ability, and never for their asceticism or religious devotion.[56] He was the first to institutionalize military excellence in the development of an Arab officer corps of professional quality. It was from Muhammad's corps of trained and experienced field commanders that the generals who commanded the armies of the conquests were drawn. Khalid Ibn al-Walid ('The Sword of Allah') and Amr Ibn al Aasi were both former Meccan enemy commanders who converted to Islam and served as field commanders in Muhammad's armies. Both became great generals during the Arab conquests.

Training and Discipline: We have only scant references to how Muhammad trained his soldiers; that he did so is almost a certainty. There are clear references to required training in swimming, running and wrestling. The early soldiers of Islam had left their clan and family loyalties behind in order to join the *ummah*. The clan-based military units typical of Arab warfare would have been impossible to recreate within the *ummah*-based armies. Muhammad's converts had to be socialized to a new basis of military loyalty, the faith, and new military units would have had to be created that contained soldiers from many clans. References in various texts suggest that Muhammad trained these units in rank and drill, sometimes personally formed them up and addressed them before a battle and deployed them to fight in disciplined units, not as individuals as was the common practice. These disciplined 'artificial clan' units could then be trained to use a wider array of tactical designs than was heretofore possible. Muhammad's use of cavalry and archers in concert with his infantry was one result. While Arab fathers continued to train their sons in warfare long after Muhammad's death, the armies of the Arab conquests and later those of the Arab empire, instituted formal military training for recruits.

Logistics and Force Projection: Muhammad seems to have had the caravaneer's concern for logistics and planning, an expertise that permitted him to project force and carry out operations over long distances across inhospitable terrain. Muhammad had been an organizer of caravans for twenty-five years before he began his insurgency. During that time he made several trips to the north along the spice road. He gained a reputation for honesty and as an excellent administrator and organizer of caravans. Planning a caravan required extensive attention to detail and knowledge of routes, rates of march, distances between stops, water and feeding of animals, location of wells, weather, places of ambush etc, knowledge that served him well as a military commander.

Unlike some other armies that he fought, Muhammad never seems to have had to change or abandon his plans due to logistical difficulties. Muhammad's armies could project force over hundreds of miles. In 630, he led an army of 20–30,000 men (the sources disagree) over a 250 mile march from Medina to Tabuk, lasting 18–20 days across the desert during the hottest season of the year. By traditional Arab standards, Muhammad's ability to project forces of such size over these distances was nothing short of astounding. Without this capability, the Arab conquest that followed Muhammad's death would have been impossible.[57]

Muhammad's concern for logistics extended to making certain his soldiers were adequately supplied with the best weapons, horses, camels and armour that he could obtain by purchase, seizing them as loot or tribute, or having them made. In the early years, Muhammad's troops were always short of everything from weapons to transport. At the Battle of Badr he had only 70 camels and 2 horses to transport 314 men more than 80 miles to the battlefield. The men took turns riding the camels, and arrived at Badr exhausted from the trek. Often his soldiers had no armour or helmets and were sometimes short of weapons.

Muhammad placed great emphasis upon having enough camels, for they were the key to the mobility and endurance of his army. All distances in the desert are reckoned by the time it takes a camel to cover them. Movement on foot is simply not possible for any distance. According to the textual accounts, when Muhammad moved against Mecca every man in his army was fully equipped with weapons, armour, helmets, shields and either a horse or camel. For an army of 10,000 men, this was no small achievement by a man who had only 4 disciples a decade earlier. It was Muhammad who taught the Arab armies how to supply themselves for long periods in the field and to ensure themselves adequate weapons and equipment. Once again, had he not accomplished this, Arab armies would have remained militarily incapable of forging an empire.

The basic conclusion that emerges from the analysis presented here is that Muhammad revolutionized the conduct of Arab warfare in ways that made possible the transformation of Arab armies from entities fit only for tactical engagements to armies capable of waging war on a strategic level, where they could engage and defeat the major armies of their day. This military transformation was preceded by a revolution in the manner in which Arabs thought about war, the moral basis of war. The old chivalric code that limited the bloodletting was abandoned by Muhammad and replaced with an ethos less conducive to restraint in war, the blood feud. Extending the ethos of the blood feud beyond the ties of kin and blood to include members of the new community of Muslim believers inevitably worked to make Arab warfare more encompassing and bloody than it had ever been.

Supporting all these changes was a change in the psychology of war introduced by Muhammad's teaching that soldiers fighting in defence of Islam were doing no less than God's work on earth, and that to die in carrying out His will earned the soldier eternal life in paradise. The usual sense of risk to life that tempers the violence of the battlefield was abandoned, replaced by a psychological doctrine that 'war to the knife', or fighting until one kills the enemy or is slain oneself, became the ideal in the conduct of war. In every respect Muhammad's military revolution increased the scale and violence of the military engagements that Arab armies were now capable of fighting.

Muhammad's Death

In June 632, Muhammad was in the final stages of planning a major attack on the Byzantine border outposts. The troops had been assembled in and around Medina and its commander, Usamah, son of Zayd ibn Harithah, appointed. All that was needed was Muhammad's final order. One night, Muhammad called to one of his companions and told him that God had ordered him to go to the cemetery and pray for the dead. He prayed at the cemetery for some time, and then returned home where he fell asleep. The next morning Muhammad was struck with a violent headache. Some sources say that he had been suffering from fever and headaches for some time, perhaps brought on by fatigue.[58] Despite his pain, Muhammad continued spending the night with each of his wives in turn. He sent for Usamah and two days later he was strong enough to perform the public ceremony of bestowing the war banner on Usamah and his troops. Ibn Ishaq tells us that 'the Apostle went out walking between two men of his family...His head was bound in a cloth and his feet were dragging.'[59] There was sufficient concern for his health that Usamah delayed the scheduled departure of the expedition to Syria.

Muhammad was moved to his wife Aisha's apartment so she could care for him. He seems to have suffered from a burning fever and a terrible headache. He instructed one of his companions to

> 'Pour seven skins of water from different wells over me so that I may go out to the men and instruct them.' We made him sit down in a tub and we poured the water over him until he said, 'Enough! Enough!'[60]

One witness told Ibn Ishaq that 'when the Apostle's illness became severe he and the men came down to Medina and he went in to the Apostle who was unable to speak.'[61] Despite these difficulties, Muhammad went to the mosque 'with his head wrapped up', where he permitted Abu Bakr to lead the prayer. On the tenth day of his illness Muhammad suffered a high fever and his body was racked with pain. Those around him thought he might be suffering from pleurisy, the symptoms of which are similar to pulmonary oedema and adult respiratory distress syndrome that sometimes accompanies long term malarial infection.[62] The next morning he arose and went to the mosque and sat down in the courtyard to rest. Then he returned to his bed in Aisha's apartment and cleaned his teeth.

At some point he asked for writing materials with which to write a document to keep the faithful from error but there is no evidence that Muhammad ever executed such a document.[63] He lay down with his head in Aisha's lap and talked to her for a while. Suddenly his head grew heavy and his eyes became fixed. 'Lord, grant me pardon', he said and slipped away into death 'with the heat of noon that day...on the very day that he came to Medina as an emigrant, having completed exactly twelve years in his migration'.[64]

There was some dispute among the Muslims as to where to bury the Prophet. Some wanted to bury him in the mosque, while others wanted him buried with his companions in the cemetery. Abu Bakr settled the matter when he claimed

> I heard the Apostle say, 'No prophet dies but he is buried where he died'; so the bed on which he died was taken up and they made a grave beneath it...The Apostle was buried in the middle of the night of the Wednesday'.[65]

And that was the end of Muhammad ibn Abdullah.

Chapter 4

Legacies of War

The object of the previous analysis was to acquaint the reader with the important, but often forgotten or deliberately ignored, historical fact that the founders of three of the four 'great world religions' were also soldiers who experienced the violence of war first-hand. I have also attempted to acquaint the reader with the cultural context of the societies and historical periods in which each of the founders lived, and to explain the nature of warfare to which the founders were exposed. The purpose of this section is to inquire as to the effect the war experience of the founders had upon the military history bequeathed to the generations that came after them. As a starting point, one can say that the military experience of the founders came to occupy a long-standing important place in all three of these great religions and changed the course of military history.

Buddha

Buddha's experience of and revulsion toward war led him to establish a religion premised upon an absolute pacifism that rejected warfare per se as immoral. Buddha extended his rejection of violence to *all* creatures and can rightly be regarded as the founder of the tradition of non-violence and pacifism that remains with us today. But as long as India remained a country of independent feudal monarchies, there was little opportunity for Buddhist doctrines to affect Indian society at large or to moderate its practice of constant conflict. It was only with the ascension of Emperor Asoka to the throne of Magdha (269 BC) and the great national Indian empire created by Chandragupta that Buddhism began to have an impact on social and military affairs.

Asoka himself converted to Buddhism and established a number of Buddhist principles as imperial policy. He instituted the principle of *ahimsa*, non-injury of men and animals; banned animal sacrifice; substituted Buddhist pilgrimages for hunting expeditions; and regulated the slaughter of animals for food, a policy that encouraged the Buddhist practice of vegetarianism. Militarily, Asoka renounced the traditional Aryan doctrine and practice of aggressive war and territorial expansion, instituting instead a policy of 'conquest by Righteousness'.[1] Asoka attempted to retain the empire by reasonable diplomacy, resorting to war only when absolutely necessary. This represented an attempt to conduct policy according to the humane ethics of Buddhism.

Under Asoka's reign, Buddhism ceased to be just another Indian sect and began its career as a world religion. A great council of Buddhist clergy was held at Pataliputra at which the great Pali Canon was finally codified and committed to writing, providing Buddhism with a definitive canon of religious beliefs and practices. With imperial support, Buddhist missions were sent throughout the empire to spread the new official state religion. Other missions were sent to parts of Asia and China, planting the seeds of Buddhism in these various realms.

The establishment of Buddhism as a state religion and its influence on military practice in India reached its highest point during the Asoka imperial period. Within a century of Asoka's death (232 BC), however, the empire had broken up into a series of feudal states that quickly returned to the Aryan practice of aggressive war. In many of these warring states, a resurgent Hinduism established itself, often by reforming its old practices and incorporating some Buddhist principles, completely eclipsing Buddhism's influence on state and social policy. The history of the post-Asokan period is one of constant struggle among regional dynasties, with the result that the cultural, political and social unity of India was lost for 2,000 years.[2]

For more than 1,000 years, India suffered the pain of foreign invaders, further preventing any attempt at national political and military unity. The invaders often brought with them rival religious creeds more in harmony with India's traditional Hinduism but violently at odds with Buddhism. The result was recurring periods of religious persecution of Buddhists, becoming most violent in the 400 year invasion and persecution by Muslim armies. During this period, most Buddhist monasteries, universities, places of worship and seminaries were destroyed, never to be rebuilt. In 1193, the Nalanda University complex was destroyed by Afghan Khilji-Ghilzai Muslims under Bakhtiyar Khalji; this event is seen as the final milestone in the decline of Buddhism in India. Khalji also burned Nalanda's major Buddhist library and Vikramshila University, as well as numerous Bhuddhist monasteries in India.[3] Those monks who were not beheaded fled to other countries were they restablished themselves and their religion, and continued the spread of Buddhism. In one of the curious paradoxes of history, Buddhism never achieved its place as a dominant belief system in India, the land of its origin, while strongly establishing itself in many other regions of Asia.

Moses

The influence of Moses's war experience on military history was enormous. Western history regards Moses as the 'father of monotheism', the founder of the world's first monotheistic religion. He was also the first to draw the famous 'Mosaic distinction', as it is called, between true and false gods, with the caveat that false gods must be destroyed to protect or promote the belief in the one true god.[4] Moses was also the first to introduce the use of violence as a legitimate means to defend the new faith, and to give the ancient world its first example of religious (and later ethnic) genocide when he slaughtered the Moabites for the crime of tempting Israelite men away from their religion. The new community of believers formed by Moses and committed to these principles and practices survives into the present day, generating a rich canonical tradition that has passed unchanged into the mainstream of Western history, becoming one of its main pillars in the process.

So strongly has monotheism entrenched itself in Western thinking over the centuries that it is almost beyond the modern imagination to think of the polytheism that preceded it, and which existed for much longer than has monotheism itself, as anything but a primitive idea on the part of intellectually unsophisticated people. It is equally tempting to believe that the polytheistic religions of the ancient world routinely distinguished between their own true gods and the false gods of others. This was not the case. In the ancient world, polytheism functioned as a vehicle of cultural translation, and drew no distinctions among deities with regard to their being true or false.

Polytheism's great contribution was to overcome the earlier ethnocentric loyalties of tribal 'enclave' religions by distinguishing many deities by name, form, and function. Names and forms of these gods varied from culture to culture, but their functions as recognizable cosmic deities were identical.[5] This made it possible for the deities of all cultures to be seen as the same gods manifested in different forms. While the cultures of tribes and nations were different, their religions provided them with a functional common ground, and served as mechanisms of intercultural transmissibility.[6] Different peoples worshipped different gods, but none contested the reality of the foreign gods or the legitimacy of foreign forms of worship. When cultures came into contact, they identified foreign gods as simply different forms of their own gods, and often incorporated them into their pantheons. This syncretism was a near universal practice among the more complex cultures of the ancient period until well after the time of Moses.[7] Moses' impact upon the religions of the ancient world cannot be fully comprehended without correctly understanding the nature of polytheism in those religions.

Unlike tribal religions, the gods of polytheistic religions are neither ethnocentric nor bounded by tribal identity as was the Yahweh of Moses. Polytheistic gods, by contrast, are international and translate *across* cultures because they possess not only names but also common functions. Function comes to supersede form from culture to culture, endowing the common functions of the different gods with common legitimacy. This ability to translate foreign gods into one's own culture was first evident in Mesopotamia about 2,500 BC, when the Sumerians produced a list of their gods in which their names appear in Akadian next to their Sumerian names. Tribal societies, like Moses' followers, were incapable of such sophistication and institutional complexity. The great achievement of the ancient polytheistic religions was their articulation of a common semantic universe to understand the divine.

Monotheism itself owes a great debt to polytheism. The idea that all gods were the same everywhere, even as their cultural forms differed, led ancient Egyptian theologians to contemplate the idea that behind all gods was one god, that the religious truths and obligations pertained to mankind and not just to a culture. It was human nature, not culture, that was truly universal. This is the early pagan concept of cosmotheism, from which monotheism necessarily sprung. The ancient polytheists saw the evidence of gods all around them in the cycles and life forms of nature, while the monotheists rejected such evidence in favour of revelation, whose content was, to say the least, not always so easily comprehensible. The unquestioning faith of the monotheist was positioned against the polytheist's belief in his own senses and reason. It was this insistence upon the 'evidence' of revelation that produced the great catastrophe of monotheism, that is, wars of religious genocide and extermination.

Even the pre-Mosaic Israelites shared this polytheistic perspective on the world where gods were everywhere and easily approachable by men. Abraham, Isaac and Jacob all lived on friendly and easy terms with their god. He gave them friendly advice, guided the tribe in its wanderings, talked to them, suggested whom they should marry and spoke to them in dreams. Occasionally, as with Jacob wrestling with El, God appeared to them in human form. The god of the pre-Mosaic Israelites was similar to the gods of other ancient cultures in these respects and radically different from the one that Moses' rigid monotheism imposed upon the Israelites later.[8]

Monotheistic religions are non-syncretic and intolerant by their very nature. Whereas the old polytheisms of the ancient world functioned as a form of intercultural translation, the new monotheism functioned as a means of cultural estrangement. The dawn of Yahwehism in Western history and its covenant with the one true God opened an immense gulf between man and God that has never been closed. Whereas in the old polytheisms the evidence of God was everywhere, comprehensible and approachable by humans, the new monotheism of Moses placed God beyond the reach of man except through precise adherence to belief and rituals whose evidence was unseen. Mosaic Yahwehism was in this sense a retrogression to the religions found among tribal ethnocentric societies, what Mary Douglas calls 'enclave religion'.[9] The distinction is reflected linguistically in Hebrew. The Hebrew word for holy is *kadosh*. In religious usage, the word does not connote, as we might expect, a sense of morality or ethics or righteousness. Instead, *kadosh* means 'otherness', connoting a radical separation between man and God.[10]

Unable to comprehend this 'otherness', monotheists are left only with obedience, an obedience often enforced by violence. To the god of Moses, humans are almost irrelevant. There is no promise of justice, mercy or compassion to its faithful. In Exodus, Yahweh repeatedly slays the Israelites over what seem to be trivial ritual infractions. The story of Job exemplifies the idea that God is his own purpose and power, and the inability of humans to discover it is irrelevant. All that is left is obedience to a deadly power that must be complied with regardless. Where the old polytheistic gods promised justice for proper behaviour, the new monotheistic god promised only death and suffering if proper behaviour was not forthcoming. This was clearly the point of the *Song of Moses* expressed in Deuteronomy 32: 39–41.

> See now that I, even I am He, and there is no god with me.
> I kill, and I make alive; I have wounded, and I heal;

and there is none that can deliver you out of my hand.
If I whet my glittering sword,
And my hand take hold on judgement;
I will render vengeance to Mine adversaries
And will recompense them that hate Me.
I will make Mine arrows drunk with blood,
And my sword shall devour flesh.

Thus, violence in service to the monotheistic deity becomes inextricably bound up with otherness that must be exterminated.

The distinction between true and false gods introduced by Moses became a primary root of Western culture, a radically new idea that changed the world. Yahwehism became the first counter-religion in the West to repudiate everything that went before it, and rejected everything outside its own experience as false. The path to truth cannot be discovered from the past, but is revealed by some traumatic event that forms the foundation of the new religion's beliefs and rituals.[11] For Moses it was the encounter with Yahweh on Sinai, for Christ it was the crucifixion, and for Mohammed it was the voices in the cave. In the new religion, the past is remembered only for its corruption against which true believers must be ever vigilant lest the past re-emerge. The past is remembered only so it may be constantly disowned as the price of one's identification with the new belief. This is, of course, precisely how monotheistic religions give birth to religious wars and violence against non-believers.

Moses did not live to reach the Promised Land, he was struck down by Yahweh who 'drew the life out of him' for yet another minor ritual offence. When at last the time came for a new generation of Israelites to enter Canaan, Yahweh ordered them to undertake a war of genocide against the Canaanites and their false idols. Yahweh commanded that all in Canaan were to be slain: 'Of the cities of the peoples that the Lord thy God giveth thee for an inheritance, thou shalt save alive nothing that breatheth.'[12] It required more than 200 years for the Israelites to consolidate their control over Palestine, and by 1000 BC the Israelites had forged a national political entity under David and Solomon. This period of consolidation was marked by frequent religious wars against the Canaanites. Joshua, Saul, Deborah, Gideon etc all fought wars whose purpose was the genocidal extermination of the non-believers.

The Israelite monarchy lasted less than a century before disintegrating into rival kingdoms, civil strife and an eventual invasion and occupation by Assyrians, Babylonians, Persians, Greeks, and Romans. Even during the period of greatest Israelite control, Palestine remained an ethnically and religiously mixed nation in which the Israelites were always a minority.[13] Under these circumstances Israelite kings had little choice but to accommodate the practice of Canaanite religions, a necessity that brought the Israelite kings into direct conflict with the new prophets who railed against idolatry and eventually precipitated the collapse of the national government. From the end of Solomon's time to the Babylonian exile, the Israelites never truly succeeded in impressing their own ethnic or religious stamp completely upon Palestine. They always remained a cultural and religious minority within the dominant Canaanite culture. After the return from Babylon, the Yahwehist monotheists continued to survive in Palestine until the emergence of Christianity, itself an offshoot of Yahwehism, which adopted the Mosaic doctrine as central to the new religion.

Monotheism and its concomitant legitimization of violence in the service of the deity gradually struck deep roots in Western culture, eventually insinuating itself into the new religion of Christianity. Under the auspices of Rome and its later Christian emperors, the Christian version of monotheism spread throughout the empire until, under Constantine, it was established as the official state religion. By the fifth century CE, the persecution of the ancient polytheistic religions finally drove them to extinction, with the result that monotheism and its innate tendency toward violence became the new religious paradigm for all of Western culture. It remains so to this day.

Muhammad

The fragile unity of the Islamic insurgency that Muhammad had managed to hold together during his lifetime began to crumble even before his death. At the time of Muhammad's death, no more than perhaps one third of Arabia had been exposed to Islam, and far less than a third of the population, perhaps no more than twenty per cent or so, had actually professed it. Once outside of Mecca, Medina, and Ta'if and the bedouin tribes in the immediate vicinity of these towns, the pull of Islam was weak if extant at all.[14] Even within the insurgency, many professed loyalty to Muhammad himself more than to the creed. In the traditional fashion of Arab covenants, upon Muhammad's death many tribal and clan chiefs no longer felt bound by their old agreements with the Prophet.

The crux of the problem was the *zakat*, the annual tax that Muhammad had imposed. Muhammad died before the tax could be collected from all but the tribes nearest Medina and Mecca. Some of the allied tribes sent delegations to Medina to negotiate new agreements with Abu Bakr who had been elected to succeed Muhammad, promising to remain Muslim and say the daily prayers in exchange for repealing the tax. Abu Bakr refused. He reckoned correctly that to accede to the tribes on the issue of the *zakat* meant the end of centralized control over the movement, opening it to schism, eventual disintegration and, perhaps, even absorption by other monotheistic religions. To prevent this, Abu Bakr declared war on all those who would not obey. The result was the Riddah or the War of Apostates.

Abu Bakr was responsible for the ultimate success of Islam by using the Arab armies to suppress all opposition to it, and to enforce conversion on all Arabia by military force. During the two year period of the wars of the Riddah, Muhammad's reformed armies operated on a larger scale over greater distances than ever before and with several campaigns taking place at once, all of them operating under unified command to implement a single strategic goal formulated by Abu Bakr. The same operational characteristics that became typical of the armies of the later Arab conquest were first revealed during the Riddah, and it was Abu Bakr, not Muhammad, who was the political and military genius behind it.[15]

The decision to attack the 'apostates' was not a popular one with many of the faithful, including some of Muhammad's field commanders. Abu Bakr removed these commanders from their positions and appointed Meccan officers who had supported his election over the opposition.[16] Once the conquest of Arabia had been accomplished, however, Muhammad's old commanders were reinstated and went on to play important roles in the campaigns against the Persians and Byzantines. Abu Bakr dispatched eleven armies, supposedly at the same time, to all parts of Arabia with the mission of subjugating the 'apostatizing' tribes.

The armies that carried out Abu Bakr's campaigns left Medina as relatively small contingents, each numbering perhaps 4 to 5,000 men or less, and were comprised of *ansar*, emigrants and tribal contingents of local Bedouin under the leadership of experienced field commanders. The size of the Muslim contingents seems to have been only large enough to engage and defeat those small clans and tribes encountered along their routes of march. These contingents were expected to recruit more manpower along the way with promises of religion and loot. If this failed, then military action could be undertaken to inflict a defeat on the recalcitrant clan, which would then make a peace agreement with the victors that required them to accept Islam and join the campaign. Once within the area of the operations of the target, Muslim commanders would seek to take advantage of local rivalries to attract additional manpower to their armies.[17] It was a technique Muhammad had used on several occasions, and it worked well for the armies of Abu Bakr.

The armies of the Arabian conquest demonstrated all the operational capabilities that Muhammad had introduced into Arab warfare. The Muslim officer corps was competent and experienced, and had acquired the skills in Muhammad's wars needed to command large armies over long distances. Abu Bakr was able to coordinate eleven major campaigns simultaneously and shift forces as needed from one front to another. The units within the armies, while mostly organized on tribal or clan lines, nevertheless operated under a unified command in which all subordinate commanders were expected to carry out the missions assigned to them as part of a larger strategic plan. Abu Bakr's campaigns demonstrated the primacy of strategic objectives in tactical planning, something which had been absent in Arab warfare until introduced by Muhammad.

Even the idea of a single tribe or political group conquering all of Arabia was inconceivable until Muhammad showed the Arabs how to think in strategic terms. Logistics and supply for large armies had improved considerably under Muhammad, and were put to good use in Abu Bakr's campaigns. There are no reports of serious shortages of water, fodder or armaments in any of the campaigns of the Riddah. Muslim morale and fighting spirit were superior to those of any tribe the armies engaged. Muslim soldiers had learned to fight as units operating within a larger tactical design, while the warriors of most tribes fought in the old manner as individuals. Finally, the quality of Muslim combat leadership, certainly at the field commander level and probably in the major subordinate units as well, was superior to their adversaries. Muslim field commanders were never selected on the grounds of piety, but always on the basis of demonstrated competence in war.

Muhammad's legacy of new operational capabilities passed intact to the armies of Abu Bakr and produced the conquest and conversion of all Arabia. By Spring 633 the Riddah was over and Arabia was an armed camp full of warrior tribes seeking new adventures and loot. An Islamic Arabia lacked sufficient resources of food and wealth to sustain itself under the limitations that the new Islamic laws placed upon the old way of life. If new sources of wealth were not found, the Muslim state that Abu Bakr's military campaigns had brought into being would soon fragment into warring tribal groups. Muhammad's earlier raids attempted against the Byzantine border provinces provided the guiding strategic concept behind Abu Bakr's decision to use the united Arab tribes as a means to an even larger conquest. In 633 Abu Bakr ordered three Muslim armies to attack the Byzantines. The great Arab conquests had begun.

The armies of the Arab Conquest were those military forces of Arabian origin that established the empire of Islam before being absorbed into the larger Muslim convert population that brought about substantive changes in the original Arab armies. The original Arab armies can be said to have existed from 622 when Muhammad first formed them to approximately 842 when the Abbasid caliph, al-Mutasim, introduced the Mamluke Institution of slave Turk soldiers who replaced the original Arab contingents in the armies of Islam. Until then, the armies of Muhammad and his immediate successors were almost exclusively comprised of Arabs from Arabia. It was these armies that invaded and conquered large segments of the Byzantine and Persian empires between 633 and 656. The Arab invasions produced a new socio-political order that eventually included the whole of the Arabian Peninsula, all the Persian lands, and the Syrian and Egyptian provinces of the Byzantine Empire. [18]

The structure of the Arab army reflected the structure of Arab tribal society. Arab society during Muhammad's day and for more than a century afterward never really developed a stable political order worthy of being called a state. There was no state per se and no administrative structure of government. Arab society remained what it had always been, a tribal society characterized by personal leadership and appointed retainers that drew no distinction between society, religion and the army. Indeed, there was never a formal army as such. Instead, there was an alliance of powerful tribal chiefs who led their personal armed retinues in battle. There was no financial system and what treasury there was came from gifts and booty obtained in raids. Government was essentially an enlarged tribal system of negotiated consensus among powerful tribal chieftains and it was these warrior chiefs who controlled the Arab populace and the army. This system of indirect rule plagued the Muslim empire until its end. Power ebbed and flowed from the centre of authority, but no caliph ever was able to retain control of the tribal and regional armies for very long. Revolts and insurrections rooted in jealousy, political interests, religious apostasy and blood feuds went on for centuries.[19]

The Arab armies that attacked Byzantium and Persia may have been infantry armies but they did not move on foot. Instead, they made extensive use of the camel in transporting their armies to the strategic objective. This provided them with superior strategic mobility, enabling them to by-pass enemy strong points and offer battle at times and places of their choosing. The guiding tactical concept was to move quickly to a favourable position, establish the infantry on the ground and then force the enemy to attack to its disadvantage. Once the horse became widely available, Arab armies continued their practice of using mounted infantry in a strategic manner.

Once established in their new lands the Arabs attempted to remain an ethnically homogeneous, warlike and religious society apart from the conquered infidels. But their numbers were not very large. The total size of the Arab armies that left Arabia could hardly have exceeded 100,000 people, including women and children, whereas the population of the conquered lands probably exceeded 20,000,000 souls![20] All Arab emigrants lived in garrison cities or military districts and were registered in the *diwan* or 'register'. The registered soldier was entitled to monthly rations for himself and his family, and received an annual cash stipend, as did his wife and children. Quarters were also provided for the soldier and his family. In return these religious warriors were available for military service at a moment's notice. When called to service, the soldier had to supply his own mount (horse or camel) and military equipment which included a lance, sword, shield, bow, quiver and armour, usually some form of mail.

The attempt to sustain a separate Arab identity set apart from the infidels was bound to fail in the long run on the grounds of numbers and conversions. Even as military manpower demands increased, the Arabs made no effort to recruit the able-bodied men of the conquered lands into their armies. Gradually native peoples were permitted to lend military service, usually ethnic or racial units serving as separate battalions. But once the conquered peoples accepted Islam, more and more non-Arabs came to serve in the Muslim armies. Over time the Arab elements of the Muslim armies came to see the military *diwan* as a social stipend, and the Arab elements became a smaller and less-used segment of the armies as the Arabs gradually were submerged into the Muslim armies of disparate peoples who had converted to the new faith.[21]

With gradual assimilation and wide-spread conversion, the old tribal armies eventually gave way to professional armies manned largely by non-Arab Muslims, although their commanders remained Arabs for many years. The regional armies of the old tribal chiefs survived for centuries, but for the most part were confined to their garrisons supported by the *diwan* and were of little use. As the Arabs were submerged in a sea of Muslims, the old tribal consensual style of government became more difficult to operate and proved insufficient to constrain tribal and personal ambitions. The result was two civil wars. The second war (684–692) forced the Umayyads to abandon the old ideal of consensual rule completely, and they governed by force supported by their professional army comprised mostly of Syrian troops. It was not until the last Umayyad caliph (744–750), however, that the armies became professionalized.

Under the Umayyads, heavy cavalry became increasingly important. Originally, Arab cavalry was divided into armoured and unarmoured horse, or heavy and light cavalry. The heavy cavalry still comprised only a small number of units and were used mostly as shock troops along Byzantine lines. Light cavalry, when not used as skirmishers and reconnaissance, was used only to complete the destruction of already disorganized or broken units. During the Umayyad period, the bulk of Arab cavalry became armoured in a transition toward the Byzantine model in mounts, armour and weapons. Unlike the Byzantines, the Arab armies retained their old infantry traditions. Byzantine cavalrymen, for example, were trained for use as shock troops fighting from horseback only. Arab heavy cavalry was trained in the old tradition of fighting first from horseback and then being able to dismount and fight on foot. Heavy cavalry never became a true arm of decision in Arab armies until much later and heavy infantry remained the central combat arm. The cavalry would deploy safely behind the infantry formations and sally forth as opportunity permitted to attack the enemy, only to retreat quickly behind its own infantry for protection. The idea of cavalry against cavalry in open combat was unknown to Arab commanders.

The Umayyad period was brought to an end by yet another civil war and the Abbasids were brought to the throne by rebel armies raised in Iran. These Iranian troops or Khurasiani were mostly horse archers, and this type of cavalry now became dominant in Arab armies. Although cavalry was now the arm of decision, infantry still played an important role on the battlefield and close infantry and cavalry cooperation remained central to the new Arab tactical design. These new troops wore clothes similar to the eastern Christian monk and wore beards and long hair. Great reliance was placed upon the bow and lance. The attack was marked by a shower of arrows as the cavalry closed with the enemy at the gallop, firing as it went. Once in contact, the lance came into play along with other weapons of close combat like the curved sword, mace, battle axe and short sword of single-edged design.[22]

The Abbasids made no effort to broaden the base of their army or government, relying instead upon those groups and tribes of mostly eastern origin that had brought them to power. The Arab armies were now mostly cavalry armies, and since horses were expensive and training took a long time, it was more efficient for the Abbasids to rely upon the natural horsemen of the Khurasiani rather than to outfit and train Arabs themselves. The reliance upon foreign troops and the failure to extend governmental participation to the powerful regional chiefs resulted in the imperial army being run more like a mafia than a military institution. The caliphs and the army became increasingly isolated from society with the consequence that the Abbasids were forced to deal with frequent revolts.

During one of the civil wars that threatened to topple the Abbasids, one of the participants, al-Mutasim (833–42), had outfitted his army with 4,000 Turkic troops whom he had purchased as slaves and then freed for military service under his command. Once al-Mutasim had become caliph, he expanded the practice of purchasing and training Turkic slaves for service in his armies, thereby bringing into existence what Muslims came to call 'the Mamluke Institution'. The essence of this institution was the systematic reliance of the caliphate upon soldiers of servile and non-Islamic origin. The use of other foreign, non-Muslim, ethnic units in the army also increased greatly. The result was that the areas of the empire under direct imperial control were policed by these slave Turks. Over time, most of the major military commands and some important governorships were assigned to Turkic officials as well. Eventually the Mamlukes carried out a military coup against the Abbasids and took control of the caliphate.

For the next two centuries the Abbasid caliphs continued to rule from Baghdad, but mostly in name only while genuine power was exercised by Turkic military commanders who continued to pay lip-service to the rule of the caliphs. In reaction to this state of affairs, the governors of various provinces, using their regional armies as leverage, broke into open revolt time and again, with one province after another seceding from the empire by force of arms. By the middle of the ninth century the old Arab empire had ceased to exist, and with it the Arab 'army of God', which had swept over the ancient Mediterranean world wielding the sword of Allah, also disappeared.

Without doubt Muhammad's most enduring military legacy was the doctrine of *jihad* or holy war. It is indisputable that divinely justified warfare became a force of major importance during the early Islamic period, remained a significant motivator for the Islamic conquests that followed Muhammad's death, and remains a primary characteristic of Islamic warfare in the present day. Pre-Islamic Arabia knew no notion of ideology of any sort, and certainly no notion of religiously sanctioned war. Pre-Islamic Arabian warfare was directly linked to the economic and social circumstances of pasturage, material wealth, and prestige, and was characterized by looting, raiding and clan and tribal blood feuds. The idea of warfare as a command of God rewarded by martyrdom and paradise was an innovation with no precedent in Arab culture, custom, or practice, brought about entirely by Muhammad's thinking and influence on events.

Setting aside for the moment the possibility of divine influence on Muhammad's thinking, where might Muhammad have acquired his ideas of holy war and martyrdom? Muhammad was a caravaneer, and had travelled to the Jewish communities in Arabia and the Christian border communities of the Byzantine Empire. Among the Jews he may have encountered the concept of *harem* or holy war against idolaters and non-believers that plays such a prominent role in the Old Testament accounts of Moses and Joshua establishing the Israelite state. Muhammad may have acquired the idea of martyrdom from the Christian communities. For three centuries (380–620) the Byzantine emperors had violently persecuted Christian heretics, events that gave renewed emphasis to the Christian notion of martyrdom. To escape persecution, the heretical sects often settled in remote border communities that traded frequently with Arab merchants.

The influence of Greek philosophy, Roman occupation, and the Diaspora put an end to the Jewish concept of holy war. The Christian ideal of martyrdom was eventually eroded by the impact of nationalism, the rise of the nation state, the Enlightenment, the emergence of American theories of secular democracy, and the Industrial Revolution, forces that shaped the secular culture of the West. These forces had little impact in Muslim lands, however, with the consequence that the Muslim idea of holy war remained essentially unchanged from the time of Muhammad. Martyrdom by death in battle in defence of the faith or proselytism became a central tenet of Islam. Muslim martyrs went directly to paradise without having to suffer the 'torment of the grave' like other Muslims who had to wait until the Day of Judgement to be resurrected.

Muhammad's promulgation of holy war may have been prompted by the political circumstances he confronted at the time at least as much as by religious zeal. It was a time of crisis for Islam. Either Muhammad would force the pagan tribes into the fold and set the stage for the religious conversion of all Arabia, or Islam would in all likelihood have remained a creed confined to the southern desert. After returning from a failed attack on Tabuk near the Byzantine border (631 AD), Muhammad had a revelation instructing him to impose an obligatory yearly tax (*zakat*) on all those, Muslim and pagan, who sought his support. He would give the tribes of Arabia one last chance to join the Islamic movement. Payment of the tax, the traditional Arab way from time immemorial of showing submission to a chief, would be the test of their loyalty. Those who refused would be killed.

This instruction is known in the Muslim tradition as *Surat al-Tawbah* or 'The Repentance', and is found in the Qur'an. The Arab world changed dramatically with its promulgation. It was now time to choose between the old order and the new, and Muhammad declared war against all non-Muslims. The idolaters were given four months' grace, after which Muhammad declared himself free of any responsibility toward them. Muslims were then commanded to 'slay the idolaters wherever you find them'. No longer would Muhammad form alliances with non-Muslims. The choice for the Arabian tribes was to join Muhammad or face 'war to the knife'.

The promulgation of the *Surat al-Tawbah* is the only example of Muhammad forcing 'conversion by the sword' under penalty of death, and it applied only to the Arab tribes within Arabia. It did not apply to those outside Arabia that later fell to the Arab conquest and not to Christians and Jews living in Arabia. These communities were not to be harmed, although as events turned out, the Jewish communities were massacred and destroyed. At least at the outset, however, there was to be 'no compulsion in religion', and conversion by the sword was forbidden.

The concept of jihad came to have many meanings over the centuries as a consequence of the influence of Muslim legalists, scholars, theologians, ambitious rulers, rebels and the violent conflicts among Sunni, Shia and Sufi Muslims. The term derives from the root *jahada* which is defined as 'exerting one's utmost power, efforts, endeavors, or ability in contending with an object of disapprobation'. However, few non-Western Muslim scholars and jurists regard the concept of jihad as only a personal inner struggle. Most subscribe to the classical evolutionary theory of holy war. In this view, what Muhammad meant by jihad depended upon the historic circumstances and needs at different times during his prophetic mission, until it was concluded that war against non-Muslims could be waged virtually at any time, without pretext and in any place. This interpretation provided the ideological justification for the Arab conquests and is very much alive in the minds of jihadists of the present day.

The history of jihad can be divided into four distinct, if overlapping, periods, each distinguished by the major combatants involved. First, the jihad of the Riddah (632–633); second, the jihad of the Muslim conquest (633–732); third, the Sunni-Shia jihads against one another (661 to the present); and fourth, jihads in reaction to Western colonialism (1700–1960).[23]

Jihad of the Riddah

Abu Bakr declared war on all those who would not obey and introduced three new elements to Islam that greatly expanded the religious justification for jihad against Muslims. First, he proclaimed withdrawal from Muhammad's coalition to be a denial of God's will and declared secession from the coalition as apostasy punishable by death. Muslims would later use this proposition to conduct jihads against other Muslims who did not follow the *sharia* law. Second, Abu Bakr declared that Muslims could not be loyal to God under any leader whose legitimacy did not derive from Muhammad, thereby laying the groundwork for the later Sunni-Shia jihads against one another over the question of who were the legitimate leaders of Islam. Third, to forestall the influence of others who claimed to be prophets who had already arisen in Arabia during Muhammad's lifetime, Abu Bakr declared Muhammad to be the last prophet that God would send. This led Muslims to regard all religions that came after Muhammad as false religions.

Although Abu Bakr's pronouncements were introduced as part of his *political* strategy to isolate and compel the obedience of the Arabian tribes and could claim no religious authority to support them, these pronouncements became important Muslim *religious beliefs* as the years passed. It was actually Abu Bakr more than Muhammad who laid what became the religious justification for the internecine jihads among Sunni, Shia and Sufi Muslims that were to follow over the centuries.

The Jihad of the Muslim Conquests

In 633, with the Riddah finished, Abu Bakr ordered the Arab armies to attack the Byzantines, beginning the first phase of the Arab Conquest that lasted until 732 and brought much of the Byzantine and Persian empires, the Mediterranean littoral and Spain under a Muslim occupation that lasted until the end of the Ottoman Empire in 1918. Jihad as a stimulus for converting non-Muslims seems to have played only a secondary role in these events, however. Once Arabia had been converted, Abu Bakr and his successor, Umar, found themselves with insufficient resources to sustain the Islamic state and its tribal coalition armies. The conquest of Byzantine and Persian lands was necessary to provide new sources of loot, booty, food, horses, land and taxes to sustain the Muslim community and its military forces. Religious jihad seems not to have been the primary motivation of the Arab armies, although it surely must have been so for many of the individuals who fought in the campaigns.

Once established in their new lands, the Arabs made no attempt to convert the conquered population to Islam, but attempted to remain an ethnically homogeneous and religious society apart from the infidels. All Arab emigrants lived in garrison cities (*ribats*) or military districts to avoid contact with infidels, lest they fall back into polytheism. All Muslims were registered in the *diwan*, or 'register', and received monthly rations, quarters and a cash allowance. The *diwan* was the primary institution for the maintenance of the army and all Muslims. The Arab conquerors took over the financial systems of the conquered lands, levied a mandatory tax on all non-Muslims, required Muslims to pay the *zakat* and exempted non-Muslims from military service.

The attempt to sustain a separate Arab identity apart from the infidels was bound to fail on the grounds of sheer numbers. The size of the Arab armies that left Arabia could hardly have exceeded one hundred thousand people, including women and children, whereas the population of the conquered lands probably exceeded twenty-million. The Arabs made no effort to recruit the able-bodied men of the conquered lands into their armies, and made no attempt at forced conversion. Voluntary conversion, however, was successful. By 825, Muslims were a majority of the population in Iran and achieved majorities in Egypt, Syria, and Iraq by 900. The Arabs gradually were submerged into the Muslim armies of disparate peoples who had converted to the new faith. The Arab tribal armies gave way to professional non-Arab Muslim armies, although their commanders remained Arabs for many years.

Jihad Against Muslims

Abu Bakr's pronouncements created serious difficulties less than a decade after his death. His pronouncements on apostasy for the first time made it legitimate for Muslims to kill Muslims. Abu Bakr's claim that only elected leaders were legitimate laid the basis for the Shia-Sunni antagonism over who were Muhammad's rightful heirs. And contrary to Muhammad's practice, religion, state and army were now inseparable. This made it inevitable that dynastic and civic conflicts would become religious conflicts, while religious disagreements became civic conflicts. The result was more than a thousand years of intra-religious jihads among Shia, Sunni and Sufi factions of Islam.

In 645, intra-religious jihad flared into the open. The appointment of Abu Bakr's successor, Uthman, as caliph precipitated a division between those who believed rulers should be selected by the Prophet's companions (Sunni) and those who believed only God could appoint the ruler (Shia) who should be a blood relative of Muhammad or his family. The Khawarij or 'Seceders' declared a jihad against the Sunni caliph on the grounds that his improper election made him a *takfir*, an apostate who must be killed. Uthman was assassinated and his successor, Ali (656–61), declared a jihad against the Khawarij. In revenge, he was assassinated in the mosque at Kufa in 661. The Sunni-Shia dispute turned increasingly violent, with each regarding the other as heretics that could be legitimately slain 'in defence of Islam'. Sufis soon joined the fray with a new mystical theory of 'jihad of the sword' that threatened everyone. From 661 to 750, Muslims fought three dynastic-religious civil wars that became the stimulus for the emergence of a formal ideology of jihad that first appeared in a treatise on the subject in 797.

It is only necessary to mention a few of the Sunni-Shia jihads to make the point. In 680, the beheading of Imam Hussein, the first Shia imam, at the hands of the Sunnis in Iraq is remembered in Shia history as the Shia Martyrdom. Jihad against infidels and Shia became the official ideology the Ottoman state used to expand its territory and control Shia and Sufi elements within it. In 1124, Shiites opposed to Ottoman rule in Iran, Iraq, and Syria formed a group dedicated to using murder and assassination to overthrow the ruling Sunni order. This group, known in the West as the Assassins, plagued Ottoman officials with violence for three centuries. In 1501, Shah Ismail Safavid, a Shia, the first ruler of the Safavid dynasty, made Shiaism the official religion of the Persian state, and launched a ten year jihad of persecution against Sunnis. Much of the centuries-long conflict between Persia and the Ottomans had its roots in the Shia-Sunni divide.

The rise of Wahabism (1744) injected an even more violent strain into these religious conflicts. The Wahabis were a fundamentalist Sunni sect originating in what became Saudi Arabia that believed most Muslims were insufficiently observant in their faith. Along with massacring fellow-Sunnis, the Wahhabis declared unrelenting war against the Shia. In 1802, they slaughtered thousands of Shiites in their holy city of Karbala in Iraq. The Wahhabis formed an alliance with the house of Saud in Arabia, and the present Saudi regime is still Wahhabist in its religious orientation. During the Iran-Iraq war (1980–1986), Iran's Ayatollah Khomeini declared the conflict against the Sunnis in Iraq a jihad. The current 'civil war' in Syria is an extension of the historical Shia-Sunni conflict, with Saudi Arabia supporting the jihadist rebels and Iran propping up Assad's Shia Alawite regime. After more than 1,400 years, it is unlikely that there is a solution to what is surely one of the world's longest running religious conflicts between adherents of the same religion. One of jihad's great paradoxes is that far more jihads have been fought among Islamic co-religionists than between Muslims and non-Muslims.

One factor contributing to the longevity of the Shia-Sunni conflict and its use of jihad is that the number of civic and religious authorities who claimed the right to declare a legitimate jihad expanded greatly over the centuries. A power originally confined to the Sunni caliphs and then the Shia imams was claimed by all sorts of malcontents for all kinds of reasons. This led to jihad being used as a justification for suppressing domestic dissent or settling domestic problems. The consequence was numerous massacres and forced conversions over the centuries, mostly against Christians and Jews living in Muslim territories. Jihad continued to serve its original purpose in justifying wars against non-Muslims, however. Jihad against polytheists was the basis for the Muslim invasion of India (1024), and the Mughal conquest of India (1507). Even the Mongols and later Tamerlane used jihad to justify attacks against fellow Muslims.

Jihad in the Colonial Period

The encroachment of Western colonial powers on Muslim territories of the Ottoman Empire provoked numerous calls for jihads to defend Islam. The Russian annexation of the Crimea in 1783, Bonaparte's capture of Egypt in 1797 and the French invasion of Algeria and

Egypt were met with calls for jihad against the foreigners. The Russian attempt to drive the Ottomans from southeast Europe in 1877 was met by a declaration of jihad, as was Russian encroachment in central Asia in 1914. In the same year, the Ottomans declared jihad against the Armenians, wherein more than a million Armenians were slaughtered. The colonial period saw jihads declared in Mali, Java, China, Sudan, Egypt, Palestine, Morocco, Sub-Saharan Africa and India. During this period, ethnic and racial minorities, Christian and Islamic sects and Jews were massacred as enemies of Islam.

World War I and the occupation of Ottoman and Persian empires by the West generally put an end to these large-scale jihads, although some resistance continued to occur until the colonial powers withdrew completely after World War II. These rebel movements were mostly led by mystical Sufi fundamentalists who opposed moderate Sunni and Shia as being equally un-Islamic. Some movements, such as in Chechnya, have persisted for more than a century.

The withdrawal of the colonial powers from most Muslim lands by the 1950s gave rise to nationalist regimes in many of the former Ottoman and Persian territories. The cultural shock following the collapse of the Ottoman Empire, the Western occupation and the establishment of Israel in 1948, followed by three wars in which Muslim forces were defeated, demoralized the spirit of Islam. The frequency of jihads declined. Muslims placed their faith in new nationalist leaders (Nasser in Egypt, Hussein in Jordan, Hafaz al-Assad in Syria, Saddam Hussein in Iraq, Mosadegh in Iran, Bhutto in Pakistan, and Daoud in Afghanistan) to protect Muslim interests. But these regimes drew support from only the small urban educated pro-Western elites, leaving the poor and rural population to the continued influence of religious leaders and the mosque schools. It was in these schools that the spirit of jihad was preserved.

By the late 1970s, the failure of the nationalist regimes to provide adequate economic improvement for most Muslims and the increased Westernization of their ruling elites provoked violent resistance from traditional Muslims. A number of events over the next two decades signalled a renewal of Muslim jihadist spirit. These events included replacement of Daoud in Afghanistan (1974), the Shia revolution in Iran (1979), the rise of Zia al-Huk in Pakistan and the creation of the Taliban (1978), the Iran-Iraq war (1980–1986), the assassination of Anwar Sadat by the Egyptian Islamic Jihad in 1981, two *intifadahs* on the West Bank (1987, 2000), the Iraqi invasion of Kuwait (1990), the renewed war in Chechyna and the North Cacausus (1994), and increased financial support by Saudi Arabia for Osama Bin Laden and other Wahabist causes throughout the Muslim world. When Saudi Wahabists crashed their planes into the World Trade towers on September 11, 2001, it was in the spirit of jihad that had already been rekindled in the Muslim world.

Muhammad's military legacy lives on in the minds of these jihadists in their memory of Muhammad as a great general and passionate revolutionary who created and fought a successful insurgency to achieve his political and religious goals. It is this legacy of Muhammad as successful revolutionary that motivates Muslim insurgents and revolutionary leaders in Iraq, Afghanistan, and elsewhere. In their portrayal of their insurgencies as divinely sanctioned movements, these modern revolutionaries are imitating Muhammad. It can scarcely be denied that at least to some extent some suicide bombers are motivated by their desire to become martyrs in the same manner that many of Muhammad's soldiers were willing to die for their faith. The Osama bin Ladens of the Muslim world, like Muhammad, speak of creating a more moral world in which to live, a community of believers living according to the instructions given by God himself. Like Muhammad, they are prepared to use violence to bring that new moral order into being.

What, then, of the historical consequences of Moses, Buddha, and Muhammad on war and military history? Buddha's revulsion of war produced a pacifistic religion that had little influence on war or military history in his native India or, for that matter, in any of the other countries where it eventually took root. There is no evidence of any Buddhist national society without a military establishment nor one willing to renounce war as an instrument of policy. The pacifism of Buddhism remains an individual practice, exactly as Buddha intended it.

The Mosaic introduction of a violent monotheism into the ancient polytheistic world brought with it a period of religious genocide largely contained to Canaan before being eclipsed by the traditionl non-violent polytheism that it had interrupted for some two centuries. The repeated occupation of Canaan by polytheistic empires – Assyria, Babylon, Persia, Greece, and Rome – insured that monotheism and its violent impulses remained suppressed and confined to the Mosaic sect settled in around Judea and Jerusalem in Canaan. The policies of these regimes greatly limited the scope and frequency of religious violence. With the destruction of the Mosaic religious establishment and the diaspora of the Judeans by the Romans following the religious inspired revolt of 73 CE., the spine of Mosaic monotheistic violence was severed. With the destruction of the Mosaic central religious authority, Mosaic religious leadership passed to a decentralized rabbinate dispersed among majority populations, with the result that its violent impulses gradually died out. Over the centuries, Mosaic monotheism gradually stopped being an enclave religion, and became a universal one, in which all human beings, not just members of the enclave, came to have moral standing. By the second century CE any tendencies toward violence in the original Mosaic monotheism had disappeared completely.

Islam took a different historical path, with the result that its brand of monotheism retained many of its original violent tendencies. Once the conquest of the Byzantine and Persian empires was accomplished, Islam had to confront no outside force that could modify its violent monotheistic tendencies. There was no continual exposure to polytheistic religions, no non-Islamic foreign conquerors, no emergence of secular national states, as in Europe, that could weaken religious loyalties in favour of nationalistic ones, and no development of secular legal codes to raise and protect the legal and moral standing of non-believers. All of these forces gradually weakened the influence of monotheism's violent tendencies during the long Christian era that followed the Mosaic diaspora in the West.

The failure of the Islamic empires to establish national secular states (as in the West) also worked to impede the development of Islamic societal structures, with the result that for a very long period, indeed, even into the modern age in some cases, Islamic societies remained tribal, severely decentralized, and strongly influenced (mullah schools) by religious elites who continue to support, propagate, and sustain the same ancient monotheism accompanied by its violent tendencies. Unlike the West where religious observance is regarded as an individual concern, in Islamic societies religious belief is a primary governmental and societal concern. The result is that there is often no discernible separation between the two, creating what are functional theocracies in secular garb. There were no forces throughout its history in most Islamic societies that worked to weaken the influence of monotheism per se, with the consequence that the violent tendencies of monotheistic thinking remain and tend to explode into violent tendencies from time to time.

In the West, the violent tendency of Mosaic monotheism found a new locus in the proselytizing Christianity that followed it as the official Roman state religion in the fourth century CE. For the next thousand years, religious wars of one sort or another plagued the West until the rise of the secular national state (Thirty Years War: 1648) put an end to them. The tendency toward violence inherent in the old monotheism was quickly replaced by various absolute nationalistic creeds in which the will of God as an object of belief was replaced by the will of the state. By the nineteenth century, even these creeds were replaced by the ideologies that accompanied wars of the twentieth and early twenty-first centuries. In this curious sense, the tendencies of monotheism to lead to violence are still with us.

Notes

Introduction

1. The Pali Canon represents Theravada Buddhism's canonical literature collected in eighty-five volumes. It existed only in oral form from the time of Buddha's life until it was finally written down in the first century BC, some four hundred years after Buddha's death.

Chapter 1. Moses: Israel's First General

1. Jonathan Kirsch, *Moses: A Life* (New York: Ballantine Books, 1998), p. 251.
2. *Ibid.*, p. 44.
3. *Ibid.*, p. 47.
4. Michael Grant, *The History of Ancient Israel* (New York: Scribner, 1984), p. 184.
5. Kirsch, *Moses: A Life*, p. 61.
6. Exodus 11:3.
7. Exodus 2:19.
8. Martin Buber, *Moses: The Revelation and the Covenant* (Amherst, NY: Humanity Books, 1998), pp. 35–36.
9. Exodus 2:12.
10. Buber, *Moses*, p. 35–36. The claim that Pharaoh would 'slay' Moses rather than turn him over to the courts sounds more like an Israelite blood feud than Egyptian justice.
11. Exodus 32:27.
12. Sigmund Freud, *Moses and Monotheism* (New York: Vintage Books, 1939), p. 45.
13. Numbers 25:5.
14. Numbers 31:13–18.
15. Numbers 31:50.

16. Kirsch, *Moses: A Life*, p. 9–10.
17. Exodus, 34:35.
18. Kirsch, *Moses: A Life*, p. 275.
19. Numbers 1:51.
20. The story is remarkably similar to a common Bedouin practice. In the spring when the new lambs are born, the winter threat has passed and the animals moved to new pasturage, the Bedouins gathered for a feast at which a lamb was slaughtered. The blood from the leg of the animal was used to anoint the doorways of the tents to ward off evil forces for the coming year. The Passover story's details may have come from the earlier experience of the Israelites when they were animal tenders.
21. Numbers 21:9. The similarity of the brass serpent with the cobra uraeus worn by pharaoh to ward off evil, a sacred amulet that later became the *tefillin* in Judaism, is obvious.
22. Kirsch, *Moses: A Life*, p. 232.
23. Buber, *Moses*, p. 37.
24. Richard A. Gabriel and Karen S. Metz, *The History of Military Medicine, Vol. 1: From Ancient Times to the Middle Ages*, (Westport, CT: Greenwood Press, 1992), p. 28.
25. William S. Barnett, 'Only the Bad Died Young in the Ancient Middle East', in *International Journal of Aging and Human Development* 21, no. 2 (1985), pp. 155–160.
26. Robert G. Boling and G. Ernest Wright, *Joshua: The Anchor Bible* (New York: Doubleday, 1982), p. 193. This source will be quoted herein as *Anchor Bible*.
27. E. A. Wallis Budge, *Osiris and the Egyptian Resurrection* (New York: Dover Publications, 1973), pp. 219–24 for the origins of circumcision and its Egyptian connection. The Egyptian origins of the practice make it unlikely that the biblical Patriarchs, who came from Mesopotamia and not Egypt, were circumcised.
28. *Ibid.* See also Richard A. Gabriel, *Gods of Our Fathers: The Memory of Egypt in Judaism and Christianity* (Westport, CT: Greenwood Press, 2001), p. 73–4. See also James H. Breasted, *The Dawn of Conscience* (New York: Charles Scribner, 1947), pp. 353–354.
29. James B. Pritchard, *Ancient Near Eastern Texts Relating to the Old Testament* (Princeton, NJ: Princeton University Press, 1955), p. 326.
30. The fact that they were circumcised in Egypt hints further at their military service of some sort in the Egyptian army.
31. Joshua 5:4–6.

32. Eric Isaac, 'Circumcision as Covenant Rite', in *Anthropos* 59 (1965), p. 444. See also *Anchor Bible*, p. 194: 'Moreover, in early Israel it is in covenant with the Divine Warrior that circumcision became important.' Exodus 15:3 describes Yahweh as a Divine Warrior.

33. B. S. J. Isserlin, *The Israelites* (London: Thames and Hudson, 1998), p. 62.

34. I am deeply indebted to Dr. Joel T. Klein, PhD in ancient languages, rabbi, psychologist, and author for helping me translate and understand the roots and derivations of the Hebrew words that appear herein.

35. See Gabriel, *Gods of Our Fathers*, 74; M. Rostovtzeff, 'The Foundations of Social and Economic Life in Hellenic Times', in *Journal of Egyptian Archaeology* 6 (1920), p. 176; and H. Idris Bell, 'Hellenic Culture in Egypt', *Journal of Egyptian Archaeology* 8 (1922), p. 145.

36. Gabriel, *God's of Our Fathers*, p. 11.

37. Rostovtzeff, 'Foundations of Social and Economic Life', in *Journal of Egyptian Archaeology* 6 (1920), p. 170.

38. Gabriel and Metz, *History of Military Medicine*, Vol. 1, Chapter 3: 'Egypt'. One of the foods regularly fed to construction workers were radishes that are effective in preventing intestinal disorders. At Passover, Jews still eat 'the bitter herb' to remind them of their days of bondage in Egypt. The bitter herb is the radish or horseradish.

39. The best works on the Amarna Period are Donald B. Redford, *Akhenaten: The Heretic King* (Princeton, NJ: Princeton University Press, 1984) and Cyril Aldred, *Akenaten: King of Egypt* (London: Thames and Hudson, 1988).

40. Breasted, *Dawn of Conscience*, p. 349.

41. *Ibid.*, see also Nicolas Grimal, *History of Ancient Egypt* (London: Blackwell Publishers, 1992), p. 219.

42. H. H. Rowley, *From Joseph to Joshua* (London: Oxford University Press, 1948), p. 55.

43. Isserlin, *The Israelites*, p. 52.

44. *Ibid.*

45. Karen Armstrong, *A History of God* (New York: Ballantine Books, 1993), p. 11.

46. Buber, *Moses*, p. 25.

47. Norman K. Gottwald, *The Tribes of Yahweh* (Mary Knoll, NY: Orbis Books, 1979), pp. 352–369.

48. *Ibid.*

49. Buber, *Moses*, p. 24.

50. Gottwald, *Tribes of Yahweh*, p. 454.

51. *Ibid.*, p. 453.

52. Buber, *Moses*, p. 24.

53. Gottwald, *The Tribes of Yahweh*, p. 454.
54. *Ibid.*, p. 408.
55. *Ibid.*
56. *Ibid.*, p. 397.
57. *Ibid.*, p. 402.
58. *Ibid.*, p. 403.
59. Nigel Stillman and Nigel Tallis, *Armies of the Ancient Near East* (Sussex, UK: Wargames Research Group, 1984), p. 83.
60. Rowley, *Joseph to Joshua*, p. 116.
61. Gabriel, *Gods of Our Fathers*, p. 54.
62. Redford, *Akhenaten*, p. 28. Asiatics were so common in Egyptian marketplaces that the hieroglyph 'to haggle' literally translates as 'to do Syrian business'.
63. Buber, *Moses*, p. 21.
64. Rowley, *Joseph to Joshua*, p. 116.
65. Breasted, *Dawn of Conscience*, p. 306.
66. Akhenaten almost certainly suffered from either Frohlich's syndrome or Marfan's disease, either of which would have made any sustained physical effort very difficult. The reliefs portraying the king as physically vigorous when he most probably was not are almost certainly propaganda. See Gabriel, *Gods of Our Fathers*, pp. 39–41 for more on Akhenaten's physical condition.
67. A. R. Schulman, 'Some Remarks on the Military Background of the Amarna Period', in *Journal of the American Research Center in Egypt* 3 (1964), p. 52.
68. *Ibid.*
69. *Ibid.*, p. 58.
70. *Ibid.*, p. 52.
71. Kirsch, *Moses: A Life*, p. 32.
72. Sir Alan Gardiner, *Egypt of the Pharaohs* (London: Oxford University Press, 1961), p. 258; Rowley, *Joseph to Joshua*, p. 132; Grimal, *History of Ancient Egypt*, p. 258.
73. H. M. Wiener, "The Historical Character of the Exodus," *Ancient Egypt* IV (1926): 108.
74. Rowley, *Joseph to Joshua*, p. 23.
75. Grimal, *History of Ancient Egypt*, pp. 248–250.
76. Eric H. Cline, *1177 B.C.: The Year Civilization Collapsed* (Princeton, NJ: Princeton University Press, 2014), chapter 1.
77. Edouard Neville, 'The Geography of the Exodus', in *Journal of Egyptian Archaeology* 10 (1924), pp. 19–25, for the locations of the two cities.
78. Neville, 'Geography of the Exodus', pp. 19–25.

79. All mercenary units bear watching. When David and his *habiru* troops arrived to help the Philistine kings against Saul at the Battle of Gilboa, the Philistines feared that David could not be trusted to fight against his own kinsmen and he was sent from the battlefield and did not take part in the battle. Interestingly, Saul did not trust David either, and left him behind to keep an eye on the Philistine route of march.

80. Peter A. Clayton, *Chronicle of the Pharaohs* (London: Thames and Hudson, 1994), p. 147.

81. *Ibid.*

82. Michael Grant, *History of Ancient Israel* (New York: Charles Scribner, 1984), p. 184.

83. *Ibid.*, p. 202. See also Josephus, *Contra Apion*, 1.82–92.

84. Jan Assmann, *Moses the Egyptian* (Cambridge, MA: Harvard University Press, 1998), p. 34.

85. Cline, *The Year Civilization Collapsed*, p. 70; see also T. R. Bryce, *The Kingdom of the Hittites* (Oxford: Oxford University Press, 2005), p. 183.

86. Steven Weingartner, 'Suppiluliuma I and his Times: Great King and Conqueror', in *Ancient Warfare* (Summer, 2014), pp. 8–13.

87. Siro Igino Trevisanato, 'The Hittite Plague: An Epidemic of Tularemia and the First Record of Biological Warfare', in *Medical Hypotheses* 69, 6 (2007), pp. 1371–1374.

88. Kerry O. Cleveland, 'Tularemia', Medscape Reference http://emedicine.medscape.com/article/230923-overview.

89. *Ibid.*

90. Josephus, *Contra Apion*, 1.82–92.

91. William H. C. Propp, *Exodus 1–18: The Anchor Bible* (New York: Doubleday, 1998), p. 487.

92. *Ibid.*

93. *Ibid.*, p. 488.

94. The modern term for un-motorized infantry is still 'leg infantry'.

95. Propp, *The Anchor Bible*, p. 414.

96. Richard A. Gabriel, *The Culture of War* (Westport, CT: Greenwood Press, 1990), pp. 39–40 for the difficulty and cost of bronze manufacture and the impact of iron on the supply of weapons in antiquity.

97. Richard A. Gabriel, *The Great Armies of Antiquity* (Westport, CT: Praeger, 2002), p. 64–65.

98. Quintus Curtis, *History of Alexander*, 5.2.7, trans. John C. Rolfe (Cambridge, MA: Harvard University Press, 1946), p. 345.

99. *Ibid.*

100. Propp, *The Anchor Bible*, p. 489.

101. *Ibid.*, p. 549.

102. *Ibid.*
103. Neville, 'Geography of the Exodus', p. 24.
104. Exodus, 8:22–24.
105. Propp, *The Anchor Bible*, p. 490.
106. Chaim Herzog and Mordechai Gichon, *Battles of the Bible* (Jerusalem: Steimatzky's agency, 1978), p. 21.
107. Diodorus Siculus, 1.30.4
108. Exodus 14:2–4.
109. Exodus 14:20.
110. Propp, *The Anchor Bible*, p. 499.
111. *Ibid.*
112. Exodus 14:21–23.
113. *Ibid*
114. Neville, 'Geography of the Exodus', p. 39.
115. Gottwald, *Tribes of Yahweh*, p. 454.
116. Numbers 10:31.
117. Exodus 17:9.
118. *Ibid.*
119. Exodus 17:13.
120. Yigael Yadin, *The Art of War in Biblical Lands in Light of Archaeological Discovery* (New York: McGraw-Hill, 1963), p. 79. See also Gabriel, *The Culture of War*, p. 44.
121. George E. Mendenhall, 'The Census List of Numbers 1 and 26', *Journal of Biblical Literature*, 77 (1958), p. 54.
122. *Ibid*, p. 55.
123. My thanks to my old friend, Colonel Reuven Gal of the Israeli Defense Force, for his explanation of this event.
124. Mendenhall, 'Census Lists', p. 59.
125. *Ibid.*
126. *Ibid*, pp. 60–62.
127. Mendenhall, 'Census Lists', pp. 60–62.
128. *Ibid.*, p. 64.
129. For the cost of maintaining chariot forces, see Robert Drews, *The End of the Bronze Age* (Princeton, NJ: Princeton University Press, 1993), p. 110.
130. Mendenhall, 'Census Lists', pp. 64–65.
131. T. R. Hobbs, *A Time for War* (Wilmington, DE: Michael Glazier, 1989), p. 78.
132. A. Lucas, 'The Number of Israelites at the Exodus', in *Palestine Exploration Quarterly* (1944), pp. 164–8.

133. Richard A. Gabriel and Karen S. Metz, *From Sumer To Rome: The Military Capabilities of Ancient Armies* (Westport, CT: Greenwood Press, 1991), p. 23.
134. *Ibid.*, 153.
135. Mordechai Gichon, 'The Siege of Masada', in *Collection du Centre des Etudes Romaines et Gallo-Romaines*, no. 20 (Lyon, 2000), p. 543.
136. As noted earlier, the Bible records six outbreaks of plague among the Israelites accounting for a total of 40,000 dead.
137. Propp, *The Anchor Bible*, p. 632.
138. *Ibid.*
139. Reuven Gal, *A Portrait of the Israeli Soldier* (Westport, CT: Greenwood Press, 1986). See Chapter 12 for an explanation of the ethical doctrine of the Israeli Defense Force.
140. Richard A. Gabriel, *No More Heroes: Madness and Psychiatry in War* (New York: Hill and Wang, 1987), pp. 87–8.
141. *Ibid.*, Chapter 4 for a history of psychiatric screening in war.
142. Gabriel and Metz, *From Sumer to Rome*, pp. 99–104.
143. A. S. Yasuda, 'The Osiris Cult and the Designation of Osiris Idols in the Bible', *Journal of Near Eastern Studies* 3 (1944), pp. 194–7.
144. For the blood taboo of the Jews, see Morton Smith, *Jesus the Magician* (New York: Barnes and Noble, 1997), p. 123.
145. For a description of the Egyptian army, see Richard A. Gabriel, *The Military History of Ancient Israel* (Westport, CT: Praeger, 2003), Chapter 2.
146. See *The Westminster Historical Atlas to the Bible* (Philadelphia, PA: Westminster Press, 1945) for a portrayal of the Ben-Hassan relief.
147. Herzog and Gichon, *Battles of the Bible*, p. 20.
148. I Chronicles 12:34.
149. Herzog and Gichon, *Battles of the Bible*, 85.
150. I Chronicles 12:24.
151. *Ibid.*, 12:25.
152. *Ibid.*, 12:9
153. *Ibid.*, 12:37.
154. *Ibid.*, 12:1–2.
155. *Ibid.*, 12:35.
156. For a description of the structure and tactics of the Egyptian army at the time of the Exodus, see Gabriel, *Great Armies of Antiquity*, Chapter 3.
157. *Ibid.*
158. Richard A. Gabriel and Donald W. Boose, Jr., *The Great Battles of Antiquity* (Westport, CT: Greenwood Press, 1990), pp. 49–50.

159. If any Israelites served in Pharaoh's personal guard (as, for example, the Shardana of the Sea Peoples served in the personal guard of Ramses II), the most likely candidates might have been members of the tribe of Benjamin. The term *yamin* means 'of the right hand', suggesting that they 'stood at the right hand' of the king, i.e. as members of his personal guard. See Joel T. Klein, *Through the Name of God* (Westport, CT: Greenwood Press, 2001), p. 237, fn. 76.
160. Exodus 32:29.
161. Michael M. Homan, 'The Divine Warrior in His Tent: A Military Model for Yahweh's Tabernacle', in *Bible Review* 16, no. 6 (December, 2000), p. 22. Homan is a professor at Hebrew University.
162. *Ibid.*, p. 28.
163. *Ibid.*, p. 55.
164. *Ibid.*, p. 30.
165. *Ibid.*
166. *Ibid.*
167. *Ibid.*, p. 55
168. *Ibid.*, p. 24
169. *Ibid.*
170. Numbers 10:11.
171. Numbers 13:17–20.
172. *Ibid.*, 13:25–31.
173. Kirsch, *Moses: A Life*, p. 307.
174. *Ibid.*, p. 308.
175. Elias Auerbach, *Moses*, translated and edited by Robert A. Barclay and Israel O. Lehman (Detroit, MI: Wayne State University Press, 1975), p. 50.
176. Gottwald, *Tribes of Yahweh*, p. 426.
177. Stillman and Tallis, *Armies of the Ancient Near East*, p. 187.
178. *Ibid.*
179. Deuteronomy 32:51–52.
180. Kirsch, *Moses: A Life*, p. 304 for Moses' suspicion that the Israelites were preparing to kill him by stoning.
181. Numbers 16:2.
182. Numbers 25:5.

Chapter 2. Buddha: The Soldier Pacifist

1. Sarva Daman Singh, *Ancient Indian Warfare* (Delhi: Banarsidass Publishers, 1997), p. 25 for the evolution of the Indian chariot and its connection to Sumer.

2. The Ashvakas, Aspasians, Assakenoi, and Asvayanas were four Aryan tribes that fought Alexander in his Indian campaign. See Richard A. Gabriel, *The Madness of Alexander the Great and the Myth of Military Genius* (Barnsley: Pen and Sword, 2015), pp. 148–9.
3. For the genetic evidence and debate see Michael Bamshad et al., 'Genetic Evidence on the Origins of Indian Caste Populations', in *Genome Res.* 11 (6), pp. 994–1004; see also Sarah Grey Thompson and Terrence Kaufman, *Language, Contact, Creolization, and Genetic Linguistics* (Berkeley, CA: University of California Press, 1991); also, in full, http://genome.cshlp.org/content/13/10/2277.
4. Bamshad et al, 'Genetic Evidence on the Origins of Indian Caste Populations'.
5. Geoffrey Samuel, *The Origins of Yoga and Tantra* (Cambridge, UK: Cambridge University Press, 2010), p. 49.
6. H. S. Bhatia, *Vedic and Aryan India: Evolution of Political, Legal, and Military Systems*, (New Delhi: Deep and Deep Publications, 2001), p. 84.
7. Richard A. Gabriel, 'Buddha: Enlightened Warrior', in *Military History* (May, 2011), pp 40–41.
8. Richard F. Gombrich, *Theravada Buddhism: A Social History from Ancient Benares to Modern Columbo* (London: 1988), pp. 33–4.
9. A. L. Basham, *The Wonder That Was India* (New York: Grove Press, 1959), p. 138.
10. Bhatia, *Vedic and Aryan India*, p. 305.
11. Portuguese traders arrived in India around 1600 and called the groups that comprised Aryan society *casta*. The term 'caste' is a variant of *casta*.
12. V. R. Ramachandra Dikshitar, *War in Ancient India* (Delhi: Motilal Banarsidass, 1987), p. 64.
13. Basham, *The Wonder That Was India*, p. 126.
14. Others immune from slaughter on the battlefield were *brahmins*, ascetics, eunuchs, the ill, the naked, persons engaged in sacrifices, musicians and hermaphrodites. Dikshitar, *War in Ancient India*, pp. 70 and 84.
15. For an analysis of Aryan rules of engagement in war, see Dikshitar, *War in Ancient India*, Chapter 2. The Laws of War.
16. Bashham, *The Wonder That Was India*, p. 126.
17. Bhatia, *Vedic and Aryan India*, p. 84.
18. The best comprehensive work on the military history of the Aryans is Major General Gurcharn Singh Sandhu, *A Military History of Ancient India* (Delhi: Vision Books, 2000). See particularly chapters 3–6.
19. Richard A. Gabriel, *Empires At War* vol. 1 (Westport, CT: Greenwood Press, 2005), p. 239 for Ravana and Aryan weapons.
20. Bisham, *The Wonder That Was India*, p. 360.

21. Singh, *Ancient Indian Warfare*, pp. 26–7 for the design of the Indian chariot.
22. *Ibid.*, p. 113.
23. *Ibid.*, p. 102, citing Herodotus, *Histories*, 7.65.
24. Arrian, *The Campaigns of Alexander*, translated by Aubrey De Selincourt (London: Penguin, 1971), 5.14–16.
25. Sandhu, *A Military History of Ancient India*, pp. 146–7.
26. *Ibid.*
27. Basham, *The Wonder That Was India*, p. 92, cites an instruction to princes contained in the famous political tract, *Arthasastra* (11.1) warning princes to be careful of the ambitions of their own offspring: 'for princes, like crabs, eat their own parents'.
28. Sandhu, *A Military History of Ancient India*, pp. 163–77 provides an excellent history of the rise of Maghda as an imperialist state.
29. *Ibid.*
30. Bhatia, *Vedic and Aryan India*, p. 83.
31. *Ibid.*
32. *Ibid.*
33. Sandhu, *A Military History of Ancient India*, pp. 163–77.
34. An overview of Indian fortifications can be found in Singh, *Ancient Indian Warfare*, pp. 120–28.
35. Arrian, *The Campigns of Alexander*, 5.14–18.
36. There is only partial agreement on the dates of Buddha's life. The parameters of the debate can be found in the following: L. S. Cousins, 'The Dating of the Historical Buddha', in *Journal of the Royal Asiatic Society* 3 (6) 1 (1996), pp. 57–63; Charles S. Prebish, 'Cooking the Buddhist Books: The Implications of the New Dating of the Buddha for the History of Early Indian Buddhism', *Journal of Buddhist Ethics* 15 (2008), pp. 23–44; Hans Wolfgang Schumann, *The Historical Buddha: The Times, Life, and Teachings of the Founder of Buddhism* (Delhi: Motilal Banarsidass), 2003.
37. Karen Armstrong, *Buddha* (New York: Viking Books, 2001), pp. 20–21.
38. Basham, *The Wonder That Was India*, p. 41.
39. Armstrong, *Buddha*, p. 23.
40. Richard A. Gabriel, 'The Sicarii', *Military History* (Winter, 2014), pp. 41–4 for a discussion of the wandering Messianists in Judea during the time of the Jewish revolt.
41. Richard A. Gabriel, *No More Heroes: Madness and Psychiatry in War* (New York: Hill and Wang, 1987), pp. 61–62.
42. For the Russian/Soviet psychiatric experience in World War I, II, and after, see Richard A. Gabriel, *Soviet Military Psychiatry* (Westport, CT: Greenwood Press, 1986), chapters 3 and 6.

43. Johannes Bronkhorst, *The Two Sources of Indian Asceticism* (Delhi: Motilal Banarsidass, 1998), p. 6.
44. *Ibid.*, p. 9.
45. The sources for the life of Buddha are a variety of different and often conflicting sources, none of which were composed during or even close to Buddha's lifetime. The earliest full biography, the *Buddhacarita*, is composed in poetic form and dates from the second century BC, almost 500 years after Buddha's death. Other partial biographies, the *Lalitavistara* (third century BC) and the *Mahavastu* (fourth century BC) are no more reliable than the first. Thus the need to rely upon the Pali Canon in what follows, most composed by Buddhist monks as a quasi-official canonical history, although they make no attempt at a formal biography.
46. J. P. Sharma, *Republics in Ancient India: 1500 B.C.–500 B.C.*, (Leiden: E. J. Brill, 1968), p. 182.
47. T. W. Rhys Davids, *Buddhist India*, (New York: Putnam,1911), p. 20. For an excellent geographical and demographic source for India in ancient times see C. C. Davies, *An Historical Atlas of the Indian Peninsula*, (London: Oxford University Press, 1949).
48. Vina Pandey, *History of Ancient India*, posted on the internet August 5, 2013, 'Sakya Clan: The Clan in Which Buddha Was Born', pp. 1–3. Rhys Davids and A. F. Caroline, *Sakya or Buddhist Origins*, (Columbus, MO: South Asia Books, reprint 1978), suggest that the population of the Sakyas may have been at least half a million strong.
49. Gabriel, 'Buddha: Enlightened Warrior', p. 42.
50. Armstrong's view that the Sakya territory 'was so remote that Aryan culture had never taken root there, and they had no caste system' is simply wrong. Armstrong, *Buddha*, p. 22.
51. Sharma, *Republics in Ancient India*, p. 19.
52. In ancient times, a tribal society could raise approximately twenty per cent of its population for military duty; in sieges, perhaps somewhat more. This rough estimate method was developed by Yigael Yadin, *The Art of Warfare in Biblical Lands in Light of Archaeological Discovery* vol 1, (New York: McGraw-Hill, 1964), p. 19.
53. Sharma, *Republics in Ancient India*, p. 19.
54. Basham, *Wonder That Was India*, p. 160.
55. Sandhu, *Military History of Ancient India*, p. 117.
56. Dikshitar, *War in Ancient India*, p. 44.
57. Basham, *Wonder That Was India*, pp. 160–161.
58. Dikshitar, *War in Ancient India*, p. 46.
59. *Ibid.*, pp. 54–5.

60. *Ibid.*, pp. 10–35 for a treatment of the psychological disposition of the *kshatriya*.

61. *Ibid.*, p. 56.

62. The *sati* custom is very ancient indeed, and we find it among the earliest kings of Ur and the Scythians. Many ancient peoples burnt a man's widow, horses and other possessions so that he might have all he loved and required in the afterlife. The practice is mentioned in one of the earliest verses of the *Rig Veda*. The term *sati* means 'virtuous woman'. In ancient times the dead were collected after the battle, heaped into a pile and set afire. Their wives would then climb onto the pile and lie down in the flames. See Basham, *The Wonder That Was India*, pp. 186–7; also Dikshitar, *War in Ancient India*, p. 54.

63. Sharma, *Republics in Ancient India*, p. 203.

64. http://www.jaibheem.com/B-page-7.htm

65. *Ibid.*

66. Sharma, *Republics in Ancient India*, p. 204; see also W. W. Rockhill, *The Life of the Buddha* (Pilgrims Book House, 2004), p. 112 for a description of the wars.

67. *Ibid.*

68. *Ibid.*, p. 152.

69. http://www.jaibheem.com/B-page-7.htm

70. *Ibid.*

71. *Ibid.*, pp. 8–9.

72. Armstrong, *Buddha*, p. 4.

73. *Ibid.*, p. 3.

74. *Ibid.*, p. 13.

75. Richard A. Gabriel, *The Madness of Alexander the Great and the Myth of Military Genius*, (London: Pen and Sword, 2015), Chapter 4 for the dynamics of psychiatric collapse in battle.

76. Richard A. Gabriel, *Soldier's Lives Through History: The Ancient World*, (Westport, CT: Greenwood Press, 200), Chapter 20: 'Injuries'.

77. The following section relies heavily upon my previous work in the area of battle stress and military psychiatry: See Richard A. Gabriel, *No More Heroes: Madness and Psychiatry in War* (New York: Hill and Wang, 1987); *Soviet Military Psychiatry: The Theory and Practice of Coping With Battle Stress* (Westport, CT: Greenwood Press, 1986); *Military Psychiatry: A Comparative Perspective*, (Westport, CT: Greenwood Press, 1986); and *The Painful Field:The Psychiatric Dimension of Modern War*, (Westport, CT: Greenwood Press, 1987).

78. Richard A. Gabriel and Karen S. Metz, *From Sumer To Rome: The Military Capabilities of Ancient Armies* (Westport, CT: Greenwood Press), p. 87, Table 4.2.

79. Richard A. Gabriel, *Between Flesh and Steel: A History of Military Medicine From the Middle Ages to the War in Afghanistan* (Dulles, VA: Potomac Books, 2013), pp. 163–5.

80. David Grossman, *On Killing: The Psychological Cost of Learning to Kill in War and Society* (Boston: Little Brown, 2009), pp. 129–30.

81. Richard A. Gabriel, 'War, Madness, and Military Psychiatry', in *Military History Quarterly*, forthcoming, 2015.

82. *Ibid.*

83. Armstrong, *Buddha*, 34. That the ancients were aware of the psychiatric symptoms caused by war is beyond doubt. See Lawrence A. Trittle, *From Melos to My Lai: War and Survival* (New York: Routledge, 2000); also Jonathan Shay, *Achilles in Vietnam: Combat Trauma and the Undoing of Character* (New York: Scriber, 1994). My own *The Madness of Alexander the Great* offers a detailed case study of Alexander's psychological collapse caused by his prolonged exposure to war.

84. Gabriel, *The Madness of Alexander the Great*, pp. 132–6.

85. Matthew Kosuta, 'The Buddha and the Four-Limbed Army: The Military in the Pali Canon', 4. http://www. urbandharma.org/udharma6/militarycannon.html

86. *Ibid.*

87. Devadatta first hired archers to shoot Buddha. When this failed, he tried rolling a boulder down a hill to crush his teacher. Finally, he obtained a drunken elephant to trample Buddha.

88. The *Mahparinibbana Sutta* of the Pali Canon is the most reliable source for the details on the death of Buddha. Mettanando Bhikkhu, 'How the Buddha died', in *Bangkok Post*, May 15, 2001, pp. 1–7.

89. Mettanando Bhikkhu and Oskar von Hinueber, 'The Cause of the Buddha's Death', in *Journal of the Pali Text Society*, 26 (2000), pp. 7–16.

Chapter 3. Muhammad: The Warrior Prophet

1. Robert G. Holland, *Arabia and the Arabs: From the Bronze Age to the Coming of Islam* (London: Routledge, 2001), pp. 3–4.

2. *Ibid.* , p. 169.

3. Yigael Yadin, *The Art of Warfare in Biblical Lands in Light of Archaeological Discovery*, vol 1 (New York: McGraw-Hill, 1964), p. 19.

4. Philip K. Hitti, *History of the Arabs* (Hampshire: Palgrave Macmillan, 2002), p. 25.

5. Qur'an, sura 14:40.
6. Hitti, *History of the Arabs*, p. 103.
7. Sir John Glubb, *The Life and Times of Muhammad* (New York: Cooper Square Press, 2001), p. 72.
8. In Muhammad's day, the relationship between men and women as regards property and children was polyandrous and not, as Muhammad later permitted, polygamous. In a polyandrous relationship, property and the children belong to the female and her family, not to the male. Khadijah's relationship with her first two husbands was likely polyandrous, accounting for her possession of wealth and property. The polyandrous system came to an end only after Muhammad permitted one man to possess four wives. He had lost so many men at the battle of Badr that permitting multiple wives was a solution to taking care of the widows and orphans.
9. Montgomery W. Watt, *Muhammad: Prophet and Statesman* (London: Oxford University Press, 1961), p. 12.
10. Glubb, *Life and Times*, p. 84.
11. *Ibid.*
12. *Ibid.*
13. Most Arabs were illiterate and writing materials and records of any sort from the period are extremely rare. The Muslim claim that the Qu'ran was written down immediately after each revelation or pronouncement of Muhammad is questionable on these grounds. More likely, the revelations and pronouncements were memorized and transmitted orally. Muhammed himself lamented after the Battle of Badr that many of the 'Qu'ran reciters' had been killed.
14. Glubb, *Life and Times*, p. 85.
15. Martin Lings, *Muhammed: His Life Based on the Earliest Sources* (Rochester, VT: Inner Traditions International, 1983), pp. 44–5, quoting Ibn Ishaq.
16. Watt, *Muhammed: Prophet and Statesman*, pp. 18–19.
17. Glubb, *Life and Times*, p. 97, quoting Ibn Ishaq.
18. Ibn Ishaq, *The Life of Muhammad: A Translation of Ibn Ishaq's Life of Muhammed* (Translated by Alfred Guillaume, Oxford: Oxford University Press, 1967), pp. 279–80. This is perhaps the most important source and most easily accessible for understanding the detail and context of Muhammad's military life.
19. *Ibid.*, Ibn Ishaq identifies Aisha as the original source of the story.
20. I wish to express my gratitude to Dr. Toby Rose, physician, pathologist and coroner in Toronto, Canada and Dr. Lucy Harvey of Montpelier, Vermont for providing me with the information on the symptoms of malaria. Dr. Peter F. Weller notes 'Clinical symptoms develop about

one to four weeks after infection and typically include fever and chills. Virtually all patients with acute malaria have episodes of fever. At the outset, fever may occur daily; over time, the paroxysms may develop the typical every-other-day or every-third day. The paroxysms of fever (as high as 41.5 degrees C [106.7 degrees F] and chills (with or without rigors) may be irregular, however. Other symptoms may be headache, increased sweating, back pain, myalgias, diarrhea, nausea, vomiting, and cough...Cerebral involvement may lead to delirium, focal disorders (e.g.,seizures), and coma. *P. malariae* organisms can persist in the blood as an indolent, even asymtomatic, infection for years or even decades.' See Peter. F. Weller, 'Protozoan Infections: Malaria', in David C. Dale and Daniel D. Federman (eds.), *Scientific American Medicine* vol. 2, sect. 7, ch. 34 (New York: Scientific American, 1999), pp. 1–6.

21. Ibn Ishaq, p. 143.
22. *Ibid.*, p. 194.
23. *Ibid.*
24. *Ibid.*, p. 203.
25. *Ibid.*, p. 204.
26. *Ibid.*, p. 213.
27. *Ibid.*, p. 213.
28. Ling, *Muhammad*, p. 35. The original source for Ling's description can be found in Ibn Ishaq, pp. 725–6.
29. Maxime Rodinson, *Muhammad* (New York: New Press, 2002), p. 279.
30. Montgomery W. Watt, *Muhammad at Medina* (Oxford, Oxford University Press, 1956), p. 321.
31. Glubb, *Life and Times*, p. 334.
32. *Ibid.* , p. 228.
33. The term is taken from James H. Breasted, *The Development of Religion and Thought in Ancient Egypt* who first used the term to describe the religious ferocity of Pharaoh Akhenaton, the ancient world's first true monotheist.
34. Ibn Ishaq, p. 157.
35. *Ibid.*, p. 131.
36. *Ibid.*, p. 106.
37. *Ibid.* , p. 227.
38. Hitti, *History of the Arabs*, p. 17.
39. See General Giap's *People's War, People's Army,* for the methods required to organize and conduct an insurgency.
40. Watt, *Muhammad At Medina*, p. 257

41. The story appears in Muhammad Hamidullah, *The Battlefields of the Prophet*, (Paris: Revue des Etudes Isalmiques, 1937), p. 40, citing Ibn Ajar Isabah, no. 8336.

42. Watt, *Muhammad at Medina*, p. 257.

43. Hitti, *History of the Arabs*, p. 95.

44. Glubb, *Life and Times*, p. 27.

45. Richard A. Gabriel, 'Charlemagne and the Franks', in *Empires at War* vol. 2 (Westport, CT: Greenwood Press, 2005), pp. 659–700.

46. Richard A. Gabriel, 'The Crusades', in *Empires at War*, vol. 3, pp. 791–836.

47. Glubb, *Life and Times*, p. 220.

48. Rodinson, *Muhammad*, pp. 223–4.

49. The information for much of this section is drawn from my previous research in the area. See Richard A. Gabriel, *Muhammad: Islam's First Great General* (Norman, OK: University of Oklahoma Press, 2007), Chapter 3.

50. V. J. Parry and M. E. Yapp, *War, Technology, and Society in the Middle East* (Oxford: Oxford University Press, 1975), p. 39.

51. Hitti, *History of the Arabs*, p. 173.

52. *Ibid.*

53. Richard A. Gabriel, 'War to the Knife', *Military History* (September, 2014), p. 36.

54. Hamidullah, *Battlefields of the Prophet*, p. 139.

55. *Ibid.*, p. 140.

56. *Ibid.*

57. Russ Rodgers, *The Generalship of Muhammad* (Gainesville, Florida: University of Florida Press, 2012), pp. 227–30 for an examination of the logistics of Muhammad's armies.

58. Rodinson, *Muhammad*, p. 286.

59. *Ibid.*

60. Ibn Ishaq, p. 679.

61. *Ibid.*

62. *Ibid.*, p. 680; see also Peter F. Weller, 'Protozoan Infections: Malaria', in David C. Dale and Daniel D. Federman, eds., *Scientific American Medicine* (New York: Scientific American, 1999), 2.5.

63. Rodinson, *Muhammad*, p. 288.

64. Ibn Ishaq, p. 689.

65. *Ibid.*

Chapter 4: Legacies

1. Basham, *The Wonder That Was India*, p. 56.

2. *Ibid.*, p. 58.
3. Mark W. Walton, George F. Nafziger, and Laurent W. Mbanda, *Islam At War: A History* (Westport, CT: Praeger), p. 226.
4. The radical ideas of monotheism and the distinction between true and false gods appeared in the theology of Mosaic Yahwehism sometime around a hundred years after the death of Akhenaten, making it almost certain that these ideas were borrowed by the Egyptianized Moses from the Atenist theology and incorporated into the new Israelite religion founded at Sinai. There is no other reasonable way to account for the appearance of such sophisticated theological ideas in Mosaic Yahwehism at this time. The incorporation of Atenist ideas into the new Israelite religion is an example of the frequent occurrence of polytheism's cultural transference between cultures throughout history. On the pre-Mosaic origins of monotheism, see Richard A. Gabriel, *Gods of Our Fathers: The Memory of Egypt in Judaism and Christianity*, Chapter 2, 'Egyptian Monotheism and Akhenaten'.
5. Jan Assmann, *Moses The Egyptian* (Cambridge, MA: Harvard University Press, 1997), p. 3.
6. *Ibid.*, p. 4.
7. Four centuries after Christ's death, paganism was still the most practised religion within the Roman Empire. In the fourth century, Byzantine emperors decided to put an end to it once and for all and for the next 200 years undertook a campaign of persecution of the pagan religions (and Christian sects declared heretical), finally destroying polytheism in the ancient world. One effect of this persecution was to weaken the empire and lose the loyalty of its population, so that when the armies of Islam attacked around 640 AD, the empire collapsed.
8. Karen Armstrong, *A History of God* (New York: Ballantine Books,1993), 14. The incident of the Kolar rebellion in Moses' camp was precipitated precisely on the grounds that 'the whole people are holy', that is, God speaks to all men, not just Moses, a view much more in line with how the Israelites traditionally saw their gods than Moses' new version.
9. Mary Douglas, *In the Wilderness: The Doctrine of Defilement in the Book of Numbers* (Sheffield, England: Sheffield Academic Press, 1993), for the idea of an 'enclave religion'.
10. Armstrong, *History of God*, p. 41.
11. Assmann, *Moses The Egyptian*, pp. 3–4.
12. Deuteronomy, 20:16–17.
13. Michael Grant, *The History of Ancient Israel* (New York: Charles Scriber, 1984), p. 87.

14. Philip K. Hitti, *History of the Arabs* (Hampshire, UK: Palgrave Macmillan, 2002), p. 40.

15. In a manner similar to how Paul of Tarsus influenced the development of Christian doctrine and helped bring about the spread and institutionalization of Christianity, so it was that Abu Bakr influenced the doctrines of Islam on critical theological points. It was also Abu Bakr, not Muhammad, who was ultimately responsible for the spread of Islam and its institutionalization as a formal religion. Richard A. Gabriel, *Muhammad: Islam's First Great General* (Norman, OK: University of Oklahoma Press, 2007), pp. 205–7.

16. Elias S. Shoufani, *Al-Riddah and the Muslim Conquest of Arabia* (Toronto: University of Toronto Press, 1973), p. 62.

17. *Ibid.*, p. 118.

18. Gabriel, 'Wars of the Arab Conquest', in *Empires at War* vol 2, p. 639.

19. *Ibid.*, pp. 642–3.

20. The size of the Arab forces and their accompanying families is a matter of some debate with estimates ranging from 100,000 to 500,000. This would place the strength of the Arab armies at somewhere between 25,000 and 125,000 soldiers.

21. Patricia Crone, 'The Early Islamic World', in Kurt Raaflaub and Nathan Rosenstein, *War and Society in the Ancient and Medieval Worlds* (Cambridge, MA: Harvard University Press, 1999), p. 316.

22. Gabriel, 'Wars of he Arab Conquest', p. 647.

23. This section draws heavily upon two sources: my own article, *Jihad: War to the Knife*, cited earlier, and Richard Bonney, *Jihad: From Quran to bin Laden* (London: Palgrave Macmillan, 2004), probably the most comprehensive source on the subject.

Bibliography

Alfred, Cyril, *Akhenaten: King of Egypt* (London: Thames and Hudson, 1988).

Armstrong, Karen, *History of God*, (New York: Ballantine Books, 1993).

Armstrong, Karen, *Buddha* (New York: Viking Books, 2001).

Arrian, *The Campaigns of Alexander*, translated by Aubrey De Selincourt (London: Penguin, 1971).

Assmann, Jan, *Moses the Egyptian* (Cambridge, MA: Harvard University Press, 1998).

Auerbach, Elias, *Moses*, translated and edited by Robert A Barclay and Israel O Lehman (Detroit, MI: Wayne State University Press, 1975).

Bamshad, Michael et al, 'Genetic Evidence on the Origins of Indian Caste Populations', in *Gnome Res.* 11, no. 60 (1996), pp. 994–1004.

Barnett, William S, 'Only the Bad Died Young in the Ancient Middle East', in *International Journal of Aging and Human Development*, 21, no. 2 (1985), pp. 155–60.

Basham, A L, *The Wonder That Was India* (New York: Grove Press, 1959).

Bhatia, H S, *Vedic and Aryan India: Evolution of Political, Legal, and Military Systems* (New Delhi: Deep and Deep Publications, 2001).

Bhikkhu, Mettanando, 'How The Buddha Died', *Bangkok Post* (May 15, 2001), pp. 1–7.

Bhikkhu, Mettanando, and Oskar von Hinueber, 'The Cause of the Buddha's Death', *Journal of the Pali Text Society*, 26 (2000), pp. 7–16.

Boling, Robert G, and G Ernest Wright, *Joshua: The Anchor Bible* (New York: Doubleday, 1982).

Bonney, Richard, *Jihad: From Quran to bin Laden* (London: Palgrave Macmillan, 2004).

Breasted, James H, *The Dawn of Conscience* (New York: Charles Scribner, 1947).

Bronkhorst, Johannes, *The Two Sources of Indian Asceticism* (Delhi: Motilal Banarsidass, 1998).

Bryce, T R, *The Kingdom of the Hittites* (Oxford, UK: Oxford University Press, 2005).

Buber, Martin, *Moses: The Revelation and the Covenant* (Amherst, NY: Humanity Books, 1998).

Budge, E A, *Osiris and the Egyptian Resurrection* (New York: Dover Publications, 1973).

Clayton, Peter A, *Chronicle of the Pharaohs* (London: Thames and Hudson, 1994).

Cleveland, Kerry O, 'Tularemia', *Medscape Reference* http://emedicine.medscape.com/article/230923-overview

Cline, Eric H, *1177 B.C.: The Year Civilization Collapsed* (Princeton, NJ: Princeton University Press, 2014).

Cousins, L S, 'The Dating of the Historical Buddha', *Journal of the Royal Asiatic Society* 3, 6 (1996), pp. 57–63.

Crone, Patricia. 'The Early Islamic World', in Kurt Raaflaub and Nathan Rosenstein, *War and Society in the Ancient and Medieval Worlds* (Cambridge, MA: Harvard University Press, 1999), pp. 312–19.

Curtius, Quintus, *History of Alexander*, translated by John C Rolfe (Cambridge, MA: Harvard University Press, 1946).

Davies, C C, *An Historical Atlas of the Indian Peninsula* (Oxford, UK: Oxford University Press, 1949).

Dharma, J P, *Republics in Ancient India: 1500 B.C.–500 B.C.* (Leiden: E. J. Brill, 1968).

Dikshitar, V R Ramachandra, *War in Ancient India*, (Delhi: Motilal Banarsidass, 1987).

Douglas, Mary, *In The Wilderness: The Doctrine of Defilement in the Book of Numbers* (Sheffield, UK: Sheffield Academic Press, 1993).

Drews, Robert. *The End of the Bronze Age* (Princeton, NJ: Princeton University Press, 1993).

Freud, Sigmund, *Moses and Monotheism* (New York: Vintage Books, 1939).

Gabriel, Richard A, *Soviet Military Psychiatry: The Theory and Practice of Coping With Battle Stress* (Westport, CT: Greenwood Press, 1986).

Gabriel, Richard A, *Military Psychiatry: A Comparative Perspective* (Westport, CT: Greenwood Press, 1986).

Gabriel, Richard A, *The Painful Field: The Psychiatric Dimension of Modern War* (Westport, CT: Greenwood Press, 1987).

Gabriel, Richard A, *No More Heroes: Madness and Psychiatry in War* (New York: Hill and Wang, 1987).

Gabriel, Richard A, *The Culture of War* (Westport, CT: Greenwood Press, 1990).

Gabriel, Richard A, and Donald W Boose Jr, *The Great Battles of Antiquity* (Westport, CT: Greenwood Press, 1990)

Gabriel, Richard A, and Karen S Metz, *From Sumer To Rome: The Military Capabilities of Ancient Armies* (Westport, CT: Greenwood Press, 1991).

Gabriel, Richard A, and Karen S Metz, *The History of Military Medicine, Vol 1: From Ancient Times to the Middle Ages* (Westport, CT: Greenwood Press, 1992).

Gabriel, Richard A, *Soldiers' Lives Through History: The Ancient World* (Westport, CT: Greenwood Press, 2000).

Gabriel, Richard A, *Gods of Our Fathers: The Memory of Egypt in Judaism and Christianity* (Westport, Greenwood Press, 2001).

Gabriel, Richard A, *The Great Armies of Antiquity* (Westport, CT: Greenwood Press, 2002)

Gabriel, Richard A, *The Military History of Ancient Israel* (Westport, CT: Greenwood Press, 2003)

Gabriel, Richard A, *Empires At War*, 3 volumes (Westport, CT: Greenwood Press, 2005).

Gabriel, Richard A, 'Charlemagne and the Franks', in *Empires At War* (Westport, CT: Greenwood Press, 2005), vol 2, pp. 659–700.

Gabriel, Richard A, 'The Crusades', in *Empires At War* (Westport, CT: Greenwood Press, 2005), vol 3, pp. 791–836.

Gabriel, Richard A, 'Wars of the Arab Conquest', in *Empires At War* (Westport, CT: Greenwood Press, 2005) vol 2, pp. 631–87.

Gabriel, Richard A, *Muhammad: Islam's First Great General* (Norman, OK: Oklahoma University Press, 2007).

Gabriel, Richard A, 'Buddha: Enlightened Warrior', in *Military History* (May, 2011), pp. 40–45.

Gabriel, Richard A, *Between Flesh and Steel: A History of Military Medicine From the Middle Ages to the War in Afghanistan* (Dulles, VA: Potomac Books, 2013).

Gabriel, Richard A, 'The Sicarii', in *Military History* (Winter, 2014), pp. 40–45.

Gabriel, Richard A, 'War To The Knife: The History of Jihad', *Military History* (September, 2014), pp. 35–40.

Gabriel, Richard A, *The Madness of Alexander the Great and the Myth of Military Genius* (Barnsley: Pen and Sword, 2015).

Gall, Reuven, *A Portrait of the Israeli Solider* (Westport, CT: Greenwood Press, 1986).

Gardener, Sir Alan, *Egypt of the Pharaohs* (Oxford, UK: Oxford University Press, 1961.

Gichon, Mordecai, 'The Siege of Masada', in *Collection du Centre des Etudes Romaines et Gallo-Romaines* No. 20 (Lyon, 2000), pp. 541–3.

Grubb, Sir John, *The Life and Times of Muhammad* (New York: Cooper Square Press, 2001).

Gombrich, Richard F, *Theravda Buddhism: A Social History from Ancient Benares to Modern Columbo* (London: Routledge, 1988).

Gottwald, Norman K, *Tribes of Yahweh* (Maryknoll, NY: Orbis Books, 1979).

Grant, Michael, *The History of Ancient Israel* (New York: Scribner, 1984).

Grimal, Nicholas, *History of Ancient Egypt* (London: Blackwell Publishers, 1992).

Grossman, David, *On Killing: The Psychological Cost of Learning to Kill in War and Society* (Boston: Little Brown, 2009).

Hamidullah, Muhammad, *The Battlefields of the Prophet* (Paris: Revue des Etudes Isalmiques, 1937).

Herzog, Chaim and Mordechai Gichon, *Battles of the Bible* (Jerusalem: Steimatzky Agency, 1978).

Hitti, Philip K, *History of the Arabs* (Basingstoke: Palgrave Macmillan, 2002).

Hobbs, T R, *A Time for War* (Wilmington, DE: Michael Glazier, 1989).

Holland, Robert G, *Arabia and the Arabs: From the Bronze Age to the Coming of Islam* (London: Routledge, 2001).

Homan, Michael M, 'The Divine Warrior in His Tent: A Military Model for Yahweh's Tabernacle', *Bible Review* 16, no. 6 (December, 2000) pp. 22–33.

Ibn Ishaq, *The Life of Muhammad: A Translation of Ibn Ishaq's 'Life of Muhammad'*, translated by Alfred Guillaume, (Oxford, UK: Oxford University Press, 1967).

Idris-Bell, 'Hellenic Culture in Egypt', in *Journal of Egyptian Archaeology* 8 (1922), pp. 141–146.

Isaac, Eric, 'Circumcision as a Covenant Rite', *Antropos* 59 (1965), pp. 442–3.

Isserlin, B S J, *The Israelites* (London: Thames and Hudson, 1998).

Josephus, *Contra Apion*, I. 82–92.

Kirsch, Jonathan, *Moses: A Life* (New York: Ballantine Books, 1998).

Klein, Joel T, *Through the Name of God* (Westport, CT: Greenwood Press, 2001).

Kosuta, Matthew, 'The Buddha and the Four-Limbed Army: The Military in the Palli Canon', http://www.urbandharma.org/udharma6/military canon.html.

Lings, Martin, *Muhammad: His Life Based on the Earliest Sources* (Rochester, VT: Inner Traditions International, 1983)

Lucas, A, 'The Number of Israelites at the Exodus', *Palestine Exploration Quarterly* (1944), pp. 164–8.

Mendenhall, George E, 'The Census List of Numbers 1 and 26', *Journal of Biblical Literature* 77 (1958), pp. 52–66.

Neville, Edouard, 'The Geography of the Exodus', *Journal of Egyptian Archaeology* 10 (1924), pp. 19–25.

Panday, Vina, 'Sakya Clan: The Clan in Which Buddha Was Born', in *History of Ancient India* (Internet August 5, 2013)

Parry, V J and M E Yapp, *War, Technology and Society in the Middle East* (Oxford, UK: Oxford University Press, 1975).

Prebish, Charles S, 'Cooking the Buddhist Books: The Implications of the New Dating of the Buddha for the History of Early Indian Buddhism', *Journal of Buddhist Ethics* 15 (2008), pp. 23–44.

Pritchard, James B, *Ancient Near East Texts Relating to the Old Testament* (Princeton, NJ: Princeton University Press, 1955).

Propp, William H C, *Exodus 1–8: The Anchor Bible* (New York: Doubleday, 1998).

Redford, Donald B, *Akhenaten: The Heretic King* (Princeton, NJ: Princeton University Press, 1984).

Rockhill, W W, *The Life of the Buddha* (London: 1984).

Rodgers, Russ, *The Generalship of Muhammad* (Gainesville, Florida: University of Florida Press, 2012).

Rodinson, Maxime, *Muhammad* (New York: New Press, 2002).

Rostovtzeff, M, 'The Foundations of Social and Economic Life in Hellenic Times', *Journal of Egyptian Archaeology* 6 (1920), pp. 161–78.

Rowley, H H, *From Joseph to Joshua* (London: Oxford University Press, 1948).

Rhys Davids, T W, *Buddhist India* (New York: Putnam, 1911).

Rhys Davids, T W, and A F Caroline, *Sakya or Buddhist Origins* (Columbus, MO: South Asia Books, reprint 1978).

Samuel, Geoffrey, *The Origins of Yoga and Tantra* Cambridge, UK: Cambridge University Press, 2010).

Sandhu, Gucharn Singh, *A Military History of Ancient India* (Delhi: Vision Books, 2000).

Schulman, A R, 'Some Remarks on the Military Background of the Amarna Period', *Journal of the American Research Center in Egypt* 3 (1964), pp. 51–70.

Schumann, Hans Wolfgang, *The Historical Buddha: The Times, Life, and Teaching of the Founder of Buddhism* (Delhi: Motilal Banarsidass, 2003).

Singh, Sarva Daman, *Ancient Indian Warfare* (Delhi: Banarsidass Publishers, 1997).

Shay, Jonathan, *Achilles in Vietnam: Combat Trauma and the Undoing of Character* (New York: Scriber, 1994).

Shoufani, Elias, *Al-Riddah and the Muslim Conquest of Arabia* (Toronto: University of Toronto Press, 1973).

Smith, Morton, *Jesus The Egyptian* (New York: Barnes and Noble, 1997).

Spencer, Robert, *Did Muhammad Exist? An Inquiry Into Islam's Obscure Origins* (Wilmington, DE: Intercollegiate Studies Institute, 2014).

Stillman, Nigel, and Nigel Tallis, *Armies of the Ancient Near East* (Worthing, UK: Wargames Research Group, 1984).

Thompson, Sarah Grey and Terrence Kaufman, *Language, Contact, Creolization and Genetic Linguistics* (Berkeley, CA: University of California Press, 1991).

Trevisanato, Siro Igino, 'The Hittite Plague: An Epidemic of Tularemia and the First Record of Biological Warfare', *Medical Hypotheses* 69, 6 (2007), pp. 1371–4.

Trittle, Lawrence A, *From Melos to My Lai: War and Survival* (New York: Routledge, 2000).

Watt, Montgomery W, *Muhammad At Medina* (Oxford: Oxford University Press, 1956).

Watt, Montgomery W, *Muhammad: Prophet and Statesman* (London: Oxford University Press, 1961).

Weiner, H M, 'The Historical Character of the Exodus', in *Ancient Egypt* IV (1926), pp. 104–15.

Weingartner, Steven, 'Suppiluliuma I and his Times: Great King and Conqueror', *Ancient Warfare* (Summer, 2014), pp.8–13.

Weller, Peter F, 'Protozoan Infections: Malaria', in David C Dale and Daniel D Federman (eds.), *Scientific American Medicine*. vol 2, sect 7, chap. 34 (New York: Scientific American, 1999), pp. 1–6.

Wright, G Ernest, *Westminster Historical Atlas of the Bible* (Philadelphia, PA: Westminster Press, 1945).

Yadin, Yigael, *The Art of Warfare in Biblical Lands in Light of Archaeological Discovery* (New York: McGraw-Hill, 1963).

Yasuda, A S, 'The Osiris Cult and the Designation of Osiris Idols in the Bible', in *Journal of Near Eastern Studies* 3 (1944), pp. 194–7.

Index